SAGE was founded in 1965 by Sara Miller McCune to support the dissemination of usable knowledge by publishing innovative and high-quality research and teaching content. Today, we publish over 900 journals, including those of more than 400 learned societies, more than 800 new books per year, and a growing range of library products including archives, data, case studies, reports, and video. SAGE remains majority-owned by our founder, and after Sara's lifetime will become owned by a charitable trust that secures our continued independence.

Los Angeles | London | New Delhi | Singapore | Washington DC | Melbourne

BETWEEN THE TWO OCEANS OF INDO-PACIFIC

BETWEEN THE TWO OCEANS OF INDO-PACIFIC

Strengthening the Myanmar–Thailand Southern Corridor

Edited by

Suthiphand Chirathivat

Charit Tingsabadh

Prabir De

SAGE | spectrum

spectrum.sagepub.in

First published in 2022 by

SAGE | spectrum

SAGE Publications India Pvt Ltd
B1/I-1 Mohan Cooperative Industrial Area
Mathura Road, New Delhi 110 044, India
www.sagepub.in

Typeset in 9.5/13 pt Century Schoolbook by Zaza Eunice, Hosur, Tamil Nadu, India.

Library of Congress Control Number: 2022945323

DOI: https://doi.org/10.4135/978-93-5479-402-5

ISBN: 978-93-5479-401-8 (PB)

CONTENTS

LIST OF FIGURES

LIST OF MAPS

LIST OF TABLES

LIST OF ABBREVIATIONS

AC	Asphaltic concrete
ACCC	ASEAN Connectivity Coordinating Committee
ACTS	ASEAN Customs Transit System
ADB	Asian Development Bank
AEP	'Act East' Policy
AFAFGIT	ASEAN Framework Agreement on the Facilitation of Goods in Transit
AFAFIST	ASEAN Framework Agreement on the Facilitation of Inter-State Transport
AGVCBP	ASEAN goods vehicle cross-border permit
AH	ASEAN Highway
AOT	Airports of Thailand PCL
ASC	ASEAN Studies Center
ASEAN	Association of Southeast Asian Nations
BCSA	BIMSTEC Coastal Shipping Agreement
BIMSTEC	Bay of Bengal Initiative for Multi-Sectoral Technical and Economic Cooperation
BRI	Belt and Road Initiative
CAGR	Compound annual growth rate
CBD	Central Business District
CBTP	Cross border transport of passengers
CEPT	Common Effective Preferential Tariff
CICTT	Centre of Information & Communication Technology Training
CIQ	Customs, immigration and quarantine
CLMV	Cambodia, Lao PDR, Myanmar, Vietnam

CLV	Cambodia, Lao PDR and Vietnam
CSR	Corporate social responsibility
CWGC	Commonwealth War Graves Commission
CYTS	China Youth Travel Services
DCA	Department of Civil Aviation
DDA	Dawei Development Association
DDC	Dawei Development Company Ltd
DFZ	Duty-free zone
DICA	Directorate of Investment and Company Administration
DOA	Department of Airport
DOH	Department of Highway
DPT	Department of Public Works and Town and Country Planning
DRR	Department of Rural Road
DSEZ	Dawei Special Economic Zone
DWT	Deadweight tonnage
EC5	Economic corridor 5
EEC	Eastern Economic Corridor
EEZ	Exclusive economic zone
EIA	Environmental impact assessment
EIRR	Economic internal rate of return
EWEC	East–West Economic Corridor
FDI	Foreign direct investment
FIRR	Financial internal rate of return
FMIA	First Myanmar Investment Airlines
FS	Feasibility study
FTA	Free trade agreements
GMA	Golden Myanmar Airlines
GMS	Greater Mekong Subregion
ICT	Information and communications technology
IMCEITS	India–Myanmar Centre for Enhancement of IT Skills

IMT-GT	Indonesia–Malaysia–Thailand Growth Triangle
IORA	Indian Ocean Rim Association
IPR	Intellectual property rights
ITC	International Trade Centre
ITD	Italian-Thai Development PCL
IUU	Illegal, unreported and unregulated
IWT	Inland water transport
JBC	Joint Border Committee
JDA	Joint Development Agreement
JICA	Japan International Cooperation Agency
KNU	Karen National Union
LDCs	Least developed countries
LOA	Length overall
MAC	Myanmar Auto Corporation
MACCS	Myanmar Automated Cargo Clearance System
MCCI	Myawaddy Chamber of Commerce Industry
MFDPC	Myeik Future Development Public Company
MIEC	Mekong–India Economic Corridor
MIL	Myanmar Investment Law
MMK	Myanmar kyat
MNA	Myanmar National Airlines
MOHT	Ministry of Hotels and Tourism
MOPF	Ministry of Planning and Finance
MOT	Ministry of Transport
MoU	Memorandum of Understanding
MPA	Myanmar Port Authority
MPAC	Master plan for ASEAN connectivity
MPC	Myanmar Pongpipat Company Limited
MR	'Myanma' Railways
MYP	Mann Yadanarpon Airlines
NACAI	Network of ASEAN–China Academic Institutes
NCs	National Coordinators
NDMP	National Disaster Management Plan

NFAT	National Fisheries Association of Thailand
NGA	NewGen Airlines (International)
NLD	National League for Democracy
NTF IV	Fourth phase of the Netherlands Trust Fund
NTMs	Non-tariff measures
OP	Operating procedures
OTP	Office of Transport and Traffic Policy and Planning
PAT	Port Authority of Thailand
PCP	Physical connectivity projects
PDF	Project Development Fund
PMTA	Prachuap–Myeik Trading and Investment Promotion Association
POW	Prisoner of war
PPC	Prachuap Pier Co. Ltd
PRC	People's Republic of China
PTTGE	PTT Green Energy
PWD	Public Works Department
RITES	Rail India Technical and Economic Service
RO-RO	Roll-on, roll-off
RVCs	Regional value chains
SCC	Siam City Cement
SCG	Siam Cement Group
SEC	Southern Economic Corridor
SEWC	Southern East–West Corridor
SEZ	Special economic zone
SGA	Southern General Army
SRT	State Railway of Thailand
SSI	Sahaviriya Steel Industries PCL
TAT	Tourism Authority of Thailand
TCCI	Tanintharyi Region Chambers of Commerce and Industry
TH	Trilateral Highway
THB	Thailand baht

TM-SEWC	Thailand–Myanmar Southern East–West Corridor
T-MVA	Trilateral Motor Vehicle Agreement
TPR	Trans-Peninsula route
TPR-MP	Trans-Peninsula Route-Myeik–Prachuap Khiri Khan
TTDC	Tanintharyi Tourism Development Committee
UNCLOS	United Nations Convention on the Law of the Sea
UNESCAP	United Nations Economic and Social Commission for Asia and the Pacific
WEC	Western Economic Corridor

PREFACE

The idea of connectivity is an integral part of regionalism in international trade and integration. In a regional block, countries come together and interact with each other on terms that are more favourable than with others outside the group. The Association of Southeast Asian Nations (ASEAN) as a regional group is a case of such a region with many intergovernmental agreements and agreed modes of operation in trade, security and sociocultural fields, as exemplified in the ASEAN Charter, namely, economic, political and sociocultural pillars defined in the Charter, and embodying the spirit of cooperation and collaboration among its 10 member states.

In this book, *Between the Two Oceans of Indo-Pacific: Strengthening the Myanmar–Thailand Southern Corridor*, we limit our focus to a specific part of Thailand and Myanmar. The focus of this book in particular is on the so-called Southern East–West Economic Corridor, which consists of the connections between the southern part of Myanmar and the western part of the central region of Thailand. It is the region defined by the line from the Salween estuary in Myanmar to the Mae Klong estuary in Thailand in the north, to Chumphon–Ranong provinces and Kawthaung in the south, to the Andaman Sea in the west and to the Gulf of Thailand in the east. The narratives in this book may help strengthen the ASEAN integration process on its way towards ASEAN Economic Community.

The book covers a diverse range of topics in the fields of geography, history, archaeology, international trade, tourism, migration and infrastructure for transportation. The information analysed in the book comprises data from published sources and is supplemented by field studies carried out from 2017 to 2018 as well as from papers presented at conferences organized by the ASEAN

Studies Center of Chulalongkorn University, Bangkok, over the same period. The authors of the chapters are from diverse fields of academic disciplines from Thailand, Myanmar and India.

The message that we want to convey is that there is a high potential to improve connectivity between the two countries, which have long been connected in the long historical past, until the end of the colonial period at the end of the Second World War. The developing context of ASEAN regionalism provides an important rationale to promote improved connectivity in this sub-region—the Southern East-West Economic Corridor—to support the integration of ASEAN with the rest of Asia.

In writing this book, we are immensely grateful to Chulalongkorn University for providing financial support. With their valuable support, we managed to organize a seminar in Bangkok and a study tour in February 2018. We are also thankful to all the authors, discussants and seminar participants for their wholehearted support to this project and for coming forward with valuable chapters. We gratefully acknowledge the copy-editing done by Ruchi Verma. Finally, we are grateful to SAGE for the timely publication of this volume.

We hope this publication will be able to fill the gap in literature, which will fulfil the need felt by the researchers and teachers in this field. Needless to say, the suggestions in this book will strengthen the policymaking process.

Disclaimer: The maps appearing in the book are not to scale. They do not represent any authentic national or international boundaries and are used for illustrative purposes only.

CHAPTER 1

INTRODUCTION

Suthiphand Chirathivat, Charit Tingsabadh and Prabir De

Regional connectivity has recently gained wide recognition as a central idea for promoting trade and regional integration among countries. In a regional block, countries come together to form a group that would allow them to interact with each other on terms that are more favourable than with others outside the group. The Association of Southeast Asian Nations (ASEAN) as a regional group is a case of such a region with many intergovernmental agreements and agreed modes of operation in trade, security and sociocultural fields, as exemplified in the ASEAN Charter, namely, economic, political and sociocultural pillars defined in the Charter, and embodying the spirit of cooperation and collaboration among its 10 member states.

Connectivity has many dimensions, not only physical but also social and cultural, which are necessary to support region-building. To realize the potential benefits of connectivity, it is therefore important to consider various elements of the concept, within the broader context of the region.

In this book, we take a practical study approach to look into specific transportation part of Thailand and Myanmar. The focus of this book in particular is on the so-called Southern East–West Economic Corridor (EWEC) that consists of the connections between the southern part of Myanmar and the western part of the central region of Thailand. It is the region defined by the line from the

Salween estuary in Myanmar to the Maeklong estuary in Thailand in the north, to Chumphon–Ranong provinces and Kawthaung in the south, to the Andaman Sea in the west and to the Gulf of Thailand in the east.

Connectivity projects between Myanmar and Thailand are unique regional cooperation initiatives in terms of geographical contiguity and access to the ocean. The Southern EWEC has far-reaching implications in terms of trade, connectivity and regional integration. Our objective is to accelerate economic growth and social progress in the Thailand–Myanmar region through joint endeavours and to cooperate more effectively in joint efforts that are supportive of and complementary to national development plans of the countries.

Greater connectivity within ASEAN and between ASEAN and India can yield numerous benefits. Larger markets can bring about economies of scale in production and enhance competitiveness. Integration of markets can facilitate the movement of production networks and attract more foreign investments along with the benefits of knowledge and technology transfer and opportunities to connect to regional and global supply chains. However, countries have to design strong implementation mechanisms to ensure that effective coordination takes place among various agencies. Such cooperation has the potential to absorb large investments in infrastructure and industry. Expanding trade is one of the many manifestations of growing economic integration. Thailand and Myanmar have to identify the connectivity projects that would trigger trade and investment. Both countries should work more closely on physical and digital connectivity and develop industrial or special economic zones, logistics and customs systems. These are essential for improving countries' competitiveness while addressing the global challenges.

Connectivity improvement in Myanmar is essential for stronger connectivity between South and Southeast and East Asia. In Southeast Asia, Thailand's connectivity with Myanmar is expected to provide cost-effective and efficient logistic services to promote trade and development.

The book covers a wide range of topics in the fields of geography, history, archaeology, trade, tourism, migration and transportation. The information analysed in the book comprises data from published sources and is supplemented by field studies carried out from 2017 to 2018 as well as from papers presented at conferences organized by the ASEAN Studies Center of Chulalongkorn University, Bangkok, over the same period. The authors of the chapters are from diverse fields of academic disciplines from Thailand, Myanmar and India.

The message to take away from the present study is that there is a high potential to improve connectivity between the two countries, which have long been connected in the historical past, until the end of the colonial period at the end of the Second World War. The developing context of ASEAN regionalism provides an important rationale to promote improved connectivity in this sub-region—the Southern East–West Economic Corridor—to support the integration of ASEAN with the rest of Asia, specifically India, in the context of Indo-Pacific and Belt and Road Initiative (BRI).

Divided into four parts, this book has a total of 12 chapters, including Introduction. The four parts of the book are as follows: History of the Region (Part I); Regional Perspectives on Southern East–West Economic Corridors (Part II); The Region in Focus (Part III); and Conclusions (Part IV). Chapter 2, written by Suchandra Ghosh, discusses the lineage of the Southern East–West Corridor (SEWC) from a civilizational aspect. The East–West Corridor is a conceptual tool for identifying common cultural processes across mainland Southeast Asia. The choice of the region is from the Northern East-West Corridor to the SEWC. It continued to be a coveted zone from the early 1st millennium CE to the early 2nd millennium CE for the monarchs, merchants and monks. The linkage was to a certain extent guided by political consideration. This chapter reviews the connected history from a few perspectives like Buddhism and the potentiality of the region for trade and artistic exchanges. There were widespread cultural and economic exchanges through this corridor.

Chapter 3, written by Thiva Supajanya, picks up the Trans-Peninsular Route, which is known as Myeik–Prachuap Khiri Khan (TPR-MP), as a case study. The TPR-MP is a communication route connecting the two great oceans—the Indian Ocean in the west and the Pacific Ocean in the east. This chapter concludes that the

TPR-MP has been popular and used for a long time. Currently, the condition of the route is usable for the entire stretch and is being improved in the territories of both Myanmar and Thailand for more efficient use and to support the opening of the Permanent Border Post, where Thailand is building government offices and other services. On the Myanmar side, though the road is still of lower standard as compared to the Thailand side, there is already a network of roads connecting the main road along the coastline from Dawei to Kawthaung, to the tip of Myanmar's territory known as Victoria Point. The opening of Dan Singkhon as a permanent border crossing point to maximize the benefits of trade between the two countries is the beginning of a new era for the old vision, after having been in use for over 350 years in the past. It is believed that this will benefit both Prachuap Khiri Khan on the Pacific Ocean side and Myeik on the Indian Ocean side.

Chapter 4, written by David Boggett, presents the historical perspectives on the development of the Thai-Burma border areas in the Second World War. During the Second World War, the Thai-Burma border areas became of critical importance to Japan, both for supplying its own troops fighting in Burma and for prosecuting further expansion of the war into India. Cross-border local trade between Burma and Thailand existed, but the Japanese had to develop these local trade routes into a modern communication network capable of supplying their armies in Burma. Several military projects were developed on these border areas, and some of these are explained in detail in this chapter.

Chapter 5, written by Mu Mu Theint, presents Myanmar's perspective on Thailand–Myanmar Southern Economic Corridor (SEC) in the context of ASEAN integration. The aim of the study is to assess the current situation in the Tanintharyi region and Kayin State by conducting secondary and primary research; to find out opportunities and challenges for the country; and to provide recommendations to improve trade flows, business performance, people-to-people contacts, employment, hotels and tourism, and social and community development of the country. Overcoming the challenges and reducing some constraints can create a better economic and business environment for the region. Therefore, strategic recommendations are added in this chapter. In conclusion, this chapter recommends that SEC and EWEC connectivity projects are strategically important for Myanmar since Dawei, Myeik, Kawthaung and Myawaddy are trading hubs. These projects will be beneficial for Myanmar, Thailand, India, ASEAN countries and Asia as a whole. Although there are many challenges for Myanmar, it is better to respond to the opportunities offered by geographical and natural advantages to have competitive advantages through the global market chain. Therefore, the economic integration depends on guidelines or policy frameworks and a strong political desire to set and agree on a common and shared vision to integrate the economies. Business collaborations between the two countries will increase opportunities for trade and investment in the region.

Greater connectivity between ASEAN and India can yield numerous benefits. Expanding trade is one of the many manifestations of growing economic integration. Larger markets can bring about economies of scale in production and enhance competitiveness. Integration of markets can facilitate the movement of production networks and attract more foreign investments along with the benefits of knowledge and technology transfer and opportunities to connect to regional and global supply chains. In view of the preceding context, Chapter 6, written by Prabir De, shares an Indian perspective on Thailand–Myanmar East–West Corridor. The chapter concludes that countries have to design strong implementation mechanisms to ensure that effective coordination takes place among various agencies. Such cooperation has the potential to absorb large investments in infrastructure and industry. ASEAN countries and India have to identify the connectivity projects that would trigger trade and investment. India and Thailand should work more closely on physical and digital connectivity and develop industrial or special economic zones, logistics, customs systems, etc. These are essential areas/issues in improving competitiveness of all the countries concerned while addressing the global challenges.

Chapter 7, written by Piti Srisangnam, presents trade and investment trends of Myeik economy and also discusses the challenges and opportunities. Myeik, formerly Mergui or 'Beik' as the locals call their home town, is the largest city in Tanintharyi Region in Myanmar, located between Dawei (the capital city of the region) on the north and Kawthaung (the southernmost part of the country) on the south. Myeik is located at the centre of the Mergui Archipelago annexe to the Andaman Sea. This chapter is divided into three parts, namely, general information of Myeik economy, production sectors and business opportunities, and challenges and policy recommendations.

Over the past few decades, there have been numerous visions and master plans around the Thailand–southern Myanmar border, but none are spot on. Some of these are at the global scale such as China's BRI, conceived by the Chinese government involving the Silk Road Economic Belt overland and the 21st Maritime Silk Road over the ocean from Asia and Southeast Asia to East Africa and Western Europe. Although somewhat stalled at present, the SEWC, a touch under the BRI's maritime path, might generate benefits in the long run. Chapter 8, written by Wiwat Sutiwipakorn, deals with the TM-SEWC and presents land, sea, air links and other considerations for improving logistics with particular reference to the Master Plan for ASEAN Connectivity (MPAC). This chapter has endeavoured to look into the present situation in this SEWC and has found that the area is in dire need of development. It has very high potential, but somehow it has been overlooked so far. Better road and rail connections will greatly enhance travel and land use and will help to facilitate intermodal transport for maritime transportation far and wide.

Chapter 9, written by Charit Tingsabadh and Suthiphand Chirathivat, presents sectoral analysis of fisheries and tourism sectors of both Myanmar and Thailand. It reviews the prospects of two important sectors that are considered to be highly promising for the development of the SEWC. In the ASEAN context, Myanmar is a major producer of fisheries products, second only to Indonesia. Marine capture is the major component of fisheries production in Myanmar. This chapter, therefore, analyses the prospects of the fisheries sector in the Tanintharyi–Tanaosri region. Next to fisheries is tourism. Tourism in Tanaosri and Tanintharyi has developed separately. Myanmar, for example, needs to strongly recognize and upgrade the importance of the Myeik Archipelago. It also needs to create value chain tourism projects in its own tourism master plan. This chapter presents the ways for future development and the Tanintharyi–Tanaosri tourism connectivity.

Chapter 10, written by Supang Chantavanich, discusses people mobility and accumulation on the Prachuap–Myeik corridor in the context of ASEAN connectivity. Prachuap and Myeik are towns in Thailand and Myanmar, respectively, which have been connected as a corridor since the 15th century. The corridor was an old trade route as well as a war route. With the ASEAN concept of connectivity and Asian Development Bank's plan and strategy on the EWEC in the Greater Mekong Subregion (GMS), this southern corridor can be an example of people-to-people connectivity and tourism development. Given the ASEAN policy on people-to-people connectivity with an emphasis on greater intra-ASEAN mobility, the Prachuap–Myeik corridor exemplifies such policy with its initiatives to enhance tourism by facilitating the immigration process and providing information to travellers. Infrastructure, particularly the 180 km route on the corridor, has been developed and renovated, thus making it faster for commodities and people to commute. Capacity building, especially language skill training and academic/student exchanges, can ensure more people mobility and connectivity. There are strong tendencies that the corridor will develop steadily and expand westward to the Bay of Bengal and link the Pacific Ocean to the Indian Ocean in the near future.

The Tanintharyi–Tanaosri region has high potential to become a strategic area for business and regional connectivity. Given the connecting border between the Tanintharyi region in Myanmar and the western part of Thailand with the advantage of linking the Andaman Sea and the Gulf of Thailand, these local entrepreneurs see opportunities to expand their existing businesses and to develop new ones. In view of the preceding context, Chapter 11, written by Suthiphand Chirathivat and Sineenat Sermcheep, presents primary survey results on Tanintharyi–Tanaosri business development. This chapter aims to find facts of business development through interviews with home-grown and well-versed entrepreneurs in both Thailand's Tanaosri and Myanmar's Tanintharyi regions. Whether they are first- or second-generation businesspersons doing business in the region, it is always interesting to learn how they started from scratch, evolved almost from nothing to build up successful business empires and solidly established all sorts of business activities despite their hardships and difficulties in the political and economic environment they had gone through years, more on Myanmar's side than on Thailand's side. While all the three entrepreneurs are operating their businesses, at least, in the scope between regions of the two countries, it is also interesting to know how they operated all kinds of activities and how they overcame barriers. The development of countries in this region, namely, Myanmar and Thailand, has contributed to further economic expansion of the region; as a result, this opens up more business opportunities for both countries.

The preceding chapters have reviewed various aspects of the Tanintharyi–Tanaosri region of Thailand and Myanmar with a focus on the Andaman Sea coastline in the context of Thailand–Myanmar relations and ASEAN connectivity. The final part of the book has Chapter 12 written by Charit Tingsabadh, Suthiphand Chirathivat and Prabir De, which presents conclusions and recommendations.

The book has carefully collated a number of dimensions that really shape up regional connectivity in ASEAN with a focus on Myanmar and Thailand. The chapters have incorporated valuable surveys of concerned literature on the respective subject matter covered, along with an in-depth analysis from existing evidence. This is a timely contribution, given the fact that ASEAN countries have been searching for new connectivity programmes that may lead to a rise in the region's competitiveness in the post COVID-19 period. In this COVID-19 era, countries are searching for new regional integration opportunities, where a stronger connectivity can not only strengthen the regional integration but also offer resilient economic recovery options. This book is an effort to understand this aspect for a better future for ASEAN as well as India.

PART I

HISTORY OF THE REGION

CHAPTER 2

CONNECTED HISTORIES

Notes towards an Understanding of Historical Relations between Lower Myanmar and Southern Thailand

Suchandra Ghosh

2.1. INTRODUCTION

Thailand and Myanmar are involved in a network of communications from very early times. In fact, as neighbouring countries, Thailand and Myanmar not only share a long border but also have a profoundly interrelated history. This network was much strengthened in and around the southern part of both the countries. The lineage of communication could be traced to linguistic commonality and, of course, Buddhism. Just as in the context of Association of Southeast Asian Nations (ASEAN) connectivity, the ASEAN Studies Center (ASC) at Chulalongkorn University is studying the potential impacts of links between the two countries so as to provide up-to-date information and support policymaking in the future. It is also possible to try and understand this linkage from a historical perspective.

The common cultural processes across Southeast Asia could be recognized with the help of a thorough study of the East–West Corridor. The choice of the region is from the Northern East–West Corridor to the Southern East–West Corridor. On the Myanmar side, we have Thaton and Mawlamyine in the north and Dawei in the south, which are major points of connectivity with Thailand. The Isthmus of Kra located to the south of the study area would also be a part of our larger study to understand the historical and cultural processes. It continued to be a coveted zone from the early 1st millennium CE to early 2nd millennium CE for the monarchs, merchants and monks. The linkage was guided to a certain extent by political considerations. We shall view the connected history from a few perspectives like Buddhism and the potentiality of the region for trade and artistic exchanges (Map 2.1).

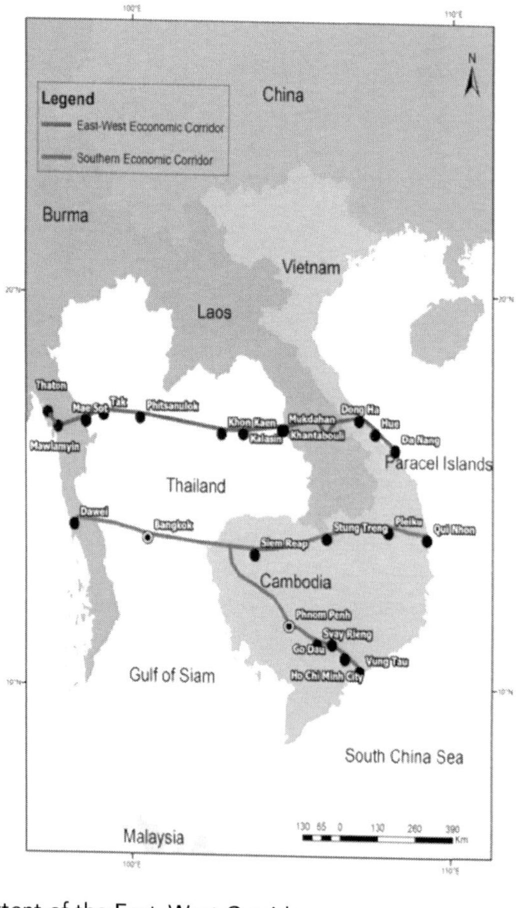

Map 2.1 Extent of the East–West Corridors

Source: The author.

Disclaimer: This figure has been redrawn by the author/s and is not to scale. It does not represent any authentic national or international boundaries and is used for illustrative purposes only.

2.2. IMPORTANT SITES IN LOWER MYANMAR ACROSS THE CORRIDOR

A significant site in the vicinity of the East–West Corridor near Mawlamyine was the place called Muttama or Martaban. The high Martaban range lies to its west. Reginald Le May mentions that in and around 2nd and 3rd century CE, Indians embarked at the port of Muttama. Some settled in the region of Thaton and the delta of the Thanlwin River and later on in the Ayeyarwady River near Bago. Others moved southwards through the Three Pagoda Pass into Siam (Le May 1954, 28–29). Thaton was a major centre of Buddhist thought and learning in lower Myanmar. Around the 5th century CE, we notice the presence of Mon Theravadin Buddhists at Thaton. It appears from archaeological context that Thaton witnessed continuous occupation and was reconstructed later.

According to a well-known inscription set up in Pegu in 1476 by Dhammacheti, the ruler of a Mon kingdom, in 1057 CE, King Aniruddha gathered together a community of priests and Pali texts from Thaton in Bagan and established the religion (Sasana; Ko 1892, 49).

Documentation of the sites by San Win and his team has led to finding of a number of stone tools and rings as well as incised black wares, which support a profile of Iron Age to mid-1st millennium CE habitation in the lowlands lying between Thaton and the Bilin egress into the Gulf of Muttama. The wave-like and criss-cross design on the pottery is similar to pieces from Sampanago (16.15 north× 97.20 east) some 20 km southwest of Thaton (Win 2005; Figure 2.1).

In Thailand, similar shards are seen at Ban Khu Mueang, Amphoe In Buri and Changwat Singburi. The Dvaravati site of Khubua also bears pottery similar to that found in Sampanago. By juxtaposing the legends and the available objects, Moore and Win (2014) offered us an understanding of the network of trade relations of the Mon State in and around late 1st and early 2nd millennium CE. Although limited physical remains have been found from Thaton, its importance in the Buddhist history of Myanmar cannot be denied. It was ideally suited to be a centre for new Buddhist visual imagery. In the opinion of Galloway (2010),

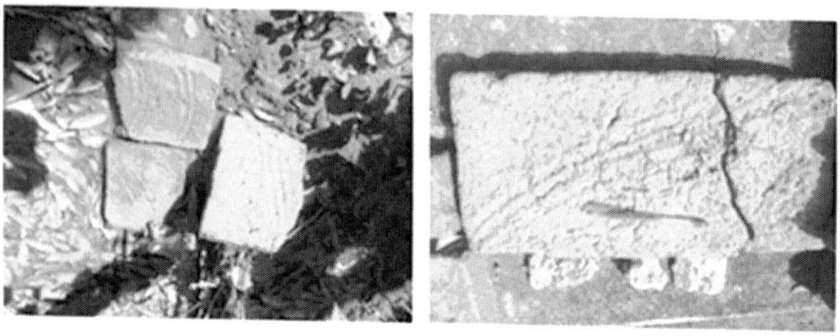

Figure 2.1 Finger-Marked Bricks from Thaton
Source: The author.

'From Thaton, these new visual repertoires could readily be dispersed both east and west where they were integrated into local styles.' Another piece of evidence that might support the view that Lower Burma was a recipient of religious practices from Pala, Kerala, India and the point of transfer of these practices eastward is a Pali chant preserved in Thailand, the verse on the eight great sites (*atthamahathana*), which are related to Buddha. The six lines of the chant begin with the word 'the first site is Lumbini where the blessed one was born, second is the ultimate tree of awakening' and ends with 'these are the great sites, I worship them from afar' (*ete attamahathane aham vandani durato*). This suggests that it was not necessary to visit in person, and it could be done mentally (Woodward 2017). Thaton also had contacts not only with Pagan but also with Bodhgaya. Thaton was located near the Gulf of Martaban, and Mon regions adjacent to the Gulf of Martaban were trading centres. Robert Wicks refers to this as numismatic connections as Mon-Pegu coins influenced Mon-Dvaravati coinage in Thailand. Coins were first introduced by the Mons in the Gulf of Martaban and the neighbouring regions. These coins were modelled on the coinage of the peninsular south. These initial coins were used as prototypes for the coinage issued by the eastern Mon kingdom of Thailand. Wicks (1985) thought that Thaton was likely the 'Mon cultural axis linking lower Burma with central Thailand'. Thaton has a large number of epigraphs and a plethora of art historical materials, particularly sculptures. A type of conch which is represented on the coins of Bago appears on the coins from

Kyontu (near Bago), Kyaikkatha (mouth of Sittaung) and some Dvaravati cultural sites in Thailand. However, these are not found on the coins from Pyu sites. A series of coins, called the Mon type, was underscored by Gutman (1978). These could be compared to those found from Nakhon Pathom. It is quite natural that the series had linkages with coins of neighbouring Thailand.

Thaton's importance in trade with early China is also evident from Chinese sources. It is important to note the celebrated passage in *Han Shu*. During the Yuan-Shih period of Emperor P'ing (1–6 CE) when Wang Mang was in power, the Chief Interpreter was sent on an imperial trade mission along the sea route to places identified as Sumatra, Thatung in Lower Burma, Pagan, Ceylon and Pulau Pisang on the southwestern end of the Malay Peninsula, taking gold and silk to exchange for pearls, beryl, curious stones and foreign exotic items. We are told that the 'trading boats of the barbarians which carried them from one place to another were also engaged in trade as well as in rapacity' making the venture very dangerous (Aung-Thwin 2005).

It took several years for these trading boats to return to China. They brought back large pearls that were almost two inches in circumference. The inclusion of 'Thatung' is significant in view of Aung-Thwin's research that no Chinese source includes reference to an 'independent kingdom or polity in Lower Burma before the very late thirteenth century' (Aung-Thwin 2005).

At the end of the Pagan period, a well-established pottery tradition prevailed in Lower Burma. By that time, in Central Burma, a glazing technique was well adopted. The ubiquitous Martaban jar received its name from Martaban that developed as a port and was well known for this kind of ceramic tradition (Figure 2.2).

Another site close to Muttama was Sampanago. According to Moore and Win (2014), the Muttama–Sampanago area includes coins, beads and finger-marked bricks. Such objects were also found in sites like Khu Bua, U Thong and early sites in Kanchanaburi. They can be dated between 6th and 9th century CE.

If we look at the political history of Martaban, we find that it was under the nominal control of the Sukhothai regime (1281–1314 CE) and under Ayutthaya roughly till the mid-15th century.

Figure 2.2 Martaban Jar

Source: The author.

Note: These jars continue to be produced with minor variations and thus cannot be properly dated.

The Martaban jars were very useful for storing condiments, water, alcohol, oil, and opium while on a long and arduous journey. Therefore, during the Ayutthayan rule when trading increased and Arab, Indian and later European merchants were frequent visitors, these jars helped them in storing commodities and carrying them in their next lap of travel.

During this period, the coastal region of the Salween River till the Isthmus of Kra was generally known as Martaban or Maritanao. The China–India porcelain trade under the Sung dynasty was gaining ground, and the two important ports on this coastline were Martaban and Mergui. From Ibn Batuta (1350 CE), we learn that a princess of Kaylukari (somewhere in Southeast Asia but not identified) gave him four 'Martabans or huge jars, filled with ginger, pepper, lemons and mangoes, all of them salted, prepared for sea voyages'. Ibn Batuta relates this even when he is talking about his journey from India to Sumatra and Java (Gibbs 1997, Chapter X, 280). One cannot but undermine the convenience of carrying useful commodities in these jars for long distance travelling both on land and over sea.

Here, we may refer to the fact that there was awareness about the potentiality of expanding trading networks down the Malay Peninsula, connecting Java and Sumatra and also along the Straits of Malacca among the southern Mon kingdoms. This gained further momentum as Kyanzittha (1084–1113) patronized the furthering of maritime interests. His appointed heir, Alaung-Sithu fostered this policy. They are praised in the Burmese chronicles for their journey across the ocean to Bengal, Sri Lanka and the Malay Peninsula.

Sidi Ali Reis, a Turkish Admiral and Commander of the Ottoman Indian Ocean Fleet, explains the name of the jars in his nautical handbook *Muhit* of 1554 during his stay in Gujarat: 'Because the porcelain Mertebans which comes to the land of Rams (Turkey) with preserves in them are produced in Merteban, a port in the province of Siam, people call them Mertebans' (Tibbetts 2002). Kalasapura, roughly identified with Martaban, is mentioned four times in a fragmentary epigraphic record from Srikshetra. In the opinion of D. C. Sircar, this could mean that there could have been a conquest or a distinctive relationship with the Pyus around the last part of the 7th century CE (Sircar 1976).

To be of economic or strategic use to the Pyus, Kalasapura would have been placed either near the mouth of the Salween River in the Martaban–Mawlamyine area or near the mouth of the Ayeyarwady. It is interesting to note that jars of the same type are still produced in Kyaukmyaung near Shwebo in upper Myanmar and used for storing water. According to Brigitte Borell, 'the potters are Mon, who were brought there as captives from the south in the mid-eighteenth century. These potters trace their origin to the Gulf of Martaban region, south of Mawlamyne' (Borell 2014).

Another significant site in Myanmar for connected history with Thailand is the site of Thagara at Dawei (Moore and Swe 2006). This section is largely drawn from their essay. Locally known as Myohaung or old city, Thagara is a large mound (c. 1,600 m × 1,100 m) that has access to the Dawei River and the Andaman Sea. The site was founded in 754 CE (116 ME), and we know about the site from the Dawei chronicles. The sea could be approached via a mountain pass, and access to the river was via a stream called the Padat Chaung on the south of the walled site. A substantial number of archaeological objects such as beads, glazed pots and bronzes were found at the site of Kayat Pyin cultivation area on the east of Thagara.

Dawei had a very alluring location and thus was attractive not only to the dominant powers of Upper Myanmar but also to Lower Myanmar and Thailand. We have another city called Weidi which was founded in 1390 CE (752 ME). Its location is significant since it is along the estuary of the Dawei River, which separated the peninsula from the mainland side connecting to Thailand.

Linkages between Thagara at Dawei and sites of Dvaravati culture and maritime polities of Sumatra and Java are evident if we study the objects; here, the case in point could be the images of Buddha (Figure 2.3), beads, urns and pots (Figure 2.4).

According to Elizabeth Moore, 'The word "Dawei" refers to the city, the region and the local dialect, a highly intonated variant of Tibeto-Burman of unknown antiquity. Dawei is both hybrid and borderland, its Buddhistic culture a stylistic and territorial puzzle.' Products of Burmese kiln, like white wares with green designs,

Figure 2.3 Buddha Heads at Thagara

Source: Author's own with courtesy Elizabeth Moore.

Dawei Glazed Vessel

A glazed vessel, possibly linked to Tak production of a somewhat later period, is a globular flat-bottomed vessel made of red clay, with a pale greenish yellow glaze (18 cm height, 8.5 cm diameter). The vessel is ovoid with the body of a small mammal draped over the top.

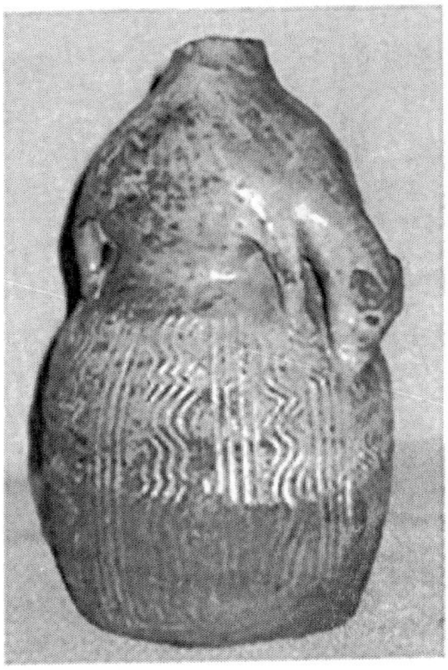

Figure 2.4 Pottery at Thagara

Source: Author's own with courtesy Elizabeth Moore.

were recovered from Thailand in Tak province. In the numismatic domain, a speciality of Dawei was the use of large tin and lead coins. These were abundantly found as there was a source of tin in Tavoy. These coins continued for several centuries, which indicates the development of international trade. From later records, we learn that the source of iron was the mountains between Myanmar and Thailand. There were villages near Tavoy where artisans knew how to process iron and tin to prepare alloys.

A vessel with clear analogies in Thailand that was used as a water-pouring vessel in the shape of a hunched man (8 cm) with a long knot of hair toting a sack was associated exclusively with Sawankhalok (Si Satchanalai) in the 15th–16th century CE. It is clearly evident from the artefacts recovered from Dawei that it was an important port having connections with other ports. In the cultural sphere, Dawei retained its uniqueness (Moore 2011).

2.3. THE POTENTIALITY OF THE REGION FOR RICH TRADE

The East–West Corridor also flourished as there was a great international demand for forest products and tin and some of the areas of the corridor were home to these items. One of the important forest products was aloes wood (also known as gharuwood or eaglewood). It had a fragrant resin. Around the 10th century, this wood became very popular in China as it was used as a perfume, medicine and ritual item in Buddhist ritual practices. It acted as a pain reliever when mixed with wine; as an ointment, it soothed cuts and open sores. It is believed that the smoke of burnt aloes wood cured wounds and ulcers. It appears that only camphor could surpass it as a coveted fragrance in China

Chau Ju-kua speaks of the gharuwoods imported from countries of Southeast Asia, and he gives an interesting classification of the best gharuwood based on the quality of the product (Hirth and Rockhill 1912). Thus, the coastal polities which produced aloes wood could accumulate a lot of wealth through this particular forest product (Ghosh 2014).

Gharuwood is found at Tenasserim in the south, which was a large region connected to the Chao Phraya plain at the Maeklong river running south along the coast until it reached Phanang Tak in Chumphon province. The Kalasin region in Thailand is also rich in gharuwood. The forest goods were transported through an intricate network of routes from the inland sites to the coast. There were passes across the Tenasserim (Tanaosri), which were used as ways of transportation across places. In this context, the Maritime Silk Route is important. It comprised a web of coastal and inland polities connected to each other through a network of port towns across the Bay of Bengal or eastern Indian Ocean and the South China Sea. Among the port towns, Dawei and the Myeik–Tanintharyi areas were perhaps important ports of call for providing commodities such as tin, lead and iron.

To the south, around Myeik (Mergui), Tanintharyi (Tenasserim) and the many islands off the coast, an early trading settlement is also indicated by the mention of minerals such as tin, lead and iron. Although finger-marked bricks have not been found, wall remains from the old port at Tanintharyi, are mentioned in 6th century CE Chinese records. Both Dawei and the Myeik–Tanintharyi areas would have been ports of call on a 'Maritime Silk Route'. Tin was an important item of trade in Thailand. The tin-bearing granite of Thailand lies in an arc of Southeast Asian metallogenetic province. The major part of this province extends from north Myanmar via peninsular Myanmar, Thailand and peninsular Malaysia to the tin islands of Indonesia. In Thailand, Phuket, Takua Pa and Ranong are the major producers of the country (Puwakool 1979). These places perhaps exported tin to Bengal, southeastern Bengal to be precise. There were profuse bronze sculptures in southeastern Bengal (present day Kumilla and Chittagong in Bangladesh). However, there was no tin production centre in the region, which was necessary for bronze. Thus, it can be assumed that there was import of tin from the tin-producing areas in the upper part of the Thai-Malay peninsula. Thus, tin was an important trading item along the trans-Asiatic route.

This could have been an incentive to vie for the control of the region around the Isthmus of Kra. Put differently, the desire to politically include the Isthmian region within their domain emanated from the fact that this would give them direct access to the vast resources. The hinterlands of the peninsula were the sources of many of the ingredients—aromatic woods and fragrances—used in Brahmanical and Buddhist rituals (Ghosh 2016a). Perhaps southeastern Bengal received its share of tin for making bronze images from Lower Myanmar and Peninsular Thailand.

2.4. THE ISTHMIAN TRACT

The area of investigation of this project encompasses Ranong that is located in the Isthmian tract (Map 2.2).

It will be worthwhile to talk about the Isthmian tract in the past. The Isthmus of Kra is the narrow neck of land linking the present-day Thailand with Malaysia; it is positioned between the Andaman Sea and the Gulf of Thailand and formed a part of the well-defined 'voyaging corridor', as suggested by Andaya, that stretched from southern India to South Vietnam (Andaya and Andaya 2014). It forms a border between Thailand and Myanmar

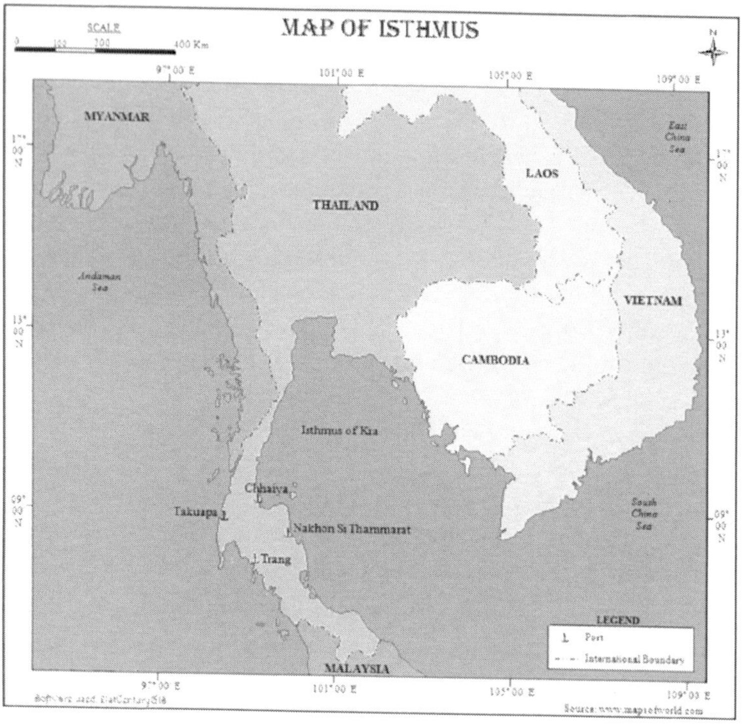

Map 2.2 The Isthmian Tract

Source: The author.

Disclaimer: This figure has been redrawn by the author/s and is not to scale. It does not represent any authentic national or international boundaries and is used for illustrative purposes only.

and a communication passage across Kra Buri, which is on the western side of the Gulf of Thailand in Chumphon province.

Situated in a strategic location between oceans, the Isthmian tract provided a halting place for traders from both directions. It is called 'crossroads of civilizations' as it has seen the presence of communities from India, Sri Lanka, Lower Myanmar, northern Sumatra, Lower Mekong (which includes the present-day Cambodia and parts of southern Vietnam), etc., and it forms a part of the extremely complex trading networks that stretched from the Mediterranean Sea to the Chinese coasts. The region around the Isthmus not only grew as a viable maritime trading zone, but it was also an important centre of Buddhist network that saw a transition from *Mahayana* to *Theravada* Buddhism around 12th century CE. The maritime and Buddhist networks provide the window to comprehend the importance of the areas around the Isthmian tract as an independent region coveted by the competing powers of Southeast Asia. In other words, as the region was dependent on trade for survival and prosperity, its emergence as an important region is linked to international maritime trade. Control of trade appears to have provided the key to political developments.

Competing powers struggled to get control of the Isthmus during the 1st millennium CE primarily for its easy east–west connectivity and for its rich natural resources that formed a part of the precious commodities in the network of exchange. Moreover, there was an exchange of ideas, rituals and technology that fostered a sense of community. Around the 11th century, in the west coast, the Burmese were gradually taking control of the region around Takua Pa, though Tambralinga was the limit on the east coast. The regional route of north Bay of Bengal was under the command of the Burmese. Considering the territorial and commercial importance of the coastal polities, Aniruddha (Anawratha), king of Pagan (c. 1044–1077 CE), embarked upon a series of campaigns to get control of Lower Burma and succeeded in getting Khabin, Pegu, Thaton, Mergui, Tenasserim and beyond. The port of Takua Pa perhaps went under Burmese control. Hall (2011, 218) writes, 'King Anawratha followed his conquest of the coasts by moving his armies south to Mergui, and from Mergui, the Burmese forces may have crossed the Isthmus and extended their control south to Takua Pa'. By dint of being a 'voyaging corridor', the importance of the Isthmus of Kra reached such a level that the region entered into a process of interaction with countries like Myanmar and southeastern Bengal on one side and Cambodia on the other side. In the 11th century, the above-mentioned interaction created a web of communication between Lower Burma and western coast of the Malay Peninsula with the eastern coast of India and Sri Lanka.

Lower Myanmar and Thailand were linked by three routes: the riverine route between Martaban and Haripunjaya, another from the Gulf of Martaban over Tak and Mae Sot, and a route over the Three Pagodas Pass to Kanchanaburi, Ratchaburi and Phetburi. In northwest Thailand, the Khmer garrison towns, namely Si Satchanalai, Sukhothai, Phitsanulok and Kamphaeng Phet, were becoming, by the 12th century, centres of silk and ceramic manufacturing that were finding an outlet in Martaban.

Two states, namely P'an-p'an and Tan-tan, are known to have provided the Chinese with Buddhist relics, leaves of the Bo tree, ivory and miniature painted stupas, sandalwood and incense as part of the trade in religious wares (Hay 2002). Such products would have travelled across the Peninsula by one of the several routes: down the Trang River valley, used as a Trans-Peninsular gateway, or along the trade route from Takua Pa across the Isthmus through Wieng Sra to Tambralinga, possibly part of P'an-p'an (Wheatley 1961, 291). In the following period, jungle products replaced these sacred objects as the main items for the Chinese market. On the basis of this international trade by the early 7th century, the peninsular 'city-states' had established their economic well-being. Wheatley's and Wang Gungwu's analyses of the evidence on these city-states during what the former has termed the 'Isthmian Age' suggests that they clustered around the coastal plains and river estuaries in the north of the Peninsula. The administration is thought to have been theocratic, imbued with Indian notions of kingship and rituals in support of a court, but hardly touching the lives of the people at large, the majority of whom were fishermen, rice farmers and collectors of jungle produce. The west coast settlements supported mining communities and cosmopolitan merchant enclaves.

Tun-sun is thought to have been a federation of five chiefdoms; others such as Kedah (Kalah), Takola and Langkasuka built their wealth from the control of the sea, but did not extend their suzerainty over all their neighbours.

2.5. BUDDHISM: AN AGENCY FOR CULTURAL LINKAGES

It will be worthwhile to mention the immense possibilities of cultural transactions among communities along with exchanges of commercial commodities, where ritual requirements complement economic needs. Buddhist networks provided such possibilities. Importance of images in the social life of Buddhism hardly needs to be reiterated. Sculptures made in stone and bronze, clay moulds

Figure 2.5 Clay Buddha Tablets at Kawgun Caves

Source: The author.

(often called votive tablets) with images of Buddha and Bodhisattvas and miniature stupas have been discovered in the cave sites and other archaeological sites of Myanmar and Peninsular Thailand. The area near Thaton yielded many clay-moulded tablets. In the Southeast Asian context, Buddhism was gradually being embedded in the society around the East–West Corridor and Isthmus of Kra (Ghosh 2016b). In Lower Myanmar, near Mawlamyine, we have the Kawgun caves where we have representations of Buddhist clay tablets (Figure 2.5). These objects are important for understanding Buddhist interactions across Asia. Tablets from Lower Myanmar and Khon Kaen region of Thailand have similarities in iconography.

An artefact known as sema stone that acts as a boundary marker in sacred Buddhist spaces was located in northeastern Thailand. In fact, the Khorat plateau bore the first archaeological evidence of such boundary markers. This has been studied extensively by Stephen Murphy who feels that these could be traced back to the origins of the religion in the region (Murphy 2014). They are dated during the Dvaravati cultural period (c. 7th–12th centuries CE; Figure 2.6).

They date from the 7th to 12th century CE, a chronological time span known in scholarship as the Dvaravati Period. In Lower Myanmar, the semas from Kalyani Sima at Thaton are finely carved with Buddhist narrative scenes of *Jataka* tales. Buddhist narrative scenes from the *Jatakas* are also represented in the sites of Muang Fa Daet. The motifs depicted compare favourably

Figure 2.6 Boundary Stones with Buddha Figures

Source: The author.

between the two regions. Thus, there is a similarity in the narrative content, but the style and compositions from northeast Thailand differ quite significantly from those at Thaton (Murphy 2014). It can be argued that the movement of motif or theme happened through the Northern East–West Corridor which was definitely active then. There might not be a direct contact between the artists, but the two regions shared similar Buddhist religious traditions (Figure 2.7); moreover, with the movement of people through the corridor, there were also exchanges of stories and ideas. The common *Jataka* stories are that of the *Mahajanakajataka*, the *Vidhura Pandita Jataka* and the *Vessantara Jataka*.

In terms of artistic exchange, the boundaries were blurred. We can take the example of Thaton from our study area. In the artistic domain, the connection between the late 'Dvaravati' sites and Thaton could be perceived. Here, we are drawing from the studies of Gutman (1978). A popular motif in the Dvaravati art of Thailand and the art of Lower Burma is the descent of the Buddha from *Tavatimsa* heaven. This refers to the time, when

Northeast Thailand

Bronze Buddha from Lower Myanmar

Figure 2.7 The Mon Connection: Similarities in Buddha Images between Northeast Thailand and Lower Myanmar

Source: The author.

after his Enlightenment, the Buddha ascended to the Heaven of the Thirty-three Gods to preach to them and to his mother Maya (who after her early death had been reborn there). After converting his mother and the gods who dwelled in *Tavatimsa*, he descended again to earth. He is nearly always depicted as having Indra to his right and Brahma to his left, the two gods who accompanied him on his descent. The descent of this triad symbolizes the incorporation and subjugation of Hindu traditions by Buddhism. Indra, the king of the gods, resided with them on the summit of Mount Meru, the mountain at the centre of the universe. Brahma, the supreme creator, is paired with Indra to emphasize the submission of the whole universe to the Buddha.

We may describe one image found at Thaton which depicts, in high relief, the Buddha, his face and headdress mutilated, standing with the right knee raised and the leg flexed, the torso bent towards the left hip in an exaggerated *tribhanga* movement, suggesting that he is walking. His right arm bends to the right shoulder, palm facing outwards, suggestive of the *vitarkamudra*, while the left arm is held out by his side, the hand again facing out. Two long garments hang open with pointed ends conspicuous near the ankles, the folds on the left side meticulously depicted, foreshadowing the style adopted in Pagan and Sukhothai. A decorated panel falls between the legs. He wears royal ornaments: a wide necklace, armlets and an ornate belt. On either side stands a much smaller figure. A haloed Indra on his right stands in a pose similar to the central figure and wears similar garments. The four-faced Brahma, who also has a halo, stands to his left, wearing a tall ornate headdress and large ear ornaments, a *dhoti*-like lower garment held with a decorative belt. Both the attendant gods, while smaller than the Buddha, come to the navel height, in contrast to the Pala type, where they merely reach mid-thigh, perhaps reflecting greater importance placed on them in Lower Burma (and Thailand). Above Brahma and Indra, on the upper section of the back-slab and in low relief are crowned figures in the attitude of obeisance seated on triple-lotus thrones mounted on pillars. Similar smaller figures sit on either side of them. These are dwellers in the *Brahmaloka* and *Devaloka* heavens from where the Buddha descends. Their pillar-mounted thrones recall similar renditions on late Dvaravati steles.

Commonality in the design of the clay-moulded tablets can be seen (Figure 2.8). Rounded clay tablets, often called votive tablets of various types (more than hundred) were recorded from the site of Winka. One type (Buddha seated within a temple structure) is common to a few recovered from Chula Pathom Chedi in Nakhon

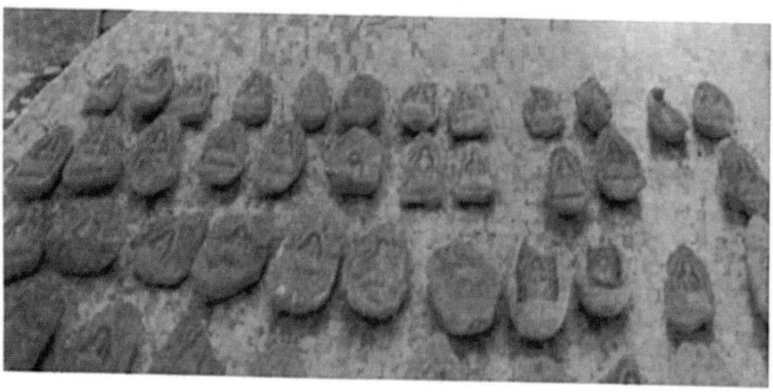

Figure 2.8 Votive Tablets Found at a Monastery in Lower Burma, Near Mawlamyine

Source: The author.

Pathom and to the one found in the Kawgun cave. Since there is a strong connection between Mon Dvaravati in neighbouring Thailand and Mon population in the area concerned, the similarity in the design of the tablets is not surprising.

2.6. CONCLUDING REMARKS

Trade routes demonstrate flow of commodities and people. This flow did not follow a single pattern or way. Reconstructing a trade route is not an easy job. One has to take into consideration a variety of sources which include epigraphy, art historical, textual and archaeological, to understand the dynamic process of trade and the route through which it functioned.

The disparate examples of threads of commonality in art, rituals and use of certain products for economic needs in a given region encompassing two countries indisputably lead us to routes, movements and mobility. Evidently, these were active routes of communication. The oldest sites in Southeast Asia where archaeologists have found evidence of contact with both China and India lie in the territory of modern Thailand. The oldest is in western Thailand at Ban Don Ta Phet where radio carbon dates cluster in the period 390–360 BCE. We learn from archaeological findings that carnelian beads were found from the Samon valley near Mandalay to Ban Don Ta Phet and Khuan Lukpad in Thailand. Actually, many unfinished beads have been found in a corridor from the Samon valley to Mawlamyine in Southeast Myanmar, and it is probable that from Mawlamyine, these reached further into Thailand. Another archaeological site from the other end of the spatial spectrum is Khao Sam Kaeo located in the upper Thai-Malay Peninsula(Bellina, 2017). Findings from this site indicate both inland and maritime exchange involving the use of complex technology in glass and hard stone working. The array of archaeological finds demonstrates that a swath of mainland Southeast Asia from Lower Myanmar to the eastern part of Thailand was already a crossroad of trade. For the Isthmus of Kra route, we have many sources. For the East–West Corridor, our sources from the past are limited. But even with limited sources, it is possible to weave in a story of the past movements across these multiple routes. If we consider the dispersed archaeological sources mentioned in this essay, the picture that emerges is that of regular movement from Lower Myanmar to central and possibly southern Thailand. Regarding the location of urban centres in Thailand across this corridor, the study of cultural heritage via satellite imagery also corroborates the archaeological findings. There were widespread cultural and economic exchanges through this corridor. The synergies of maritime, riverine and overland interchange between lower Myanmar and Thailand in the past cannot be lost sight of. This chapter has concentrated only on the study area of the project. Further study can be extended to understand the implication of the network in the context of South Asia.

REFERENCES

Andaya, B. W., and L. Y. Andaya. 2014. 'The "Sea of Malayu": An Ocean Perspective on Early Southeast Asian History'. In *The Dynamics of Cultural Counterpoints in Asian Studies*, edited by David Jones and Michel Marion, 208. New York: SUNY Press.

Aung-Thwin, Michael. 2005. *Mists of Ramanna: The Legend That Was Lower Burma*. Hawaii: University of Hawaii Press.

Bellina, Berenice, ed. 2017. *Khao Sam Kaeo, An Early Port-City between the Indian Ocean and the South China Sea*. Paris: Ecole Francaise D'Extreme-Orient.

Borell, Brigitte. 2014. 'A True Martaban Jar: A Burmese Ceramic Jar in the Ethnological Museum in Hydelberg in Germany'. *Artibus Asiae* LXXIV, no. 2: 257–297.

Galloway, Charlotte. 2010. 'Ways of Seeing a Pyu, Mon and Dvaravati Artistic Continuum'. *Bulletin of the Indo-Pacific Prehistory Association* 30, no. 76: 70–78.

Ghosh, Suchandra. 2014. 'South-East Asia and the Eastern Sea Board of India through the Lens of Zhao Rugua'. In *Convergence: Rethinking India's Past*, edited by Radhika Seshan, 41–54. Delhi: Primus Books.

———. 2016a. 'Early Peninsular Thailand and Eastern India (Including Bangladesh): Understanding the Buddhist Milieu through an Archaeological Lens'. In *Interpretative Studies on Southeast Asian Culture*, edited by Withaya Sucharithanarugse, 227–245. Bangkok: Institute of Thai Studies, Chulalongkorn University.

———. 2016b. Between the Oceans: The Isthmian Tract, Cross Roads of Civilizations between East and West. *Journal of Indian Ocean Archaeology* 12: 117–128.

Gibbs, H. A. R., trans. 1997. *Travels in Asia and Africa* (reprint). New Delhi: Asia Educational Services.

Gutman, Pamela. 1978. 'The Ancient Coinage of Southeast Asia'. *Journal of the Siam Society* 66, no. 1: 8–21.

Hall, Kenneth R. 2011. *A History of Early Southeast Asia, Maritime Trade and Societal Development, 100–1500.* Plymouth: Rowman and Littlefield Publishers.

Hay, Stuart Munro. 2002. *Nakhon Sri Thammarat: The Archaeology, History and Legends of a Southern Thai Town.* Bangkok: White Lotus.

Hirth, Frederic, and W. W. Rockhill, ed. and trans. 1912. *Chau Ju-kua: His Work on the Chinese and Arab Trade in the Twelfth and Thirteenth Centuries*, Entitled Chu-fan-chih. St. Petersburg: Imperial Academy of Sciences.

Ko, Taw Sein. 1892. *The Kalyani Inscriptions Erected by King Dhammaceti at Pegu in 1476 A.D.: Text and Translation.* Rangoon: Government Printing.

Le May, Reginald. 1954. *Culture of Southeast Asia.* London: George Allens Union.

Moore, Elizabeth. 2011. 'Dawei Buddhis Culture: A Hybrid Borderland'. *Myanmar Historical Research Journal* 21 (June): 1–62.

Moore, E and Than Swe, 2006. 'Early Walled Sites of Dawei, Thagara and Mokti', In Uncovering Southeast Asia's Past, edited by L. Bacus, I. Glover, V.Piggott, Singapore:Singapore National University Press, pp.271-282.

Moore, Elizabeth H., and San Win. 2014. 'Sampanago: City of Serpents and Muttama (Martaban)'. In *Before Siam, Essays in Art and Archaeology*, edited by Nicolas Revire and Stephen A. Murphy, 217–237. Bangkok: River Books and The Siam Society.

Murphy, Stephen A. 2014. 'Sema Stones in Lower Myanmar and Northeast Thailand: A Comparison'. In *Before Siam, Essays in Art and Archaeology*, edited by Nicolas Revire and Stephen A. Murphy, 353–371. Bangkok: River Books and The Siam Society.

Puwakool, Suchit. 1979. 'Review of the Potential and Exploration of Tin in Thailand'. *Bulletin of the Geological Society of Malaysia* 11: 323–331.

Sircar, D. C. 1976. 'Indological Notes. 21: R.C. Majumdar's Chronology of the Pāla Kings. 22: Two Inscriptions from Prome and Vesali in Burma'. *Journal of Ancient Indian History* 9: 200–218.

Thai Ministry of Science and Technology. 2017. *Thai Heritage from Space.* Bangkok: Geo-Informatics and Space Technology Development Agency, 240–291.

Tibbetts, G. R. 2002. *A Study of the Arabic Texts Containing Material on South-East Asia*. London: Routledge.

Wheatley, Paul. 1961. *The Golden Khersonese: Studies in the Historical Geography of the Malay Peninsula before A.D. 1500*. Kuala Lumpur: University of Malaya Press.

Wicks, Robert S. 1985. 'The Ancient Coinage of Mainland Southeast Asia'. *Journal of Southeast Asian Studies* 16, no. 2: 195–225.

Win, San. 2005. 'The History of Suvannabhumi in Kyaikto and Bilin Townships, Mon State: Results from fieldwork 27 April–07 June 2001 (in Myanmar)'. In *Myanmar Historical Commission Golden Jubilee Collected Articles*, 258–285. Yangon: Ministry of Education.

Woodward, Hiram. 2017. 'Image and Text in Eleventh-Century Burma'. In *India and Southeast Asia: Cultural Discourses*, edited by Anna L. Dallapiccola and Anila Verghese, 98–124. Mumbai: The K. R. Cama Oriental Institute.

CHAPTER 3

THE TRANS-PENINSULA ROUTE*

Myeik–Prachuap Khiri Khan

Thiva Supajanya

3.1. INTRODUCTION

The Trans-Peninsula Route, which is also known as Myeik–Prachuap Khiri Khan (TPR-MP), is a communication route connecting the two great oceans—the Indian Ocean in the west and the Pacific Ocean in the east. It straddles the middle part of the Tenasserim Region, which lies at the upper part of the Indo-China Peninsula (also known as the Southeast Asian Peninsula). It covers the area from the Isthmus of Kra, the narrowest part of the peninsula, where the Kraburi River flows into the Andaman Sea, northwards to the Chao Phraya River plains. Here, the route connecting the Gulf of Thailand to the Andaman Sea at Dawei has been an important communication route for trade and military strategy from ancient times. At present, the route is being revived as part of the national development project to connect the Eastern Economic Corridor (EEC) and the Western Economic Corridor (WEC). An industrial estate will also be developed as part of the project. This will be the fourth time of settlement in the area. Evidence of past developments can be seen at the Prasat Muang Singh Historical Park, Kanchanaburi Province (Map 3.1, Figure 3.1), which is a walled and moated city on the eastern bank of the Khwae Noi River

* This chapter is translated by Charit Tingsabadh.

Map 3.1 Prasat Muang Singh on Trans-Peninsula Route: 'Dawei–Kanchanaburi–Ratchaburi'

Source: The author.

Disclaimer: This figure has been redrawn by the author/s and is not to scale. It does not represent any authentic national or international boundaries and is used for illustrative purposes only.

Figure 3.1 Plan of the Town of 'Prasat Muang Singh'

Source: The author.

on the mountain pass over the Tanaosri Mountain Range to the Andaman Sea at Dawei, and the route along the Khwae Noi River northward through the Three Pagodas Pass to Mottama. The first settlement period was the human settlement, the second was the construction of the city's wall and moat and the third was the expansion of the city wall and the construction of a stone temple at the centre of the city. On the old city wall and moat stands a stone statue of King Jayavarman VII, 1724–1762 BE, as the Avalokiteswara Bodhisattva. The TPR will thus be the fourth wave of development.

3.2. Strategic Significance

The Tenasserim Region has the Tanaosri Mountain range running north—south down to the Isthmus of Kra as the watershed acts as a dividing line marking the boundary between Myanmar, sloping down to the Andaman Sea to the west, and Thailand, sloping down to the east to the Gulf of Thailand. In Myanmar, the Tanaosri River flows in the Dawei watershed parallel to the mountain from the west of Dawei town to the sea at Marid (Myeik in Myanmar language). The river is joined at Tanaosri town by the Little Tanaosri River, which flows from the south. The town of Tanaosri was an important town of Thailand in the Sukhothai–Ayutthaya periods (Map 3.2).

The TPR-MP route is an important trade and strategic military communication route connecting the two towns and the oceans on either side—Myeik to the west on the Indian Ocean and Prachuap Khiri Khan town on the Pacific coast in the east.

'Muang Marid' (Myeik in Myanmar language) is a Thai name that appears in documents from Sukhothai and Ayutthaya periods. The foreign name 'Mergui' is used in ancient maps and on the internet today, as in the 'Mergui Archipelago'. It is believed that the old Thai name sounds like 'Muang Gui', which is the Guiburi district located about 30 km north from Prachuap town. Maps label this part of the peninsula as 'Kui'. The 'Kui people' in the northeast region of Thailand are skilled in handling elephants, and this region is a habitat for many elephants, so much so that it was a major port for sending elephants to India for a long time in the past. The name is common between the two sides of the peninsula. The word 'Kui' also means a 'port'.

Map 3.2 The Tenasserim Region

Source: The author.

Disclaimer: This figure has been redrawn by the author/s and is not to scale. It does not represent any authentic national or international boundaries and is used for illustrative purposes only.

In terms of geography, Marid town is located at the estuary of the Tanaosri River. With many islands situated across the bay area, Marid suffered little damage during the tsunami. It is suitable as a port and it has been the case in the past. When it was a river port, ships could travel up to Tanaosri town, which was the administrative centre located hundreds of kilometers inland.

Marid has a long history as a port city on the Trans-Peninsula Marid–Prachuap route. From the documents related to the founding of Marid town, it was a walled and moated city on the right bank of the Tanaosri River, located downstream from Tanaosri town at 7.5 km. The wall and the moat are round in shape for storing water around the raised ground. It is a pre-Buddhist era town, and its importance declined when Tanaosri town, at the confluence of the Tanaosri and the Little Tanaosri Rivers, built city walls and moats with a rectangular shape with rounded corners and became a strong administrative centre. A governor ruled over the region under the influence of Thai, Myanmar and British governments.

During the reign of the Thai King Narai, (2199–2231 BE), Marid was an important port city on the Andaman coast for the Ayutthaya kingdom, trading with places overseas in the Indian Ocean through the Trans-Peninsular Myeik-Prachuap route. The city declined with the decline of the Ayutthaya kingdom until the Burmese invasion in 2310 BE. Before that time, the coming of King Alaungpaya in 2302 BE saw Myanmar spread its influence down the Andaman coast until it captured Marid and sent an army marching on the TPR to subdue towns on the Gulf of Thailand and lay siege on Ayutthaya. The Myanmar king died from an accident in the battle, when a canon that was used to bombard the Ayutthaya city wall exploded and killed him. Marid was ruled by the British when Myanmar became a British colony (2367–2491 BE). Throughout this period, Marid was an important trading and strategic military centre for the British, which was independently administered from the rest of Myanmar, with the idea of occupying the Andaman coastline from Myanmar to Malaysia. It was also an important centre when the boundary line between Myanmar and Thailand was drawn up, under the Bowring Treaty (2411 BE).

'Muang Prachuap Khiri Khan' was the name given to the Thai end of the TPR. King Rama IV saw the importance of establishing the communication along the Gulf of Thailand coast, from Koh Kong at the eastern end of the Gulf of Thailand (now in Cambodia) to this town. The pair of city names, Prachuap Khiri Khan and Prachan Khiri Khet, were bestowed on these places. Other names for Prachuap are 'Narang', which means deserted fields; Koh Lak, the bay where the Koh Lak Island is located; Klong Pla Wan or Hua Wan, now the district of Klong Wan, lying further south; and Bang Nang Rom, after the waterway that flows into Prachuap bay. The location of the town was given by the order of King Rama II, as a defence post against enemies coming through from the Singkhon Pass (Map 3.3).

The geomorphology of Prachuap Khiri Khan, which covers the Muang district of Prachuap province and measures 860 sq. km in area, is a narrow strip of land between the Gulf of Thailand coastline and the Tanaosri mountain range, and it serves as the border between Thailand and Myanmar. The narrowest part measures 11 km and the widest is 22 km, extending down the

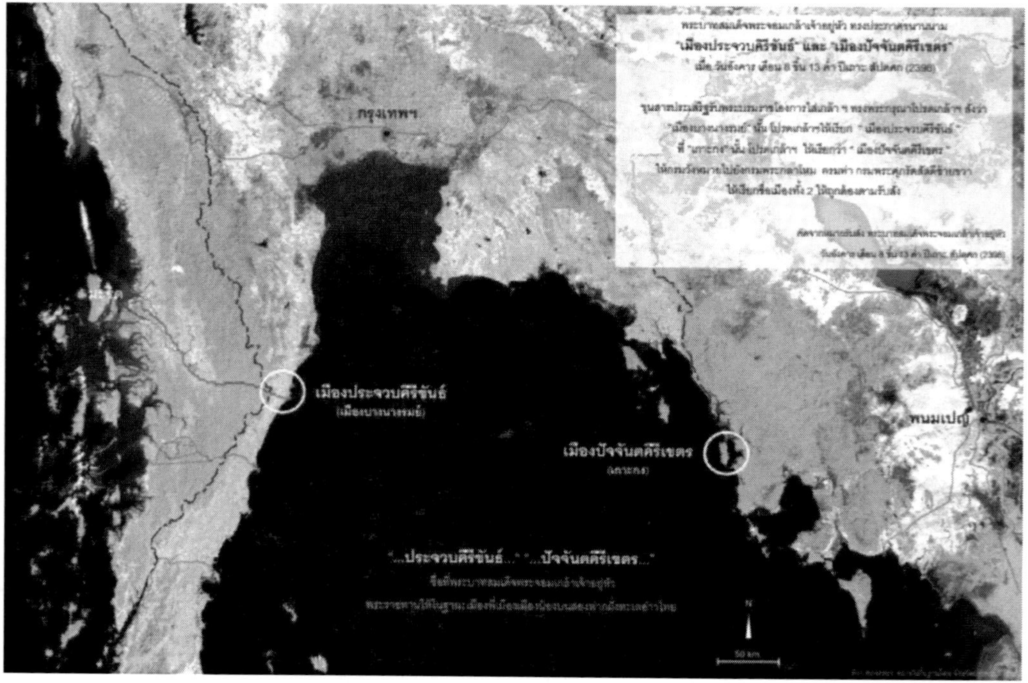

Map 3.3 Muang Prachuap Khiri Khan (Bang Nang Rom) and Prachan Khiri Khet (Koh Kong)

Source: The author.

Disclaimer: This figure has been redrawn by the author/s and is not to scale. It does not represent any authentic national or international boundaries and is used for illustrative purposes only.

coast for 67.5 km. Prachuap has a popular name of 'the Three-bay City' as it is bestowed with an amazing coastline made up of three beautiful bays, namely, the Ao Noi, Ao Koh Lak or Ao Prachuap and Ao Manao. Each bay is separated by a sandy ridge reaching till the rocks at the seafront, which were once islands in the sea. The hill to the north of Ao Koh Lak or Ao Prachuap is called 'Khao Ta Mong Lai', and the hill to the south is called 'Khao Lom Muak'. The cape area is the location of Squadron 5 of the Royal Thai Air Force, and the other end has a small island shaped like Chinese whiskers, where there is a small shrine with a statue of the Chinese king. Based on old local legends, the Ta Mong Lai tale reflects the port function of the city, with the names assigned to the different landmarks for navigation purposes. The important one mentioned is the 'Nang Yom Doy', a beautiful girl that foreign seamen long to see (Map 3.4).

To the south is Ao Manao, which is the base for Air Squadron 5. It is a semi-circular bay, like a split lemon. It serves as a recreational area for the families of air force people and is open to the public to support tourism in the province. It has won awards for good site management from the Tourism Authority of Thailand (TAT) and aims to reach the standards of the Association of Southeast Asian Nations (ASEAN) management in the future.

In summary, it can be said that the TPR-MP route is an important trade and strategic route connecting the two sides, the Indian Ocean to the west and the Pacific Ocean to the east, located at about the middle of the Indo-China Peninsula. Historical and archaeological evidence confirms our understanding that this route is an important connecting route even before the Buddhist era to the present. Historical evidence shows settlements along the coastline, located in relation to the TPR. This is evident from the walled and moated cities of Mow Tone, Tanaosri and Singkhon, located along the TPR (Map 3.5), and from the maps recorded in the annals; foreign visitors' accounts; Thai literature such as the *Khun Chang Khun Phaen* tale, which mentions the Simok horse at Tanaosri town; journals of ambassadors to Thailand; and the story of the English adventure 'Samuel White' who was promised the post of Prime Minister if his plot was successful.

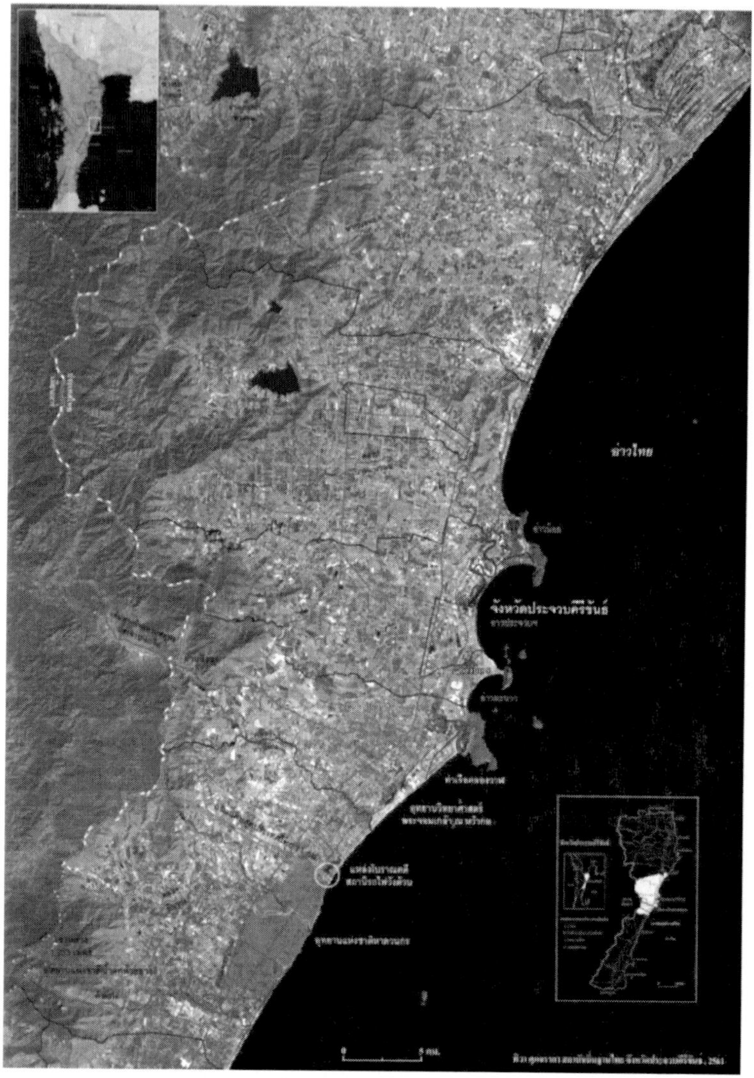

Map 3.4 Muang District of Prachuap Province

Source: The author.

Disclaimer: This figure has been redrawn by the author/s and is not to scale. It does not represent any authentic national or international boundaries and is used for illustrative purposes only.

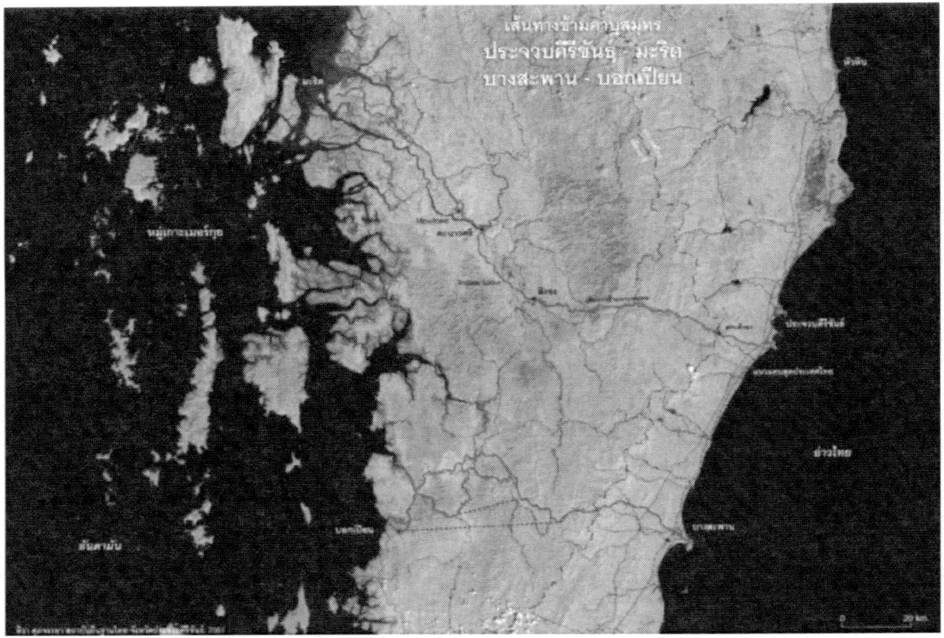

Map 3.5 Trans-Peninsula Route: 'Myeik–Prachuap Khiri Khan'

Source: The author.

Disclaimer: This figure has been redrawn by the author/s and is not to scale. It does not represent any authentic national or international boundaries and is used for illustrative purposes only.

The area around Ban Wang Duan, where the railway station Wang Duan is located, is the narrowest part of Thailand, which measures only 11 km across from the coastline to the Myanmar–Thailand border on the Tanaosri watershed line (Figure 3.2). Here, archaeological evidence of early settlements can be found.

Further evidence from sites located inland shows human settlements over time. Some important pieces of evidence include the walls and moats of cities located along the route, as Mow Tone, with the round wall and moat, located on the right bank of the Tanaosri River, 54 km from Marid city, and Singkhon town located at the confluence of the Sai Khao River and the Little Tanaosri River, with a rectangular wall pattern that was built later, and the corners of the walls were rounded before this. Such walls and moat patterns (Map 3.6) lead us to hypothesize that these ancient settlements were established at different times, from the pre-Buddhist era to later, around the time of King Jayavarman VII of Cambodia, and indicate that the TPR has been in use to connect the two oceans from a very long time.

Historical records mention Marid as an important port city on the Andaman coast. Gold leaf inscriptions are found in Tanaosri town. In the Sukhothai Inscription Pillar No. 1, 1855 BE, we can read:

> Supannabhumi, Ratchaburi, Petchaburi, Sridhammarat
> (are) on the coast
>
> To the west Muang Rod, Muang Chod, Muang …
> Hongsawaddi on the coast and boundary.

Many other inscriptions record stories in the annals showing the times when the route was used for communication for both trade and military strategy.

The Japanese army of the East Asia landed on the Ao Prachuap and Ao Manao beaches, and this is the origin of the 'Honouring the Heroes' day in the Prachaup Khiri Khan province. The landing was meant not just to block the communication route to the south of Thailand, but it was also aimed to capture the TPR to the Andaman Sea, and to this day, the road through the Singkhon Pass is called the 'Japan Road'.

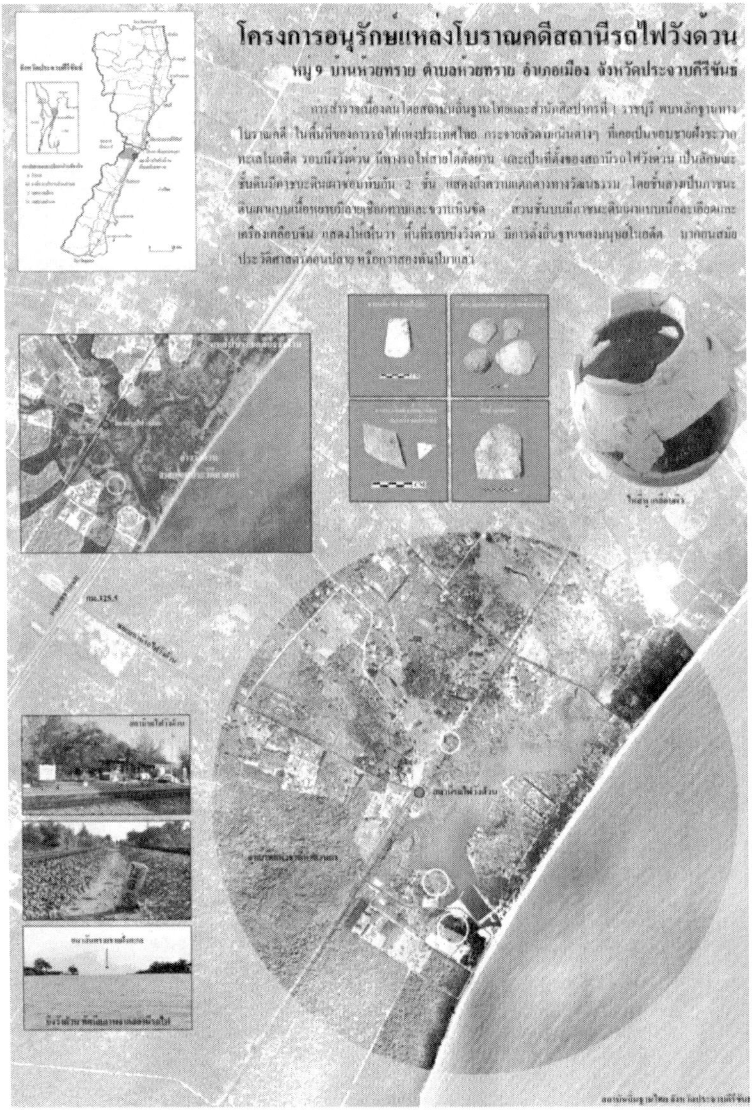

Figure 3.2 Archaeological Conservation Project of the Wang Duan Railway Station

Source: The author.

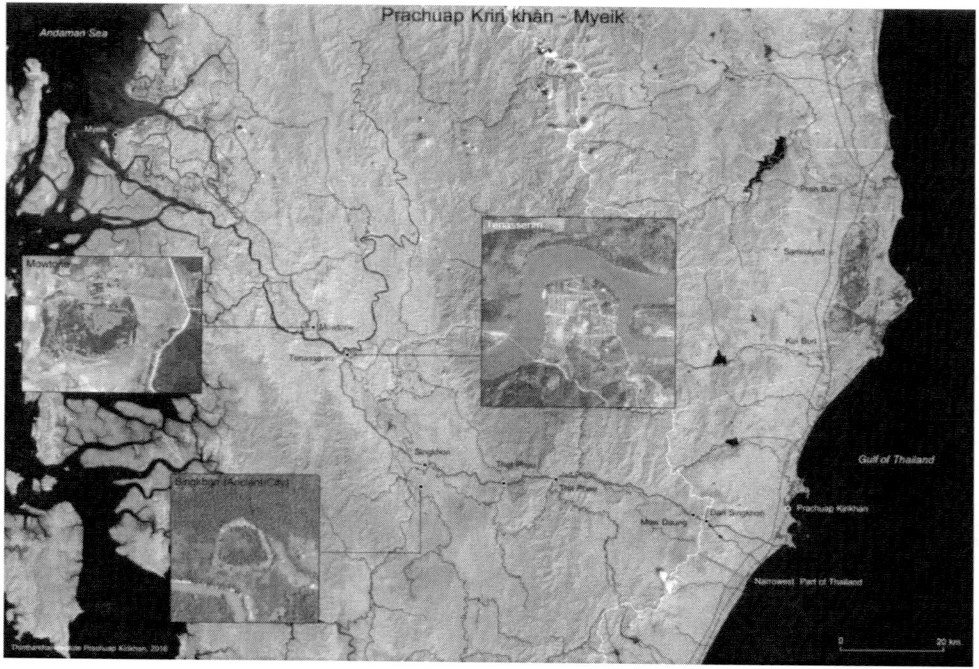

Map 3.6 Ancient Settlements along the Trans-Peninsula Route: 'Myeik–Prachuap Khiri Khan'

Source: The author.

Disclaimer: This figure has been redrawn by the author/s and is not to scale. It does not represent any authentic national or international boundaries and is used for illustrative purposes only.

3.3. CONCLUSIONS

It can be concluded that the TPR has been known and used for a long time. Currently, the condition of the TPR is a road that is usable for the entire stretch and is being improved in the territories of both Myanmar and Thailand for more efficient use and to support the opening of the Permanent Border Post where Thailand is building government offices and other services. On the Myanmar side, although the road is still of lower standard as compared to that on the Thai side, there is already a network of roads connecting the main road along the coastline from Dawei to Kawthaung, to the tip of Myanmar's territory known as Victoria Point.

The opening of Dan Singkhon as a permanent border crossing point to maximize the benefits for trade between the two countries is the beginning of a new era of the old vision, after having been in use for over 350 years in the past. It is believed that this will benefit both Prachuap Khiri Khan on the Pacific Ocean side and Myeik on the Indian Ocean side. Significantly, it also contributes to the China's policy of 'One Belt One Road', connecting to the Pacific Ocean in a more effective manner.

CHAPTER 4

DEVELOPMENT OF THE THAI-BURMA BORDER AREAS IN THE SECOND WORLD WAR

David Boggett

4.1. INTRODUCTION

During the Second World War, the Thai-Burma border areas became of critical importance to Japan, both for supplying its own troops fighting in Burma and for prosecuting the further expansion of the war into India. The latter led to the disaster of the Imperial Japanese Army's defeat in the Imphal Campaign of early 1944, in which the Japanese are alleged to have suffered 55,000 casualties from an invading force of 65,000 (including 15,000 deaths). Most of these casualties did not occur on the battlefield itself, but rather on the disastrous retreat in which Japanese soldiers desperately tried to return to 'friendly' Thailand.

But the Japanese military had other reasons to regard the—Thai-Burma border areas as essential to their interests. Only six months after the attack on Pearl Harbour, Japan had suffered a serious naval defeat at the Battle of Midway Atoll (immortalized in the 1976 movie, *Midway* starring Charlton Heston and Henry Fonda. At Midway, Japan lost four of its large aircraft carriers (Akagi, Kaga, Soryu and Hiryu—all part of the six-carrier fleet that had attacked Pearl Harbour a few months earlier). Japan was never able to recover from its losses at Midway, and the defeat in the Midway battle probably presaged the inevitability of its later loss of the overall war. Paradoxically, it was the defeat at distant Midway that forced the military to reassess the importance of the Thai-Burma border areas.[1]

Despite a sortie into the Indian Ocean (by several of the vessels subsequently sunk at Midway) shortly after the fall of Singapore, the Japanese navy seems to have concluded that control of the Indian Ocean was futile and that Japan simply did not have the resources necessary for such a venture. After attacking Colombo and Trincomalee, the Japanese fleet had simply withdrawn, never to return.[2] The defeat at Midway left the Japanese army perilously exposed in Burma, which had been occupied since February 1942.

Put simply, it was impossible for Tokyo to supply its armies in Burma by sea. This would have involved a long sea voyage through the Straits of Malacca and exposed all Japanese vessels to the serious risk of attack by the British navy in the Indian Ocean. Other means had to be devised to supply, maintain and provision the Japanese forces in Burma. Shipping from Japan to Bangkok was still relatively safe and secure because of Japan's continued control of the western Pacific sea lanes to Southeast Asia. It was simply necessary to ensure the transport of sea supplies received in Bangkok, overland through Thailand to Burma. Cross-border local trade between Burma and Thailand existed, but the Japanese would have to develop these local trade routes into a modern communication network capable of supplying their armies in Burma.

Several military projects were developed on these border areas:

1. **The Thai-Burma Railway** (commonly known as the 'Death Railway'), a 415 km railway line linking Nong Pladuk (on Thailand's Southern Railway line, built by the British) with Thanbyuzayat on Burma's Southern Railway.
2. **The Kra Railway**, a 90 km rail link from Chumphon to Ban Khao Fa Chi (from where goods were to be transported by boat

[1] https://en.wikipedia.org/wiki/Battle_of_Midway
[2] https://en.wikipedia.org/wiki/Indian_Ocean_raid

down the rivers La-Un and Kra to Ranong and Victoria Point (Kawthaung).

3. **The Khun Yuam–Toungoo (Taungoo)Road**, a full-scale military road for transporting supplies, around 150 km as the crow flies.
4. **The Chumphon-Mergui (Myeik) Road**, a roughly constructed road, over a distance of around 200 km as the crow flies at the very end of the war when the Japanese had few resources to spare. The road was possibly intended for use as an escape route from Burma, rather than a supply road. (Editor's Note: This road is described more fully in this report and should be called Prachuap–Myeik since the starting point is in Prachuap Kiri Khan province.)

All these projects required construction through areas of wild jungle, bedevilled with mosquitoes and other wild fauna, far from any human habitation and medical facilities. It would be the miseries of being forced to work in these appalling conditions that would be remembered after the war, whether by Allied Prisoners of War (POWs) or impressed Asian workers who laboured on these projects under the supervision of Japanese (and Korean) soldiers. Largely forgotten are the considerable achievements in terms of engineering that these projects engendered; so great were the technical innovations that these Japanese military projects rightly deserve to be considered the first modern infrastructure projects in these (still) inhospitable border areas. After the war, all these projects were abandoned. The British regarded Thailand as an 'enemy' country and had no intention of encouraging either trade or human interaction between the Thais and their newly recovered colony. The British army removed the tracks of the Thai-Burma Railway in order to repair railways damaged by the war in Burma, and then selling the much depleted remains to the Thai government as 'war reparations' for an exorbitant price. The Kra Railway had been abandoned by the Japanese before the end of the war due to heavy Allied bombing raids (the line ran through very exposed territory). The Khun Yuam–Toungoo road is barely passable even by four-wheel drive vehicles or military trucks, and only today is the Myeik Road being considered for possible construction.

4.2. THE THAI-BURMA RAILWAY ('DEATH RAILWAY')[3]

The best-known Japanese project to connect Thailand with Burma was, without doubt, the Thai-Burma Railway, the subject of David Lean's popular and widely successful 1957 movie *The Bridge on the River Kwai*. It has been the subject of numerous diaries and memoirs penned by the Allied POWs whose labour was used in its construction. The original steel bridge is still widely visited as a tourist attraction in Kanchanaburi; and the graves of the soldiers who perished in the ordeal are carefully and tastefully maintained by the Commonwealth War Graves Commission (CWGC), two in Kanchanaburi and one near Thanbyuzayat. This railway has become so embedded in the popular conscience as the representative par excellence of Japanese brutality in Southeast Asia that it has continued to this day to be the subject of memoirs, novels, documentaries and movies with varying degrees of accuracy (Figure 4.1).

Figure 4.1 A Japanese C56 Class Locomotive Passing the Chungkai Cutting, Near Kanchanaburi

Source: The author.

[3] This chapter is a digest of some 13 articles (see Boggett 2000).

4.3. THE ASIAN WORKERS

Our perceptions of this railway, despite all the publicity, remain deeply flawed. Because the reality is rather different. The POW workforce of some 60,000 Dutch, British, Australian and American POWs is but a small fraction of the railway's victims, and the around 13,000 corpses laid out neatly in the CWGC's cemeteries, but a tiny portion of the deceased. The Japanese conscripted (forcibly and otherwise) a huge number of Asian workers from their colonies; Allied post-war counts of the Asians are usually listed as 270,000, but this number is probably underestimated. The total Asian workforce may have been anything between that figure and half a million.

Arguably, despite the appalling events described in POW diaries, the conditions facing the Asian workers were much worse than for the POWs who, being part of a military unit, could alleviate their circumstances with their military disciplinary structure, being commanded by their own officers with their own military doctors, nurses, priests, etc.

By contrast, the Asian workers had been randomly rounded up from their various local villages; largely poorly educated, they were totally unstructured and could not even speak each other's languages (let alone English or Japanese). Australian POW, Hugh Clarke introduces the sections on 'Conscript Asian Labour' of his work as follows:

> The Japanese at the end of 1942 resorted to many ruses to recruit an additional labour pool of over 270,000 civilian labourers. They included Chinese, Burmese, Thais, Indians, Malays and Eurasians. As POWs began moving north the Japanese placed advertisements in Malayan newspapers seeking labourers for work periods of up to three months in Thailand. Free rail travel, housing, food and medical services were offered together with pay at a rate of one dollar a day. The response was negligible so the Japanese resorted to press-gang methods. Free picture shows were advertised at various theatres around Malaya and when full, the doors were locked and all males in the audiences put aboard trains and railed to Thailand. Later, as all civilians had to register to receive their rice rations the Japanese were able to assess the male population and began demanding 50 to 70 per cent

> of males in villages for their labour force.... As pressure for the completion of the railway built up it became increasingly difficult for the Japanese to replace people dying in Thailand. Java was then exploited with even more attractive rates of pay promised, as well as advances of up to 100 dollars for the three-month-contract. Similar methods were used in Burma. Needless to say, three-month contracts proved valueless as no labourers returned to their homes during the first 18 months. Once they reached Thailand and Burma, they found themselves herded into unhygienic, half-built camps with no medical facilities, inadequate rations and yoked to a relentless grind in which nothing mattered but completion of the railway. (Clarke 1986, 49)

British POW Doctor Robert Hardie's 'Secret Diary' has some of the most graphic accounts of the Asian *romusha* (workers). Dr Hardie had been a plantation manager in Malaya; he was an admirer of Malay culture and seems to have been more sensitive than most to the plight of the people, whether Malay, Tamil or Chinese. Summarizing an entry on Asian labourers on 14 August 1943, he mentions, 'When one hears of these widespread barbarities, one can only feel that we prisoners of war, in spite of all the deaths and permanent disabilities which result, are being treated with comparative consideration' (Hardie 1983, 109).

The diary contains several lengthy entries describing the Asian camps, usually of those workers from Malaya where Dr Hardie had previously resided. The first such entry bears the date 6 July 1943:

> A lot of Tamil, Chinese and Malay labourers from Malaya have been brought up forcibly to work on the railway. They were told that they were going to Alor Star in northern Malaya; those conditions would be good—light work, good food and good quarters. Once on the train, however, they were kept under guard and brought right up to Siam and marched in droves up to the camps on the river. People who have been near the camps speak with bated breath of the state of affairs—corpses rotting unburied in the jungle, almost complete lack of sanitation, frightful stench, overcrowding, swarms of flies. There is no medical attention in these camps, and the wretched natives are of course unable to organise any communal sanitation. (Hardie 1983, 102)

The lack of medical care and prevalence of diseases in the Asian camps is a recurring theme throughout the diaries, but Dr Hardie's perceptive comments spell out most dramatically the ghastly conditions prevalent among the *romusha*. A further note of 21 July 1943 reads:

> The conditions in the coolie camps down river are terrible, Basil says. They are kept isolated from Japanese and British camps. They have no latrines. Special British prisoner parties at Kinsaiyok bury about 20 coolies a day. These coolies have been brought from Malaya under false pretences—'easy work, good pay, good houses!' Some have even brought wives and children. Now they find themselves dumped in these charnel houses, driven and brutally knocked about by the Jap and Korean guards, unable to buy extra food, bewildered, sick, and frightened. Yet many of them have shown extraordinary kindness to sick British prisoners passing down the river, giving them sugar and helping them into the railway trucks at Tarsao. (Hardie 1983, 106)

A British POW who was severely tortured, Eric Lomax, in his moving personal record, 'Railway Man', published much later (some 45 years after his own experiences) notes,

> At about the same time the first civilian labourers arrived. At first there were thin columns of Asians; Chinese, Indians, Malays, Indonesians, struggling along the main road from Ban Pong towards Kanburi (Kanchanaburi). Unlike the POWs, however, the labourers had no organisation. They were individuals, or families, with no structure or chain of command. It was possible to guess that these pathetic labourers would die in enormous numbers and be the biggest victims of the railway. (Lomax 1995, 105)

That many of the Asian labourers, believing in the Japanese promises of workers' paradise, brought wives and children with them is borne out by the sketches of British POW artist, Ronald Searle. One of Searle's sketches, entitled 'Natives 'going up' Thailand jungle, 24 August 1943', clearly depicts an Asian woman (possibly a Tamil?) with a young child accompanying the labourers. Other hurried jottings of Asian workers also include women (Searle 1986, 116; Figure 4.2).

Figure 4.2 The Book Cover of *Thai-Myanmar Railway: A Personal Memoir*

Source: The author.

The most harrowing accounts in the POW diaries, however, are those of disease, sickness and ultimate deaths in the Asian *romusha* camps (in no small measure due to the complete lack of medical personnel and facilities). One of the sketches by another British POW artist, Leo Rawlings, is entitled 'Dying natives'; it depicts several Asians slouched under trees, lying prone on the ground or in makeshift shelters, near to death. In the foreground, an Asian figure is crawling on hands and knees trying to beg food from nearby Western POWs (Rawlings 1972, 86). In a particularly vivid description of Asian labourers, in his memoirs, *And the Dawn Came Up Like Thunder*, Rawlings (1972, 64) records:

> (We) were duly dispatched to a transit camp. It was teeming with dying natives, all in the throes of dysentery and cholera. Coloured and white slept together in the same huts. Clad in rags or even naked, we huddled together during the cold wet nights. Natives and POWs alike unable to control themselves, emitted vomit and excreta everywhere. Each day a number of POWs who could still walk were detailed to carry out those natives who had died during the night. The smell of death was everywhere, an almost sweet, sickly smell that defied description.

Then of a later camp transfer, he continues,

> In this new camp were many natives; Indians, Malays, Chinese etc., dying from dysentery. There are no cooks in this camp but a quantity of rice and a few vegetables. Two others in our party and myself set to work to make a crude meal. We made more than was needed for ourselves and then distributed the remainder to our native fellow sufferers. At night we slept alongside them, oblivious of any fear of contaminations, simply dead weary and exhausted. By morning many of our native companions were dead. That was the only time I ever cooked rice—I hoped it was my last. (Rawlings 1972, 85)

Such meagre medical attention as was afforded the Asian labourers appears to have been provided entirely by the medical staff among the Allied POWs. Dr Hardie's entry for 22 July 1943 reads:

> More stories filter in about the coolie camps, where, at least in some, British medical officers are working. Before a coolie can report sick at all to the British medical officer he must obtain permission from the Japanese guards, who do not of course often give it. Even when he sees the medical officer, generally very little can be done for him, as the medical officers are not supplied with drugs or dressings. Men with cholera are taken out to makeshift shelters in the jungle and left there. If they have friends who will look after them, these do what they can. If they have not, so much the worse. A fatigue of officers at Kinsaiyok goes each morning to the Tamil lines and carts away for burial anyone who has died during the night. (Hardie 1983, 108)

Hugh Clarke mentions that it was not until June of 1943 that, at last recognizing the seriousness of the situation in the *romusha* camps, the Japanese authorities formed two teams of medically proficient Allied POWs—doctors, medical orderlies, etc.—from among the POWs held in the Changi Prison in Singapore. Known as 'K' and 'L' Forces, they were sent up to the railway camps. He writes:

> The role of both these parties was to provide belated medical care for survivors of the army of civilians then working and dying on the railway… Attached in ones and twos to civilian camps the men of 'K' Force embarked on a soul-destroying

> period of improvisation and daily toil from dawn to beyond dark. In spite of their dedication, the Asian labourers continued to die in hundreds. (Clarke 1986)

He also adds, '(The Asian labourers) were appreciative of any efforts made to help the sick and showed great generosity with gifts of food and items from their piteously few possessions. Through their kindness the majority of 'K' Force escaped the more extreme forms of vitamin deficiency' (Clarke 1986, 50–51).

Like Dr Hardie, Sir Edward ('Weary') Dunlop, an Australian POW surgeon who—after the war—became something of a national hero in Australia, met colleagues from these medical parties and notes in his diary on 30 July 1943, 'These are all acting as MOs (medical orderlies) to the Tamil camps without medical stores and presumably with little to do except to make hygiene rules and bury the dead' (Dunlop 1994, 306).

The Japanese military seems to have entertained a pathological dread of contracting cholera. Sir Edward Dunlop notes in his diary entry of 14 June 1943:

> Okuda came up to our lines to tell us that there was a serious outbreak of cholera in one of the coolie camps. 200 cases. The Nipponese are in a flat-tailed spin about cholera and some are actually walking about the camp in masks.... Jack Clarke and Billie Wearne saw Kanomi at Konyu today and intimidated him with talk of 'chorrera', causing him to sweat freely each time the word was mentioned. (Dunlop 1994, 281)

Dunlop does mention in his account instances of cholera vaccine being made available to POWs, but it is clear that none was ever given to the Asian *romusha*. The Japanese dread of the disease, however, can hardly excuse the frequently reported occurrence of victims (usually, but not always, Asian labourers being buried alive, presumably in an effort to escape the contagion). The most horrifying description occurs in Dr Hardie's 'Secret Diary' entry of 4 August 1943:

> A British bombardier, Royal Artillery, who has arrived at this camp after being in a POW party cooking for the droves of Tamil and Chinese labourers being marched up the river

under guard to work, told me this morning of the terrible treatment these poor wretches get from the Japanese. Many are contracting cholera; often of course it is quickly fatal, but if there is any delay in a man's dying, the Nips try to get the British POWs to bury them before they are dead. On one occasion they forced them at the point of loaded rifles to lay them in shallow graves; but the British (they were only a handful of other ranks, no officers) steadfastly refused to do any more. The bombardier reported that the Japanese themselves—terrified as they are of going near cholera cases—covered the bodies. Other dying men were taken out into the jungle and dumped there to die, the Nips compelling other coolies to do this act at the point of the bayonet. At all the camps cholera cases are treated as untouchable (except by British POWs, who are heavily sprayed with disinfectant before they are allowed to approach the Nips again), and the permanent camps which are sometimes quite near are not allowed to do anything for the wretches. There is no-one to give them water. They are left to rot, their bones a memorial to the arrival of the New Order and a comment on the attitude of the Japanese to their fellow Asiatics of other races. (Hardie 1983, 109)

It is only from Burma that writings by a labourer himself have been published. The late Lin Yone Thit Lwin was a volunteer labour organizer for the Japanese. Even though his situation would have been a little better than the compulsorily drafted workers, Lin Yone Thit Lwin and his friend, Then Tha Sin, escaped from the horrors of the Railway, eventually returning to their homes. After the war, Lin Yone Thit Lwin became a well-known novelist and essayist in the days of the Ne Win government and wrote a book describing his escape from the Railway and the terrible conditions faced by the other Burmese workers, entitled *The Thai-Myanma Railway: A Personal Memoir*. It was published in Rangoon in 1968, sometime after the end of the war, by which time the author's reputation as a writer had already been established (Figure 4.2).

The Japanese forcibly recruited over 170,000 labourers from all over Burma. In order to get the necessary number, township administrative officers cooperated with some politicians in the recruiting. Only a few far-sighted and brave politicians defied this duty. People aged from 13 to over 60 and 70 fled their homes to avoid the recruiting drive. They hid in jungles, pagodas and monasteries. Some starved for days at a time.

Recruiting forced labour was like capturing people in every district. Well-to-do people used their wealth to protect their sons, brothers and nephews from becoming part of the labour force. Some bribed the Japanese soldiers, while others paid money and found someone to go for them. At that time, the going price for a substitute labourer was anywhere from 300 to 500 kyat. All in all, the majority of the labour corps constituted village people and unemployed townsmen.... Meanwhile other group leaders from nearby barracks came with more bad news. More labourers had died (from cholera) and there were problems in burying them. I was shocked when I saw the dead bodies of the labourers in all positions of death. Since we could not keep these bodies exposed any longer, we started to bury them. Some labourers dug a big pit for a mass grave. At the same time the bodies were tied together with creepers and vines. While they were doing that we moved to another barrack. I saw three or four bodies being carried out into the forest for burial. Some held torches and accompanied them. Until dawn we had to keep the fires burning and bury the dead bodies. (Lwin 1968 cited in Kratoska 2006, 42 and 53)

The following is an edited version of an interview with the last surviving Malay worker then still living in the Nam Tok (Tha Sao) area. The late Lung ('Uncle') Yu Chalawankumphi, then in his late seventies, eventually married locally in Thailand and settled in Nam Tok.

I was brought here from Kota Baru in Kelantan when I was fifteen years old. I was picked out at random by the Japanese. It wasn't voluntary; they simply took one out of three males. After we arrived, I was split up from the friends who'd been rounded up together with me. I was put to work immediately. I started at Nong Pladuk and worked right up to the Burmese border. The area was virgin jungle then; very wild. I was working more than two years. We had been promised pay at the rate of 600 a month. I can't recall the currency unit but it was certainly 600 a month![4] The unit

[4] The unit of '600 per month' is rather problematic. Clarke (1986) mentions that, in Malaya, promises were made 'with pay at the rate of one dollar a day'. He adds that later, in Java, 'even more attractive rates of pay (were) promised as well as advances of up to 100 dollars for the three-month contract'. Dunlop (1994) also mentions promises to Tamils from Malaya 'their rate of pay to be $1 a day plus food' and a later entry about a newly arrived group of 'about 500 Malay, Chinese and Thai coolies' reads 'They say their pay is $1 a day, although they

doesn't matter because we never actually received anything at all; no pay at all for all those months' labour!

We were given food three times a day. Well, it was edible, at least—if we didn't eat it, there was nothing else! We couldn't understand what the Japanese or (Koreans) were saying. We had to work every day, regardless of the weather; in the monsoon rains or the fierce sunlight.

We didn't have to work through the night though, as nobody could see anything. We slept in rough attap huts with a considerable number of people together; I think as many as a hundred people to a hut. We did have some clothing and mosquito nets, but only very rough sandals for footgear. There was no medicine available in those days. Even when sick, we were forced to work. So many people died, especially of dysentery and cholera. Many also died of malaria. The dead bodies were just thrown into huge holes. That was all!

After the war, I didn't go back. Indeed, many never returned; they remained scattered here and there along the course of the railway. Here at Nam Tok alone there were about 20 or more of us Malays. I was very depressed at that time and so sad. I'd wanted to return but I couldn't even contact my mother! Much, much later I was able to contact my family in Kota Baru; they've been to visit us here and I've been to visit them too. But by then I had settled locally and I had my sons here, so in the end I no longer dreamed of returning (to Malaysia). I have often talked about my

have not got it yet… Contrast with our pay of 25c a day'. Another reliable source, Kratoska (1998, 182–186) states, 'Dependents of Malayan labourers received an allowance of $15 per month, plus a gratuity of $120 and a certificate of service if a labourer died, but the allowance was stopped if the labourer absconded… The allowance for dependents also seems not to have been paid regularly… As Malaya's labour surplus turned into a labour shortage, the Japanese found it increasingly difficult to obtain workers. In 1943 the administration paid $1 per day with free food and lodging, but by 1945 the rate had increased to $20 per day with food and lodging, and there were few takers'. The 1945 figure of US$20 per day (in Japanese military scrip) would give US$600 per month, the amount mentioned by Lung Yu, but from his account about working on the early stages of the railway from Nong Pladuk, it is clear that Lung Yu was brought to Thailand before 1945. Other accounts mention pay in terms of Thai baht; 'The labourers recalled that they were paid a salary of 1–10 baht, but none told the student researchers what happened to the money' (Ahmad, 2000, 55).

experiences with my sons and it has saddened them. But we have already forgotten the past; for them, dwelling on the past is not healthy—there's no point!

4.4. THAI LABOUR AND THE BAN PONG INCIDENT

The important topic of Thai labour on the Thai-Burma Railway must not be neglected, even though estimates of the numbers involved are highly suspected and no known accounts survive of the experiences of the participants themselves. Although the Japanese destroyed most records pertaining to the Asian workers at the war's end, whatever military statistics have survived indicate that there were considerable numbers of Thais involved. Statistics for the 4th Battalion of the 9th Railway Regiment listed 8 per cent of the total labour force as Thai (Toshio 1971, 237).[5] Thai labour was used in the construction of the first section of the railway, from Nong Pladuk (the junction station with the main Southern Line), through Ban Pong, to Kanchanaburi (Figure 4.3).

Figure 4.3 Lung Yu at the Santi Restaurant, Nam Tok Station

Source: The author.

[5] Other figures were Malay 67 per cent and Chinese 25 per cent.

> With Thailand … the planners of the new line had to proceed with a little more respect for the diplomatic niceties. Although the country had been attacked and practically occupied by Japanese forces, it still remained technically independent throughout the war… Indeed, part of the reason for the delay in starting the railway project at the Thai end was the opposition of local Siamese landowners who had to give up property to make way for the new line. Negotiations were necessary and a series of conferences was held in Bangkok between Thai government representatives, Thai National Railways and the Japanese authorities…. An agreement was finally reached according to which Thailand provided the land for the Japanese right of way and also agreed to undertake some of the work at the south (and much easier) end of the projected line. The Thais were to help with the railway roadbed construction between Ban Pong and Kanchanaburi, where the line was to run parallel with a motor road already in existence and for the continuation of the motor road from Kanchanaburi to Wan Yai which lay some 120 kilometres to the North West of the line's projected starting point. With Thailand bearing some of the cost and supplying a portion of the labour and materials, it appeared that the Japanese construction task would be eased considerably. (Kinvig 1992, 38)

Japanese military statistics for Thai labour probably underestimate the number of Thai personnel. Both (Thai-) Mons and (Thai-) Chinese seem to have been included under the 'Mon' or 'Chinese' categories rather than 'Thai'.

> When it became necessary in 1942 to build the Thai-Burma Railroad, the Japanese Embassy's chief liaison man, Fujishima, prompted the Chinese Chamber of Commerce (located then, as now. on Bangkok's South Sathorn Road) to establish a joint stock company (Manho Yogen Koshi) that played a crucial role in supplying gravel and other materials for the project. In 1943, the Chamber raised 1.2 million baht for labour recruitment and signed up 16,000 Chinese coolies by offering twice the normal wage for the hazardous construction work. (Reynolds 1994, 177)

Japanese historian, Murai Yoshinori, has found that

> 12,968 Thai Chinese romusha (labourers) were to have been received by the Japanese, but only 5,641 reached the labour

> camps; others ran away en route. The number of Thai romusha is unknown. For the construction of the railway between Nong Pladuk and Kanchanaburi about 5,000 (Thai) romusha were registered (September and October 1942). In Kanchanaburi prefecture about 700 romusha were hired by the Japanese (October 1942). On 18th December 1942, Thai romusha and some policemen attacked the Japanese military base of Ban Pong. After this, Thai people became very reluctant to become romusha. (Yoshinori 1993, 62)

Considering the importance of this Thai labourers' attack on the Ban Pong military camp, its omission from many accounts of the railway is curious. As Thailand had never been a Western colony and was regarded (at least by Britain) as a war-time Japanese ally, the fate of Thai labourers working on a military project within Thailand itself was never a subject of Allied concern. Nevertheless, the Ban Pong riots were of sufficient significance to force the Japanese army to seek civilian labour from occupied Southeast Asian countries outside Thailand and to restrict the recruitment of Thais. On their part, ordinary Thais indeed became increasingly resistant to work on the railway project, not only due to news of the Ban Pong events but also due to the persistent rumours about the appalling conditions pertaining to those Thai workers who had been contracted by Thai companies to assist in the construction of a Japanese military railway in the Kra Isthmus.[6]

The best description of the Ban Pong Incident is that given by E. Bruce Reynolds in his pioneering study.

> The fall flooding had slowed construction, and by mid-December only 13 kilometres of track had been laid. Considerable tension had developed between the Japanese, who mistrusted their allies, and the local residents. A Thai police lieutenant, Sisuk Mahinthorathep, recalled that the Kempeitai conducted searches, arrested people, and tortured

[6] Although started after the Thai-Burma Railway, construction of the Kra Railway finished earlier. The Kra Isthmus Railway was built to link Chumphon (on the Bangkok Southern Line) to Victoria Point (now renamed Kawthaung), the most southern town of Burma. The railway ran from Chumphon through Kraburi to a terminal at Khao Fa-Chi-on the La-Un River, where goods were transferred by boat to Ranong and Victoria Point in Burma. This railway is more fully described later.

suspects without regard to Thai law. It seemed to him that the bullying Japanese were about to take over the whole district.

This mutual hostility flared into violence on 18th December when a Japanese sentry struck a Thai monk after a dispute about his presence in a restricted area. The Thai consider the head the most sacred part of the body and even a Thai monarch must treat a monk respectfully. Thus, when the monk complained to a group of Thai laborers that he had been slapped in the face, they were outraged. After nightfall they formed into an angry mob that attacked and killed a Japanese sentry with bamboo sticks and knives. Other Japanese soldiers heard the commotion and ran to the aid of their comrades. Chaos ensued. The Thai officials and the commander of the Japanese guards sought the assistance of the Kempeitai, which sent out a call for reinforcements. As 'the sound of gunshots and battle cries echoed in the night air', would-be peacemakers reached the scene of the melee, now involving several hundred people. After about 20 minutes' effort, the authorities from the two sides were able to break up the fight. Accounts indicate that at least two Japanese were killed.

Lt. Sisuk, who had been left in command of the police headquarters in Ban Pong, was not sure what had happened, but fearing an imminent Japanese attack, he deployed 30 men, armed with rifles and two machine guns, around the building. They watched nervously as several trucks loaded with armed soldiers passed by from the direction of Kanchanaburi and headed toward the Japanese camp. Next, a black car and two trucks loaded with more than 20 armed soldiers slowed at the roundabout in front of the station. Although Sisuk claimed that the Japanese dismounted and opened fire with a machine gun, the Japanese contended that they were fired upon without provocation. They later concluded that a nervous Thai policeman probably opened fire at a Japanese who emerged from one of the vehicles. In any event, the shooting continued for several minutes before Thai officials and the commander of the Japanese guard arrived and intervened. Two contemporary Japanese accounts placed their toll at four dead (including a military doctor) and two seriously wounded.

From the next day the local people's attitude was extremely bad', a Japanese officer noted in his diary. A series of anti-Japanese incidents ensued, including the destruction of a mile of railway track, an attack on Japanese soldiers by armed Thais and stone throwing by Thai women. A Japanese show of force restored a surface calm, but in the officer's view the atmosphere remained 'oppressive', and the surroundings 'disagreeable'. (Reynolds 1994, 138–139)[7]

Several details differ slightly according to various sources. Even the date of the incident itself is unclear and the figure of deaths disputed.[8] Just as the Ban Pong disturbances have often been ignored, their importance and long-term effect on wartime Thai-Japanese relations have likewise been underestimated. Settlement of the affair was complicated by the demands of the Japanese Southern Army which, though headquartered in distant Saigon, retained direct command of all operations related to the railway's construction. Thai Prime Minister, Field Marshal Plaek Phibunsongkhram, in an attempt to calm the situation had ordered the Ban Pong and Kanchanaburi districts to be cleared of foreign residents within 7 days.[9] It is probable that the Japanese military was unimpressed as it appeared that the order also applied to Japanese civilians.

> The Southern Army soon confronted him (Phibun) with a series of demands so sweeping that they aroused concern in the Greater East Asia Ministry (in Tokyo) that Phibun's authority could be undermined if he were forced to accept them. These involved execution of 'criminals' involved in the Ban Pong incident, the transfer of policemen and discharge of officials involved, reparations ranging from 20.000 baht for each dead officer and 1,000–3.000 baht for each injured soldier, a formal apology, and various preventative measures. Among the latter were a vigorous public re-education effort

[7] The Japanese officer's diary quoted towards the end of the lengthy description was taken from Ken (1978). A Thai account of the incident was written under the pseudonym Khamsan (1982). A useful contemporary Japanese account is Kametaro (1987, 169–171). An account based on Thai sources available in Bangkok's National Library is Yoshikawa (1994).

[8] Reynolds (1988, 169), in which the number of Japanese deaths is recorded as six. In a footnote, Reynolds explains, 'Murashima Eiji has found a Thai Foreign Ministry document confirming the date as 18th December' (Murashima, Mektrairat and Wanthana 1991).

[9] Similar orders had been issued for other 'sensitive' military or security-related areas from May 1941. In January of 1942, several of Thailand's northern provinces were cleared of non-citizens. The measures were probably primarily intended to remove ethnic Chinese. It has been discussed elsewhere in a preceding context. Full details appear in Skinner (1957, 270–275).

> to eliminate anti-Japanese attitudes, and special training for policemen. (Reynolds 1994, 139)

Execution was also demanded for the monk whose head had been hit by the Japanese guard—the alleged 'ringleader' of the affair—despite Thai insistence that no matter what the crime, a monk could not be given the death penalty under the country's legal arrangements.

> The language barrier between the two peoples contributed to misunderstandings, and quarrels were often intensified by economic inequities or simple jealousies. The Thai were feeling the economic effects of the war for the first time, but Japanese, whether they came from the homeland—where a four-year conflict had already forced severe austerities—or chaotic China, found life in Thailand very pleasant. In fact, to soldiers in transit from one grim battlefront to the next, Bangkok seemed a veritable oasis.... Free-spending Japanese pleasure seekers, who benefitted from the devaluation of the baht, became the favored clients of night spots and brothels, much to the irritation of local patrons. Japanese messages had expressed concern about quarrels between their soldiers and Thai civilians as early as May 1942, and (Japanese Ambassador) Tsubokami reported in August 'numerous incidents of friction between Thai officials and the Japanese residents and military groups', 'frequent skirmishes', and an increase in thefts and robberies. (Reynolds 1994, 136–137)

Some Allied POW accounts mention the ill-treatment frequently experienced by the local Thais. Passing through the Ban Pong camp a month or so before the incident, the British POW Charles Fisher records:

> Ban Pong provided a final surprise in the course of our one-day stay there. On our arrival we had noticed a bunch of about a dozen scared-looking Thais lined up outside the guard room, as we trooped in. It now appeared that they had been caught carrying on a highly illicit trade in bananas and other equally dangerous goods with the prisoners, and were to be punished accordingly. One by one, they were dragged forward, and thrown to a waiting gang of Japanese toughs who alternately pummeled, punched and slapped them, or kicked them in unmentionable but proportionately painful places. Then each

> of four guards seized a leg or an arm of each of the victims in turn and swung the wretched men wildly to and fro in the air for a few minutes to gain momentum, before flinging them into a stinking puddle. For most of us this was the first sight of naked brutality on the part of the Japanese, and it was horrible. (Fisher 1979, 65–66)

The Ban Pong affair had important ramifications, one of which was the establishment of a newly organized Bangkok Garrison Command under the leadership of General Nakamura Aketo.

> Arrogant attitudes displayed by both military and civilian Japanese in the heady early stages of the war made matters worse, setting the stage for the eruption of violence at Ban Pong in December 1942. Coming at a time when the Japanese high command had been shaken by setbacks in the Guadalcanal campaign, the Ban Pong incident was a warning signal that alerted Tokyo to the seriousness of the problems in Thailand. This led to the dispatch of General Nakamura (Aketo) to head the new Thailand Garrison Army, a real turning point in Japanese-Thai relations. Not only were Nakamura's warm personality and his ability to understand the Thai. While Ambassador Yamamoto exerted his influence to avert any military action against the Thai in the final months of the war, given the Japanese army' s well-known capacity for independent action, Nakamura deserves particular credit for the fact that the Japanese-Thai alliance did not end in a bloodbath. (Reynolds 1994, 234)

4.4.1. Bones of Asian Workers Found in Kanchaburi

Unlike those of the Allied POWs who sleep in the neatly arranged graves of the CWGC's cemeteries, the spirits of the Asian dead have hardly rested peacefully. 'Grisly Find: Mass Grave Unearthed' were the headlines of the *Bangkok Post's* 18 November 1990 edition which announced the discovery of some 400 labourers' bones in Kanchanaburi. The find was allegedly occasioned by recurring troublesome dreams experienced by Sompong Chawangal, a local bike shop proprietor. The latter contacted a nearby teacher and owner of the two-acre plot of sugar-cane field near his residence,

Ananya Watanayaem, who said he had earlier come across skeletons when ploughing his field (Brooke 1995, 105).[10]

> Ananya's elder sister, Lek Pailom, then 75 years of age, recalled that when she was about 20 years old, field hospitals for sick Indian, Malayan and Singaporean prisoners of war or slave workers were located on a large piece of land where the Kanchanaburi provincial hall and business area are now located. 'Every morning the Indians dug a hole in this area to bury dead bodies in the evening. The bodies were simply thrown into the pit and covered with dirt. Some days, 2 or 3 bodies were buried; some days more than 5'. (*Bangkok Post* 1990)

A Chinese organization was called in to investigate the grave and re-inter the bones in an appropriate manner to placate and enable the release of the angry spirits.[11] Concerned at the haphazard and hardly professional nature of the excavations, the Thai Government's Fine Arts Department appointed the Director of nearby Muang Singh Historical Park, Sathapon Khwanyun, to take over and supervise the site. The latter published a full report of his findings in the *Sinlapawathanatham* (Art & Culture) Magazine's February 1991 issue. The report stresses that this was by no means the first time that such graves had been unearthed in the area: such discoveries had been a common occurrence, and usually the excavated bones had been quietly cremated by such (Chinese) spiritual organizations as the *Jin Siang Tung*. Excavations established beyond doubt that the bodies were those of Asian labourers, most probably Indian, and that several women and children were among the victims (Figure 4.4). Information was also gathered from the local community. Maj Ruanisak Chaigomin stated that the Japanese had referred to the victims as 'kulito' (possibly derived from the English word, 'coolie'), the term they invariably used for Asian labourers. Urai Bosap (65 years of age) stated:

---

[10] Brooke renders Sompong's surname as Charoenchai. I have referred to him as Chawangai, following a literal transcription of the Thai letters found in Khwanyun (1991; also see Figure 4.4).

[11] The *Sinlapawathanatham* report lists the organization's Chinese name as 'Jin Siang Tung'.

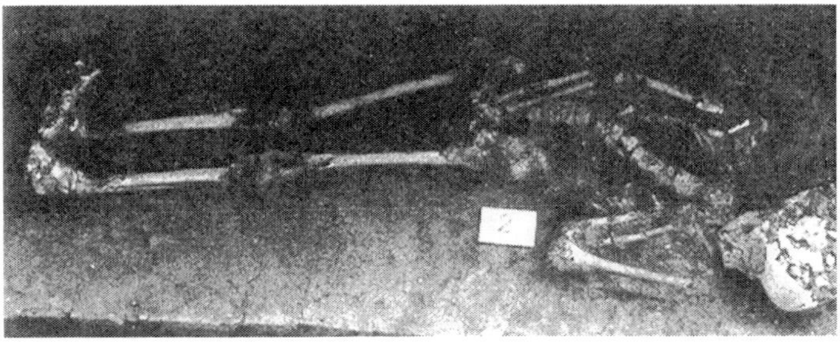

Figure 4.4 Sathapon Khwanyun: 'A Newly Discovered Second World War Graveyard in Kanchanaburi' (in Thai)

Source: Khwanyun (1991).

> They made a huge pit for the burials. After a few bodies had been tossed in, they would add white lime (to avert unpleasant odours) before piling in further layers of the dead. The grave was finally covered with earth. The people were all very dark-skinned and must have been Indians. (Khwanyun 1991, 90–102)[12]

A later report again carried an interview with Lek Pailom, who talked of the 1943 cholera epidemic:

> Lek Pailom … had been 28 in 1943 … and remembered that hundreds of Malayans and Indians had been held during the war in a slave camp located on the land where the remains were found… 'I saw Japanese soldiers digging huge graves into which bodies were dumped. Some were sick but still alive'. (Brooke 1995, 105)

Micool Brooke, then a *Bangkok Post* journalist, visited the site in the very early stages of excavation. He writes:

> The excavated hole measured about 20 metres square and was located in a sugar cane held about half an acre in size…. I approached the edge of the grave, unknowing what I expected to see. And yet I also felt a strong sense of embarrassed shame

[12] Urai Bosap uses both the words, 'Indian', as well as the Thai word, 'khaek' (see Figure 4.5), when referring to the victims. I am indebted to Thanawalai Jaroenjandang for translation assistance.

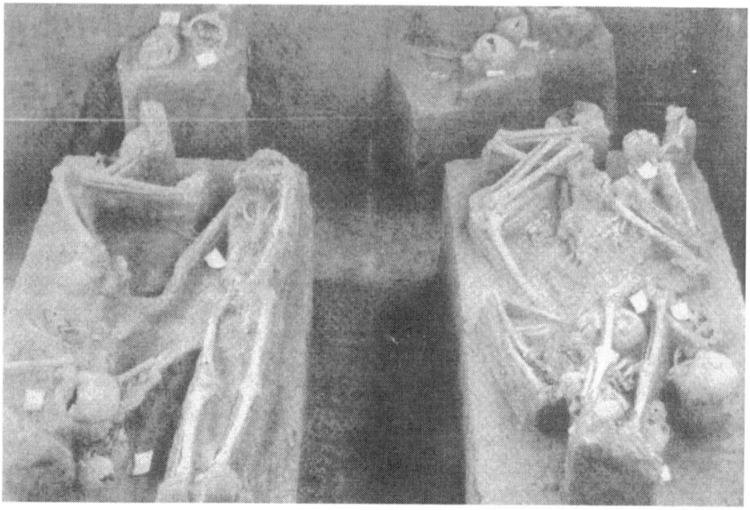

Figure 4.5 Photo from Sathapon Khwanyun: 'A Newly Discovered Second World War Graveyard in Kanchanaburi' (in Thai)

Source: Khwanyun (1991, 90–102).

> at intruding upon the sorrow-covered grave. And sorrow and remorse did overwhelm me when I looked down and saw hundreds of skeletons pressed together, their arms reaching out. They had tried to crawl out of the grave before they finally suffocated to death. (Brooke 1995, 107)

4.5. THE JAPANESE MILITARY MEMORIAL

Upon completion of the railway on 17 October 1943, the Japanese military authorities determined to erect a memorial to the people who had lost their lives during the railway's construction. This unusual monument still survives today, at Tha Makham, some 100 m downstream from the famous bridge. Artistically, it is hardly a particularly attractive monument, being a cenotaph-type structure made of the rough concrete that had sufficed for the railway's construction. Usually unvisited and ignored by the regular tourists to Kanchanaburi, this monument is nevertheless of considerable significance and importance in memorializing the tragedy of the railway.

Forming the four corners of a square at some 10 m distance from the cenotaph itself, are four wall-like structures, bearing memorial plaques of marble inscribed in the languages of those who had lost their lives in building the railway.[13] One corner structure (two tablets) records a poem in classical Chinese (a literary form known as *kanshi* in Japanese). At another corner, inscriptions appear in both Vietnamese[14] and the peculiar 'reformed' Thai script in use during the era of Thai Prime Minister Plaek Phibunsongkhram. The third corner structure was bombed during an Allied air raid on the bridge, after which only the English language tablet memorializing the Western POWs was restored. (The second, now missing tablet possibly contained an inscription in Burmese). The final corner bears memorial inscriptions in the Indonesian/Malaysian[15] and Tamil languages. A further Japanese language inscription on the rear of the cenotaph itself mentions the deaths of Japanese military personnel. The memorial's importance lies in the fact that so many Asian languages appear; this has given the Japanese army's wartime memorial the distinction of being the *only* monument of the war era in the Kanchanaburi area to recognize the existence and enormous sufferings of the Asian labourers.[16]

---

[13] One western POW account states that the marble slabs had been obtained by forcibly confiscating marble tables (a common Sino-Thai item of furniture) from the local Chinese community, but I have regrettably been unable to locate the description in question.

[14] The Vietnamese language inscription reads, 'A memorial to the spirits of those Vietnamese labourers (lit. Romusha) who died constructing the Thai-Burma Railway'.

[15] The national languages of both Indonesia and Malaysia (*Bahasa Indonesia* and *Bahasa Malaysia* respectively) are the same, the language of Sumatra having been selected as independent Indonesia's national language, rather than Javanese, the language of the majority of the population. The language of Sumatra and that of the Malayan Peninsula, being populated by essentially the same peoples, was, to all intents and purposes, identical. The inscription reads. 'Paying our respects to the souls of Moslems who worked her; Allah rewards you'. Translation by Murai Yoshinori from his article 'Asian Forced Labour (romusha) on the Burma-Thailand Railway' in McCormack and Nelson (1993, 61).

[16] More recent serious museum displays, especially those of the Australian Government's Hellfire Pass Memorial Museum and the Thai-Burma Railway Center's museum in Kanchanaburi itself, devote considerable display space in their exhibits to introducing the horrific situation faced by the Asian labourers. Another less reputable 'war' museum, run by local business interests and conveniently located by the side of the famous bridge to attract as many tourists as possible, contains a rather distasteful memorial to Asian workers, displaying

Those involved in the railway's construction hold widely different opinions about the validity of the monument. Opinions expressed by former Allied soldiers (POWs) have been fairly negative, with some notable exceptions. Cornelis Evers, a former Dutch POW, writes of the railway's completion in his own account, 'Death Railway'.

> A holiday was declared for October 25 (1943) and on that day a gaily festooned train arrived at the camp, which unloaded extra rations for the Japanese troops and even some for the prisoners. All the Japanese and Koreans who had collaborated on the construction of the track received a medal. And we learned that a memorial to the Allied troops who had 'contributed' to it, was going to be erected near the bridge on the river Kwai. This did not interest us very much at the time. It was only after the war when we came face to face with the monument that the cynicism of the Japanese in commemorating those whom they had driven, mercilessly and callously, to their deaths, struck us in full force. (Evers 1993, 60)

Eric Lomax, a former British POW, points out that the monument has often been defaced by stones thrown by former Allied prisoners visiting Kanchanaburi, such is the hatred that they still bear towards Japan as a result of their cruel treatment.

> The Japanese War Memorial which POWs were forced to build some time in 1944, is a sadder and more neglected place. A cenotaph now showing blotches of weather and stress was erected in a compound surrounded by low trees: it is ill-kept and deserted. The cenotaph incorporates plaques to the dead of other countries, like an afterthought. Some ex-POWs, who can never forgive, throw stones at the memorial when they come here: the scars are visible on the stained concrete. (Lomax 1995, 268)

The projectiles thrown by visitors have done rather greater damage than Lomax indicates. Several of the inscriptions on the marble tablets have also been defaced. Although damage to the Malaysian/Indonesian language inscription was repaired by the Japanese Association, that of the Tamil language still renders a part of the

actual skeletons and bones, questionably obtained from the excavation of mass graves in Kanchanaburi.

text illegible. Former Japanese *Kempeitai* (Military Police) official, Nagase Takashi, is more specific:

> It is true that there is a memorial tower which was built by the Japanese Arm [sic] But there are very few visitors partly because of the difference in religion of the Thai. It has even become the object of hatred from the ex-prisoners who visited the Kwai. They throw stones at the memorial, (and) pull out flowers offered, candles and incense sticks to stamp on. The ex-POWs still have deep-seated resentment towards the Japanese. In the construction of the tower the British POWs were made to design it and carry cement for it. They still say in anger. 'Why did we, the victims, have to build the memorial tower for our own comrades?' (Takashi 1990, 70)

Opinions about the annual memorial services held at the site by the Japanese army also differ considerably, depending on a prisoner's perspective and memories. A particularly negative impression was recorded by Rohan Rivett.

> On arrival at Tamarkan (Tha Makham) we found a gang of British captives engaged in building a memorial to those who had died on the railway. The Japanese chose a point midway between the camp and the Tamarkan Bridge across the river for this memorial, which had commemorative tablets at its four corners and a tall cenotaph in the center. On 21st March, Brigadier Varley, together with a selected number of officers and men, was marched over to the memorial to witness the opening service. Representatives of the various native races and sects employed on the railroad were present, while gold-braided officers of the Thai army, navy and air force sat with the Japanese officers under a specially erected marquee. The Japanese, sublimely unconscious of the irony of things, decked out the whole memorial as if for a harvest festival, the cenotaph and oblation stone before it being covered with many types of the fruit and vegetables for lack of which the prisoners had died. While newsreel photographers filmed us from every angle, various Asiatic representatives delivered speeches which were received with absolute apathy by the natives present, who looked as if they had been shanghaied into attendance. The Japanese and Thai officers fidgeted and looked grim and bored throughout the whole ceremony. Finally, Brigadier Varley read out a statement emphasizing that the conditions under which prisoners had worked would

> be investigated after the war. The entire ceremony was an insult to God and man, carried through with a blatant hypocrisy and a lack of sincerity which no Japanese took the trouble to conceal. At the end, they lined us all up black, white, yellow and brown, and solemnly presented each person with a tin of biscuits—a gesture apparently meant to suggest that all was now forgiven and forgotten. I have never been present at a function so patently meaningless to everybody concerned. Prisoners and Asiatics alike, knowing the Japanese by bitter experience, knew that this was merely a gesture required by the demands of face. The only real point of interest was that on the memorial the Japanese admitted 76.000 deaths among the fellow Asiatics whom they were 'redeeming from Anglo-Saxon bondage'. (Rivett 1946, 315–316)[17]

It would be interesting to know the opinions of the 'representatives of the various native races and sects' but, needless to say, none of these were ever recorded. A rather different view of the same ceremony is, however, provided by Sir Edward Dunlop in his 12 March 1944 diary entry;

> Up betimes and on parade and ready to go to Takanoon. There is a most impressive monument to those who have lost their lives in making the Thailand/Burma Railway. A party to attend consists of 20 British, 10 Dutch, 10 Australians and we were told to send well-dressed soldiers! This we did by free borrowing. We marched across between two rivers almost two miles to the monument—a tall, substantial cenotaph of concrete with some marble slabs for inscription set in a square of approximately 20 metres with four right-angled corner bastions of stone and cement, each inscribed on the inner side with languages of the people concerned: Nipponese, Thai, Hindu, Malay etc. The English caption read, 'May they rest in peace', which indeed they deserve. The monument was adorned with fruits and vegetables, bottles of saki (sake), lampangs of tobacco and such good things. A table in front with a white cloth had upon it a brass urn in which three sticks smoked. Also, some candles. We were drawn up before the monument with a hollow square arrangement, an N (Nipponese. i.e., Japanese) general and higher staff officers on the left; Many other N of high rank and many Thai officials and higher service officers on the right. In the center were the various

[17] The grounds for Riven's assertion of 76,000 Asian deaths are unclear.

> native groups to the right, the British, American, Dutch and Australians on the left; a N priest, a 2-star private with bayonet at side, did most of the initial ceremony which was complicated and impressive. The N general then approached and read a scroll with his message and this was interpreted in several languages. Thai officials and many Japanese officers paid more respects than persons from any other religion who approached the monument. Brigadier Varley also read a scroll after advancing and saluting the cenotaph. 'They shall grow not old as we that are left grow old. In the morning and at the going down of the stat, we will remember them'. Many pictures were taken, including cine films. Huge numbers of colourful wreaths were grouped about the central cenotaph. It was extremely hot and this interesting ceremony took about two hours. I wish I understood more of it. Afterwards, all men were given a tin of biscuits and allowed to go to the Tamarkan camp for lunch. (Dunlop 1994, 384–385)

After the end of the war, the monument's maintenance passed from the (now defeated) Japanese Imperial Army to the Japanese Association of Thailand, an independent group run by Japanese residents to address the various needs of the substantial community of Japanese residing within the kingdom. Some years ago, the same association actually purchased the title to the land on which the monument stands, to prevent it from being appropriated by and incorporated within the neighbouring dubious 'war museum' near the bridge, mentioned above.[18] The same association has continued to hold an annual memorial service for the railway's victims every March. The Japanese Shingon priest who, re-ordained according to Thai Theravada Buddhist rites, is the resident monk at the Japanese Ossuary located in Bangkok's Wat Liab Temple and customarily leads the service. The solemn prayers and sutras recited at the service make ample and clear reference to both the Western and Asian victims (Figures 4.6 and 4.7).

[18] The same museum had previously purchased rights to the land on which lay the remains of the approaches to the (subsequently bombed) wooden bridge across the river, which was pictured in Part VI of this series. The photo was taken before the museum in question was constructed. The track and flimsy riverside approach to the wooden bridge now feature as one of the Museum's exhibits. Despite verbal undertakings to the contrary (and the illegality of such riverside construction), the same museum built an extension blocking the Japanese monument's view of the river.

The Vietnamese language inscription.

Repainting the Vietnamese language panel.

The Malaysian/Indonesian language inscription.

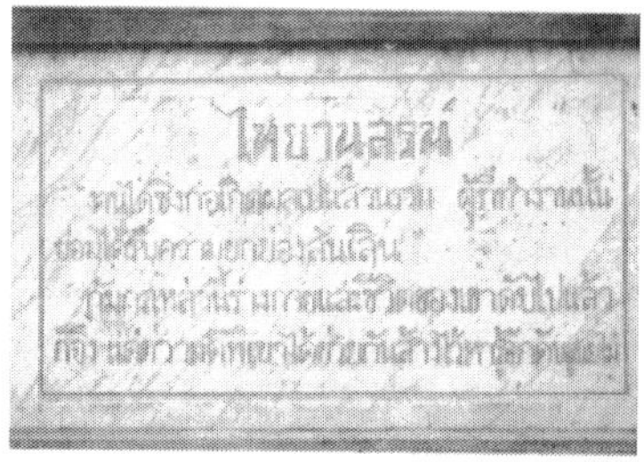

The Thai language inscription.

The defaced section of the Tamil language panel.

English language panel memorializing the POWs.

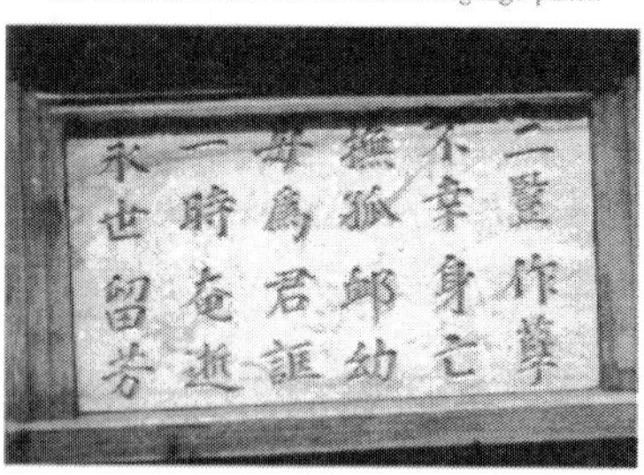

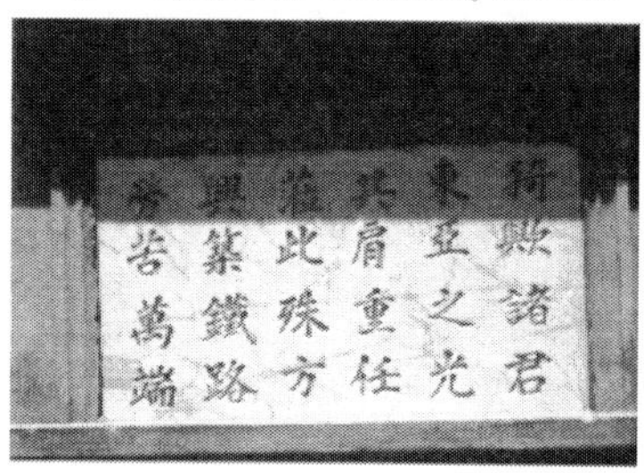

The two sections of the Chinese language poetry *(kanshi)* inscription. Both Japanese and Chinese would have been able to understand the characters.

Figure 4.6 Inscriptions from the War Memorials in Kanchanaburi, Various Languages

Source: The author.

Figure 4.7 The 2000 Memorial Service at the Monument Erected by the Imperial Japanese Army Near the Famous Kanchanaburi Bridge.

Source: The author.

Note: Rev Sasaki Kojun reads Japanese Sutras at the service which is organized by the Bangkok Association of Japanese Residents.

4.6. THE KRA ISTHMUS RAILWAY

The Thai-Burma Railway was not the only railroad constructed by the Japanese military to link Thailand with Burma. The first completed attempt to link the two countries' railroad systems was the much shorter Kra Isthmus Railway, extending some 90 km from the main Southern Line station of Chumphon to the village of Ban Khao Fa Chi on the small river La-Un. From this Thai rural village terminal, goods were to be loaded on to small river boats for trans-shipment along the river La-un and the larger river Kra to Ranong, and thence to the southernmost town of Burma, then called Victoria Point (Figure 4.9). Today, this sizable Burmese town has

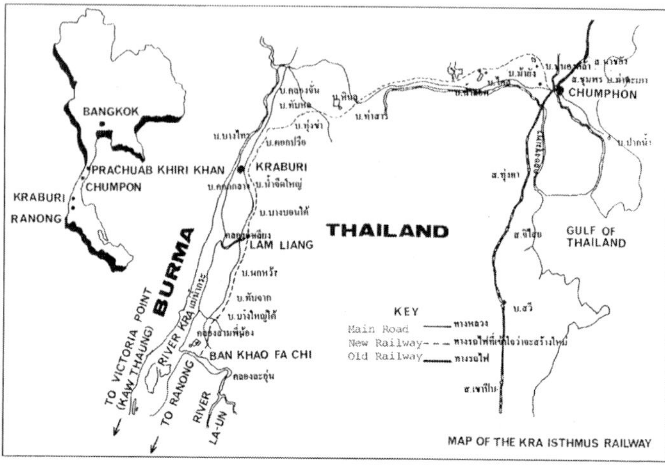

Figure 4.8 This Map of the Kra Isthmus Railway Based on Praphan Phonsawek

Source: Phonsawek (1991, 107).

Disclaimer: This figure has been redrawn by the author/s and is not to scale. It does not represent any authentic national or international boundaries and is used for illustrative purposes only.

been renamed Kawthaung and is known to the Thais as Ko Song.[19] Construction of the Kra Railway was started later than that of the Thai-Burma Railway but was completed first, and, indeed, this railway had been intended as only a temporary measure to address the problems of transporting goods into Burma posed by the slow pace of the former's construction.

Chumphon is located in Southern Thailand, in an area where the peninsula separating the Gulf of Thailand from the Andaman Sea is, in some places, only a little more than 50 km wide. On the Andaman coast, the present town of Ranong (historically a somewhat Chinese-oriented town) still carries on a regular trade of goods and tourists to Victoria Point (Kawthaung) in the neighbouring Burma. Construction work on the Kra Isthmus

[19] The present military government not only changed the country's name from *Burma* to *Myanmar*, it has also renamed most of Burma's cities, towns and villages, causing considerable confusion to outsiders unfamiliar with the country. For the sake of clarity, this chapter retains the old names commonly used in documents covering these events. Wherever possible, the new names have been inserted in brackets.

Figure 4.9 Photos of Parts of the Kra Isthmus Railway

Source: Author's own based on various secondary sources.

Railway began in June 1943, and the line was completed by the end of November of the same year, but it only operated for some 11 months before intensive Allied bombing of the extensively exposed track forced the Japanese to abandon it and concentrate their efforts on the larger Thai-Burma Railway project. Much of the steel track was at that time removed from the Kra Isthmus Railway to be used on the Thai-Burma Railway and elsewhere. What little remained after the war was taken up by the British army that briefly occupied Thailand.

As a result of its strategic importance to the railway effort, the sleepy town of Chumphon was transformed into a major construction and engineering base. Even today, the approaches to Chumphon's sizable station are lined with spacious old housing for railway officials, built in a semi-colonial Western style popular at that time, and humbler wooden tenements for railway workers. The station boasts a large marshalling yard, engineering workshops and—for that time—a rather advanced water system to fuel the steam locomotives, a system built by the Japanese. Outside the station, three old steam locomotives are on permanent display, attesting to the station's former importance in the saga of Thailand's railway system.[20]

This was not the first time that the Japanese war effort had impinged upon the lives of Chumphon's citizens. On 8 December 1941, a detachment of the invading Japanese army had landed at one of Chumphon's many inlets, only to encounter resistance from a Thai student military unit raised from the students of the Sriyaphai High School. Their regular commanding officer, Col Thawin Niyornsaen, lost his life in the ensuing skirmishes at the Tha Nang Sang Bridge and the nearby Wat Tha Yang Tai temple. Col Thawin's second-in-command, Lt Samran Kuanphan (then a sergeant) also lost his right arm up to the elbow. Sometime after the war, Lt Samran contacted the youth brigade's leader, Thepthai Chaisomkhon, who gathered the other former student soldiers in order to erect a small memorial to those involved in opposing the Japanese army's landing. In 1981, with financial assistance from the Chumphon local government and Col Thawin's son, the memorial was restored, enlarged and moved to its present location beside the old Tha Nang Sang Bridge. The gist of the commemorative inscription on the monument begins,

[20] The locomotives displayed at Chumphon are (a) A 4-6-2 Baldwin Pacific built in the USA in 1926, (b) A 4-6-0 engine built by the North British Locomotive Co. in 1919 and (c) A small 0-6-OST engine built at Bristol (England) in 1897. The Kra Isthmus Railway apparently used the same locomotive types as were employed on the later Thai-Burma Railway. These would have included, besides C56 locomotives from Japan, both British-built 4-6-0 engines already in use on the Thai railways and 4-6-2 types moved by the Japanese from Malaya. Interestingly, there are two C56 locomotives formerly used in Thailand but now in Japan: both were found at the Chumphon yards. C5631 (Japanese wartime number) is now displayed at Yasukuni Shrine in Tokyo, the controversial site that enshrines the spirits of Japan's war dead (including Class A war criminals). The other, C564, is still operating on the privately owned *Oigawa Tetsudo* (River Oi Railroad) in Shizuoka Prefecture (Figure 4.9).

> A youth brigade in the uniform of the Chumphon military cadets demonstrated their bravery before all the people when, despite their small numbers, their courageous stand delayed the invading (Japanese) army from entering Chumphon Province. This is a glorious history and will not be forgotten.... (This monument) is dedicated to their courage and valour that it will he [sic] forever remembered by all.[21]

Few records of the railway's construction survive; the only substantial account of the railway being that (in Thai language) by Praphan Phonsawek which appeared in the June 1991 edition of the *Sinlapawathanatham* (Art & Culture) Magazine. Praphan traces the process of negotiations which led to an agreement between Col Yamada (presumably Military Attaché of the Japanese Embassy in Bangkok) and Phisit Disaphong Ditsakul representing the Thai government to build the railway. The negotiations were held in Yamada's house on Wireless Road. Under the agreement, Thailand was to prepare the earthworks for the rail course, build bridges and undertake the necessary drainage system to prevent the heavy monsoon rains from flooding the track. The Japanese were to provide the labour for laying the sleepers, the track itself and construction of related facilities. Japan also undertook to provide the steel rail track from the Malayan railway system in Kelantan and provide technical staff (also from Malaya) to operate the railway when finished (Phonsawek 1991, 104–113).[22]

---

[21] Details about the Chumphon Youth Brigade Memorial are taken from a Thai-language book issued to mark the 50th anniversary of the war and published by the Nakhon Sri Thammarat local administration. The Chumphon Monument is explained in detail in a chapter entitled 'Anuson Sathan' (Memorial Sites), pp. 158–161. I am indebted to Thanawalai Jaroenjangdang, formerly a student of both Seika and Chiang Mai Universities, for translation assistance, and to Viwat Sritrakul (Seto Masao) of the Bangkok *Asahi Shimbun* (newspaper) office for obtaining copies of this important document. The fighting in Chumphon and other areas of the south ended when Thai Prime Minister Plaek Phibunsongkhram returned from his most famous 'absence' to Bangkok, ordered a ceasefire and went on to negotiate various friendship treaties and agreements with Japan.

[22] I am again indebted to Thanawalai Jaroenjangdang for translation assistance and to Charnvit Kasetsiri, former Rector of Thammasat University, for obtaining copies of this article, the best overall description of the Kra Isthmus Railway to date. Details on the negotiations and agreements about the railway as well as

The agreement was formally signed by Thai Prime Minister Plaek Phibunsongkhram and General Nakamura Aketo of the (Japanese) Bangkok Garrison Command. Interestingly, anticipating Thailand's agreement, the Japanese had already made a thorough survey of the railway's projected course. It seems that the Japanese side was somewhat elated, having obtained Thailand's agreement to undertake rather more of the construction work than had at first been anticipated. The Thai government immediately contracted their share of the work out to private (Thai) contractors who endeavoured to employ chiefly Thai-Chinese labour. Although conditions for those workers employed by the Thai contractors were infinitely better than that of labourers conscripted by the Japanese army, Thai company officials nevertheless had great difficulty in persuading their workers to stay longer than one or two months and were constantly seeking new recruits.

The Japanese, for their part, had determined that not only the rail track and operating technicians were to come from Kelantan, but also that the labour for track-laying and construction of the related railway and port facilities would be obtained—voluntary or otherwise—from Malaya; most informed estimates vary between 60,000 to 120,000 persons. Information from local informants suggests that, in a harrowing prelude to the excesses of the later Thai-Burma Railway, unencumbered by the niceties of any international agreements and not fearing post-war reprisals for their treatment of Asian civilians, the Japanese were quite prepared, if necessary, to work their Malayan labourers literally to their deaths.[23] Praphan Phonsawek's informants repeatedly state that work continued on a 24-hour day basis, that there were neither doctors nor medicines available, that the food was totally inadequate and that distressed Malayans—knowing neither the local

---

the Thai companies who received the Thai government contracts are all taken from this important article.

[23] Although local informants believed that only Malayans had been used in the construction work, Kiattisahasakul (2011) in her book states, 'The Japanese Army requested from the Thai Government some 10000 Thai labourers. The Thais provided 3,630 people from Surat Thani, Nakhon Si Thammarat, Pattalung, Narathiwat, Pattani, Yala & Songkhla. Also 1,221 people from Phetchaburi, Nakhon Pathom, Pathum Thani, Ayudhya, Chonburi, Chachoengsao & Nakhon Nayok'.

nor the Japanese language—who tried to abscond, were severely dealt with. The numerous dead were simply buried in shallow holes by the side of the rail tracks.[24]

In January 2003, a research visit to the area and travel along the length of the old railway course confirmed that the rail track had run, by and large, alongside the present main road from Chumphon to Ranong: the old rail course was easily established from local informants, although—due to post-war internal migration to other parts of Thailand—very few people in the area today have direct memories of construction. The railway had not at first utilized the river port facilities that existed in the town along the Kra River, and trains stopped here only briefly to replenish supplies of fuel and water. But after the first few months of operation, when trains could no longer hazard the journey to the remote terminal of Khao Fa Chi due to Allied bombing, the terminal was moved back to Kraburi, and port facilities were constructed there. At Lam Liang village, a small rush mat and thatch-making factory sits astride the old rail line: an elderly local resident indicated the old bridge which had been bombed (the only old road bridge still in existence, for the bomb had failed to explode). Now disused, a more modern structure carries today's traffic to the side of the old bridge site (Figure 4.9).

At the railway's terminus in Khao Fa Chi village, the local administration has tried to reconstruct some sites connected with the railway. Efforts have been made to preserve some of the old warehouse sites at the Kra River port (for larger boats) and the harbour for smaller craft at the River La-Un terminal. An old steam locomotive has been positioned here to recreate the atmosphere of the old rail terminal. However, somewhat paradoxically, the engine is a Japanese 2-8-2 'Mikado' class locomotive—far too large to have run on the narrow, winding and rather tortuous course of the Kra Isthmus Railway—and was in fact shipped to Thailand from Japan after the war, probably under a GHQ plan to assist the resurrection of Japanese industry and at the same time to 'compensate' and aid Thailand's post-war development (Figure 4.10).[25]

---

[24] An edited form of remarks made by Lung (Uncle) Gi Suwawichien (then 68 years of age) to Phonsawek (1991, 109).

[25] Identification and verification of every steam locomotive preserved in Thailand can be achieved by consulting the thorough and complete listings in Ramaer

Figure 4.10 2-8-2 'Mikado' Class Locomotive

Source: The author.

Note: A 2-8-2 'Mikado' Class Locomotive (Japan, 147) now stands at the river La-un railway Terminal in Khao Fa Chi Village. Although some 12 Mikados were supplied by Japan during the war in 1942, this particular engine was delivered in 1947, under the direction of the Allied Occupation Authorities in Tokyo. They were too large to run on the Kra Railway.

At the small Khao Fa Chi village administrative centre, 66-year-old Sabiang Chuchat, son of the wartime village headman, recounted his memories of the railway as a young boy:

> Well. I was only 6 years old or so at the time, but I used to be terribly afraid of the Japanese soldiers. I used to see them hitting the workers regularly: they were always beating the workers. These workers had to carry earth from the Khao Fa Chi hill to prepare the ground for the railway terminal, the warehouse buildings and the port. Later they had to load all those heavy goods on to the boats.... The death toll was enormous So many died and there was much fever and sickness.... The dead were just thrown into holes: there were no burial services or cremations.... Nobody recorded the deaths; they were such a common occurrence. Many Thai people were arrested by the Japanese allegedly for stealing something. Several Thais were put in prison and some died there.... Some of these Thais hadn't actually stolen anything; they were just accused of stealing. I heard some were shot while trying to escape.

The local village office has also started a small collection of artefacts found along the rail course to develop into a memorial museum. Among these are some pottery bowls of Islamic design (Figure 4.11), thought to have been used by the Malayan workers. Sanan Bainrung, an assistant to the village office, has often guided visitors around the old sites near the Kra River. He is able to locate the old drainage pipes still lying under the railway embankments and is also familiar with the site of the old Japanese military camp near the Bang Kaew police station. There had been some 1,200 troops stationed here at any moment of time, and the remains of old gun emplacements are still clearly visible. A tunnel in the hillside behind the camp had probably been used as a military hospital. In a

(1994). This invaluable work has been used to verify the histories of all the locomotives mentioned in the article. The locomotive displayed at the Khao Fa Chi terminal by the La-Un River is a Japanese-built 'Mikado' 2-8-2. Although some 12 *Mikados* were supplied by Japan in 1942 (later Thai National Railway engine numbers 367–378), this particular locomotive was delivered after World War II in 1947. The post-war Allied Occupation authorities arranged for Japan to supply a further (modified) 70 *Mikados*—as well as some 30 *Pacifics*—to Thailand. (The engines were supplied as 'war reparations'). By 1950, it is estimated that there were a total of 98 *Mikados* in use on the Thai National Railway system.

Figure 4.11 An Islamic Patterned Bowl Used by Workers from Malaya Preserved at Khao Fa Chi Village Office

Source: The author.

local restaurant, by the side of the La-Un River, an old well built by the Japanese military is still in use, and the wreck of a small boat used to transport the rail goods on to Ranong and Victoria Point has been discovered in the La-Un River—it has been examined and recorded by the government's Fine Arts Department. But other efforts to commemorate the railway's existence and the preparation of sites and their detailed description are to be commended and deserve a wider recognition. Few tourists, however, visit the area and even people in nearby Chumphon are largely unaware of the village's attempts to reconstruct the saga of the Kra Isthmus Railway (Figure 4.12).

Clouded in oblivion though the construction of the Kra Isthmus Railway may be, its demise has been clearly recorded. In November 1944, 20 Allied bombers attacked the railway and both the La-Un and Kra River piers. A raid by 30 aeroplanes on 19 March 1945 sealed the railway's fate; the damage was so severe that it was completely abandoned, and its steel rails taken up for re-use elsewhere (Phonsawek 1991, 111).

> With many bridges destroyed along the Kwai Railway, Colonel Alness, on 19th March 1945, led 37 bombers from

Figure 4.12 A Local Artist's Depiction of Wartime Khao Fa Chi.

Source: The author.

Note: The River La-Un is in the foreground, flowing into the larger Kra River at the top of the sketch.

> the tour squadrons on a 2,700-mile flight to the rail line on the Kra Isthmus. All bombers were in the air over 18 hours, and bridges and track in that area were destroyed (Fritsche n.d., 26)

Likewise, the human aftermath of the railway has also been recorded. Sir Andrew Gilchrist, first a student interpreter at the British Embassy in Bangkok who had later attained the rank of consul before the outbreak of war, was one of the first British officers to reach Chumphon. In a letter to his wife, he records the human devastation he encountered:

> I began to realise that I had quite another problem on my hands in the shape of thousands of sick and starving and dying labourers whom the Japanese had brought up from Malaya and Sumatra and Java and Singapore, to work on roads and railways in the Kra Isthmus area and had now been abandoned to their own devices. From their working camps those creatures now came walking and crawling in search of food and help… .I am being pressed to put some of the Japs in on war crimes charges: indeed, I have actually named the ones I think most responsible for leaving the Malayan slave-labourers to die…. (Regrettably at this important point several key paragraphs were omitted from Gilchrist's publication)…. These people crawling along the roads were bad enough, but next day I visited some of the dispersal camps, including a place which the Japanese called a hospital. It was nothing hut [sic] a ghastly charnel house; a series of small rotting huts in heavy jungle with 30 serious cases and a few corpses huddled together on filthy wooden floors. The smell was intolerable: the commonest diseases were tropical ulcers and dysentery—many people had four diseases, ulcers, dysentery, beri-beri and malaria, while scabies, typhoid, pneumonia, syphilis, gonorrhea and cancer were also well represented. The only medicine on view was a kind of weak red disinfectant; no bandages were available and paper dressings, sometimes actually made of what looked like toilet paper, either adhered by themselves or were gummed down round the edges. Food consisted of rice and vegetable soup, in the most meagre quantities. Sanitary arrangements were non-existent, and all the patients were indescribably filthy and verminous… The Japanese attitude was not so much one of obstruction as of total incomprehension: they could not understand why anyone

took so much interest in those miserable creatures. (Gilchrist 1970, 224–225)[26]

Gilchrist included several photographs of these Asian workers in his letter home, five of which are included in his book. They show barely living skeletons, some on the verge of death. One photo caption reads 'When I removed the blanket to take the photograph the man was alive: when I bent down to put it back, he was dead'. Another photo of a skeletal Tamil woman is labelled, 'A Tamil woman describes the whereabouts of yet another horror camp'; that under a photo of an emaciated young man, 'Newly collected from a jungle charnel-house', and yet another, "Dysentery corner in the hospital'. It is clear that he was personally considerably shocked on encountering these survivors (see Figure 4.13; other photos in Figures 4.14–4.17).[27]

---

[26] The likelihood that Gilchrist was responsible for the arrest and trial of any Japanese military officials for war crimes is, however, rather small. Following his earlier repatriation from Thailand, Gilchrist spent most of the war in Calcutta, where he worked on supporting and supplying the *Seri Thai* (Free Thai) Movement that opposed the Japanese presence within Thailand. (His diplomatic career in Bangkok had brought him into contact with—and he was well liked by—both the movement's leader and Regent of Thailand, Pridi Phanomyong and his remarkable wife.) Gilchrist was considerably more ambivalent about the issue of war crimes than the excerpted quotations might suggest. During his lengthy Calcutta sojourn, he had personally witnessed the horrific war-time famine that occurred there due to the negligence of the British colonial authorities, and which had likewise greatly affected him. He was later moved to write, '...if the Japanese had captured Calcutta while the war-time famine was at its height, with innumerable weightless corpses lying about the streets at a moment when no British soldiers were short of rations, might they not have felt justified in putting British commanders on trial as being responsible for this appalling situation?'

[27] It has not been possible to determine which people—if any—were arrested on war crimes charges for their treatment of these Asian workers. However, the Vice Chief of Staff of General Nakamura's Bangkok Garrison Command, Lt General Hamada Minoru committed ritual suicide on 17 September 1945. Hamada's death is the subject of Appendix E ('Chumporn & the Death of Hamada') in Gilchrist (1970, 222–231). A more helpful and informative account of Lt General Hamada's death can be found in Reynolds (1988, 189). An excerpt of the latter reads,'The war crimes issue hung like a black cloud over the Japanese, largely because of the mistreatment of 55,000 Allied prisoners of war (POWs) during the construction of the Thailand–Burma Railway. Nakamura's command had assumed administrative control over the POW camps only in 1945, but Vice Chief of Staff Attaché Hamada had served as head of the POW

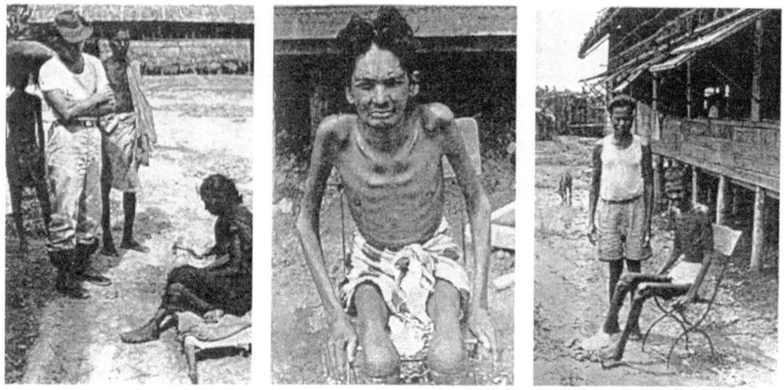

These 1945 photos of Asian labourers taken in Chumphon by Sir Andrew Gilchrist attest to the appalling conditions in which he found the labourers' camps. The photos were later published in his book, *"Bangkok Top Secret"* (Hutchinson) 1970. *(Above Left)* "A Tamil woman describes the whereabouts of yet another horror camp". *(Center)* "Newly collected from a jungle charnel house". *(Right)* "A male nurse of the British forces with a patient outside the camp hospital. *(Photos Below: Left)* "Dysentery corner in the hospital". *(Right)* "When I removed the blanket to take the photograph the man was alive: when I bent down to put it back he was dead".

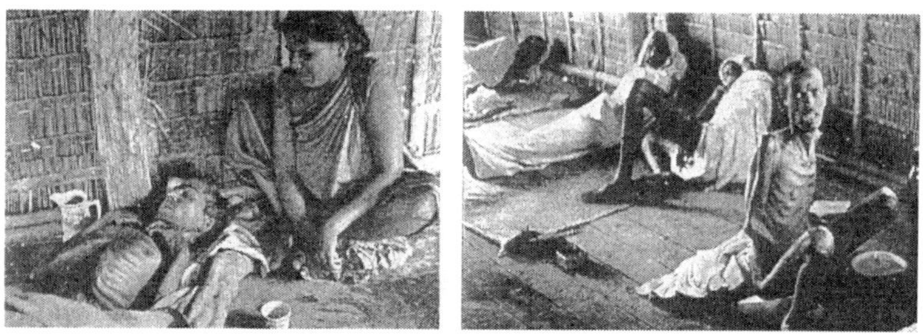

Figure 4.13 These 1945 Photos of Asian Labourers Taken in Chumphon by Sir Andrew Gilchrist Attest to the Appalling Conditions in Which He Found the Labourers' Camps

Source: Author's own collection based on several secondary sources.

Information Bureau in Tokyo at the height of the construction and seemed a prime candidate for indictment. Perhaps with this in mind—or as Nakamura interpreted it—to take responsibility for his failure to push through POW camp improvements he had personally advocated—Hamada committed seppuku (ritual suicide) on September 17th'.Note 104 of the same work contains more details on Hamada's background: 'Tojo had sent Hamada to inspect conditions on the Thailand-Burma Railway in the Spring of 1943 and what he saw greatly distressed him. As a means to better the situation, he proposed putting the entire railway project under Nakamura's command. Nakamura, aware of the problem, agreed to the idea and lobbied for its acceptance with the Railway Section Chief of Imperial General Headquarters when he accompanied Tojo

Chumphon Station, located on the main Southern Line and terminal of the Kra Isthmus Railway, became an important engineering and supply base for the new railway's construction. Much of the wartime railway workers' housing still remains, as does the advanced water supply system. Several steam locomotives on display outside the station attest to Chumphon's importance for Thailand's railway system.

Housing for railway workers, Chumphon Station.

A 4-6-2 Baldwin Pacific (USA, 1926) outside Chumphon Station.

A 4-6-0 type locomotive (UK, 1919) outside Chumphon Station.

Figure 4.14 Views of Chumphon Railway Terminal

Source: Author's own based on several secondary sources.

Figure 4.15 Asian Workers Being Transported to the Railway

Source: Wartime photo © Ao-sha Publishing Co., Nagoya, Japan

Figure 4.16 The Ao-sha Photos Include Some of the Asian Women and Children Involved in the Railway Camps

Source: The author.

Today, the Ban Khao Fa Chi local authorities have erected plaques in Thai Language, describing the village's wartime experience.

---

to Bangkok. However, the SGA (Southern General Army, head-quartered in Saigon, Vietnam) refused to relinquish its long distance direct control'.

Figure 4.17 (Left Column) Wartime Photos of Asian Workers Being Transported for Railway Work and (Right Column) Asian Workers on the Railway

Sources: (Left Column) © Home Phu Toey Resort Museum. (Right Column) © Ao-sha Publishing Co., Nagoya, Japan

> The construction of the railway began on June 1st, 2486 BE. Colonel Sugihara Masaharu was the military corps leader, and Kawahashi the controlling engineer. There were some 20,000–25,000 Chinese, Malay and Indian workers transported from Malaya. Workmen were divided into gangs, the Kinjo, Nishimoto, and Kago gangs, to work day and night to speed up the construction. The railway ran in parallel with the Chumpon-Ranong Highway, with 31 bridges, and 7 stations. Japanese troops brought the iron tracks dismantled from Kelantan in Malaya ... work was finished on November 24th (Ineligible) [sic]. Now the locomotive is placed at Ban Khao Fa Chi, Tambol Bang Keo, District La-Un, Ranong province.[28]

[28] I am grateful to Dr Charit Tingsabadh for drawing my attention to the existence of this more recent memorial and for his English translation of the Thai text. It should be mentioned that the estimated number of workers brought from Malaya is rather lower than the 80,000 commonly used.

4.7. THE KHUN YUAM–TOUNGOO ROAD

The town of Mae Hong Son is a remote mountain resort for Bangkok's elite (and, of course, not-so-elite foreign tourists, both Western and Japanese) being connected by air with daily flights to both Bangkok and Chiangmai. Apart from the air links, however, the province is remote and considered somewhat 'exotic' by most Thais. Only about 2 per cent of the province's population is 'central Thai' (mostly concentrated in Mae Hong Son town), whereas around 50 per cent are Tai Yai (or ethnic 'Burmese' Shan), the remainder of the figure (somewhat over 40%) being made up of numerous hill tribe groupings. To the west and north the province borders on Burma, the lower western border being marked by the Salween River. Mae Hong Son was relatively inaccessible by road until the opening of the Mae Sariang 'loop' road in the late 1960s. This Mae Sariang 'loop', Highway 108, proceeds due west from Chiangmai to Mae Sariang, near the Salween River border with Burma, and thereafter turns due north to Mae Hong Son. It takes about 10 hours of continuous driving and passes through some of the most spectacular mountain scenery in Thailand (resembling northern or central European scenery, and occasionally that of Japan). Morning mists cloud the valleys for part of the year. In the early 1990s, however, a shorter Highway 1095 was constructed from Chiang Dao (north of Chiangmai) to Mae Hong Son through the town of Pai. Highway 1095 follows precisely the original route of the old Japanese military supply road.

> The 1095 was originally laid out by the Japanese in World War II as a way of supporting their war effort in Burma. It was to take another fifty years before this tortuous dirt track through the mountains and jungle was to become properly serviceable (Goodden 1996, 63).

Highway 1095 meanders on to Mae Hong Son town and then turns South (following the course of today's Highway 108) as far as Khun Yuam. A few kilometres beyond Mae Hong Son, in Pha Bong village, is an extensive hot spring, advertised as having curative powers for a wide range of diseases. The official explanatory notice board (in Thai language only) states that the hot springs were found and developed 'by the Japanese soldiers during the era of World War II'.

The early surveying work for the Khun Yuam–Toungoo Road appears to have been done by a Japanese photographer resident in Chiangmai, Tanaka Morinosuke (1905–1961; married to a Thai wife with whom he had a daughter, Tanaka was never repatriated to Japan and continued to live in Chiangmai until his death in 1961).[29]

Khun Yuam was an important centre for the road-building project. The sleepy, undeveloped town now hosted a sizeable garrison of several thousand Japanese troops. Employment was readily available in servicing this military base. Indeed, Khun Yuam had never been so prosperous. The Japanese period is still looked upon by the town's inhabitants with considerable affection. From Khun Yuam, the road turned due west and crossed over the Burmese border. A museum of exhibits connected with Japan's 'Burma Road' was opened in Khun Yuam in 1996.[30] The exhibits included around 1,000 items of tools, military equipment, guns and personal belongings of Japanese soldiers involved in the road's construction. An impressive array of contemporary photographs records the road's progression; Japanese soldiers drilling in the nearby Shan (Tai Yai) temple grounds of Wat To Phae,[31] and Japanese soldiers tending elephants (allegedly treated better than human labourers, in that they were permitted alternate days of rest!). More ominously, a contemporary notice (in Thai) reads,

---

[29] English language information about Tanaka Morinosuke's life can be found on the website of Hak Hakanson, http://www.lanna-ww2.com/pages/z02200-CNX_city/y02235%20Tanaka/y02235-001_page_01.html. I am also grateful to Mr Seto Masao (Viwat Sritrakul) of the Asahi Newspaper in Bangkok for further information, chronology and notes.

[30] A Kyodo news service report, datelined Khun Yuam and published in *The Japan Times* on 12 November 1996 reads, 'A museum displaying some 500 Japanese items from World War II has opened in this North-west Thailand town… Pakdee Chompooming, governor of Mae Hong Son Province who presided over the ceremony, explained that many Thais in Khunyuam District were forced under brutal circumstances by the Japanese army to construct a road into Myanmar. "Tens of thousands were forced to construct the road aiming to link Thailand and Myanmar from the northern capital of Chiangmai", the Governor said. "They couldn't complete the construction before the surrender of the Japanese Imperial Army, but thousands of people died of malaria"'.

[31] Wat To Phae, an elegant Shan (Tai Yai) style temple is chiefly noted today for its possession of a rare 19th century Shan Buddhist tapestry from Burma and two excellently preserved carved teak toilets.

'Mosquitoes are more dangerous than tigers', continuing in small print to depict the dangers posed by malaria. A further leaflet, evidently dropped from allied aircraft, bears the US flag and exhorts the local populace to assist any parachuting soldiers in distress in order to aid the *Seri Thai (Free Thai) Movement.*[32] More recently, the late Lt Col Cherdchai's modest museum was replaced by a rather grandiose structure now termed 'The Thailand-Japan Friendship Memorial Hall', though many of the artefacts collected by him are still on display (Figure 4.18).

Although there had been many casual liaisons with the Japanese troops, Kaew Chantasima believed that hers was the only official marriage to a Japanese soldier. Her husband, a certain Fukuda (given name forgotten) from Tottori Prefecture, was well known in the town. This Fukuda had not himself worked on road construction, but he had evidently been attached to a technical division which had set up the first electricity-generating station in Khun Yuam. Their son, Bunat, is today a teacher in the local school. At the end of the war, the husband, Fukuda, being married

Figure 4.18 The Present 'Thailand–Japan Friendship Memorial Hall' at Khun Yuam

Source: The author.

[32] Although the Phibun government was officially allied with Japan, a *Seri Thai* (Free Thai) anti-Japanese guerilla movement had grown up under the support of the then Regent Pridi Phanomyong, and with the knowledge of both the USA and Britain (see Wiriyawit 1997; Wyatt 1982; also see Haseman 1978).

to a Thai, had chosen to try to remain in Khun Yuam, but had been arrested while working in the rice fields and taken to Bangkok. Fukuda had been interned there awaiting repatriation to Japan. Kaew had been unsuccessful in her attempts to contact her husband during his confinement and was subsequently verbally informed by the Thai police that her husband had died during captivity. Kaew was indignant that, as the legal wife of a Japanese citizen, her attempts to find information about her (late) husband had led nowhere and that she had received no aid whatsoever from the post-war Japanese authorities to support their eldest son (who was one year old at the time of the end of the 'war). The Japanese—she claimed—had shown no interest whatsoever in trying to determine the fate of her husband and had given her an honorarium of a mere 2,000 baht (at that time worth about 10,000 yen or less) for her televised interview. 'That's all I ever got from Japan', she retorted '2,000 Baht to bring up my children of a Japanese father!' One cannot help but wonder, however, whether the truth might have been even less palatable, for, as no written evidence confirming 'Fukuda's death was ever presented, the possibility remains that the said Fukuda might—after all—have returned alive and well to Japan.[33]

The Khun Yuam—Toungoo Road apparently became a serious issue of contention between the Japanese and Thai governments in 1943:

> In September the Japanese had to return (to the Thai Government) with a request for an additional 20.4 million baht. This money was to be used mainly for the construction of a military road connecting Thailand and Burma through the Thai border town of Mae Hong Son, a route considered

[33] Kaew Chantasima's memory was not too good, presumably due to her age (75 years). She had never had any photo of her husband, Fukuda, and she clearly did not use his given name, though she remembered that he was from Tottori Prefecture. It is also unclear how many children she had with him. She subsequently had married again but her second husband (by whom she also had children) was something of a 'playboy' (her words) and again left her after a year or so. (She thinks this may not have been unrelated to her having children by her previous marriage.) Although it is clear—and widely known in the town—that her first child, Bunat, was with her first (Japanese) husband, she appears also to have had a younger daughter by the same marriage.

> vital to the support of a planned Japanese offensive. Although (Japanese ambassador) Tsubokami appealed for prompt action when he met Phibun on 23rd September, in early October the two sides remained at loggerheads. (Reynolds 1994, 212)

Japan's 'Burma Road' was still serviceable at the end of the 'war. But it did serve one totally unintended function. As with the better-known Thai-Burma Railroad, the Khun Yuam—Toungoo road had been intended not only to back up 'Japan's wartime occupation of Burma, but also to supply the Japanese army in its disastrous Imphal Campaign, an attack into British-occupied northeast India overland from Burma. The fiasco and defeat of the Imperial Army at Imphal and the hardships and loss of life in the disorderly retreat, first from India and later from Burma, are well documented. Paradoxically, the Thai-Burma Railroad and the Khun Yuam—Toungoo Road, rather than supplying victorious Japanese campaigns, became the chief routes for retreat or escape for the badly battered Japanese soldiery (Michio 1966).

> In the north, small groups of soldiers in tattered rags stumbled eastward via the Thai border town of Mae Hong Son, along the supply road that the Japanese had improved from the latter half of 1943. The retreating troops sometimes were forced to trade their equipment or personal belongings for food, or simply to beg for it. (Reynolds 1994, 212)

Many of the Japanese military returnees struggled through Mae Hong Son to Chiangmai, where they were eventually impounded by the Allies at the end of the war. The plight of the hapless Japanese soldiers occasioned some sympathy from the locals: several informants in Chiangmai have related how they were sent by their families to take scraps of food to Japanese soldiers impounded in Wat Meun San, one of Chiangmai's temples.

Despite providing a means of escape for the Imperial 'Army's disillusioned soldiers at the end of hostilities, 'Japan's 'Burma Road' would remain a dirt-track until the construction of Highway 1095 nearly 50 years later. Beyond Khun Yuam, across the Burmese border to Toungoo, the road still continues to be used today for trade by merchants of both towns. Other visitors (whether Thai or foreign nationals) are discouraged, and special permission is required to enter the military reserved areas near the Thai border. A small border check post is maintained by Thai and Burmese soldiers, and beyond this border post, the road seems somewhat better maintained on the Burmese side of the border. A large Thai army base is located a few kilometres into Thailand, and the remnants of the site of old gun emplacement can be seen on the hill overlooking the border.[34]

So much for the road, but the fate of those involved in its construction or those who had used it as an escape route from Burma was somewhat less fortunate. Between the townships of Pai and Wiang Haeng—today still connected only by a dirt track—lies the small village of Sala Muang Noi, nestling on a bend in the river Pai.[35]

> When the (Sala Muang Noi) health center had been built a year or two earlier workers had unearthed the mass grave of Japanese soldiers who had been massacred in World War II. They were probably killed by Karens as the Japanese withdrew from Burma back into Thailand at the end of the war. In 1945 Karen and Karenni underground forces, organised and armed by the British, killed an estimated 12,500 troops of the Japanese 15th. Army, as it retreated in disarray through Burma's eastern hills and back across the Thai-Burmese border'. (Goodden 1996, 60; Figures 4.19 and 4.20)

This information was recorded in Christian 'Goodden's guidebook to the area. 'Goodden's informant was a young Karen from Mae Haat hamlet of Wiang Haeng, Witit Terkae. He had been an employee of Wiang 'Haeng's small hospital, usually working in the Mae Haat village clinic, but frequently travelling around the area when involved in various hill tribe development schemes.

> Witit recounted details his mother had told him about the Japanese in Wiang Haeng during World War II. They had press ganged local people to act as porters in their invasion of Burma from Thailand. But they could not have had things all

[34] Photographs from a visit to the border in 2016.

[35] Sala Muang Noi is approachable, even in the dry season, only by four-wheel drive vehicles. As my own transport is a saloon car, I was unable to visit the village personally. Information on Sala Muang Noi is taken from Goodden (1996).

Figure 4.19 The Border Checkpoint on the Khun Yuam–Taungoo Road and the Road on the Burmese Side of the Border

Source: The author.

> their own way in this isolated area. Recently a mass grave of Japanese soldiers had been unearthed at nearby Sala Muang Noi... It was a Karen village halfway between Wiang Haeng and Pai. (Goodden 1996, 54)

Ba Maw, the Prime Minister of Japanese-promoted 'independent' Burma, recorded the difficulties surrounding the minority peoples' situation during the war. Regarding the Karen people, Ba Maw writes,

> In fact, a large number of (Karens) believe that a Burmese-dominated nation to which they are indissolubly tied will mean their gradual extinction as a community.... (The British) consequently decided to give such protection to the Karens as they did to the minority races in India.... They also gave the Karens military training in the British army in Burma, whereas the Burmese ... were kept out altogether.... When the war came, the Karens as a community remained loyal to

Figure 4.20 The Border Post at Huay Ton Nun and a Japanese Gun Emplacement Site

Source: The author.

> the British, and Karen troops in the British army remained loyal to the end. (Maw 1968, 187)[36]

One elderly Karen leader reported to Ba Maw,

> (The Japanese officer) questioned me about Karen loyalty to the British. He wanted to know the reason for it. I told him quite simply. The British had always protected the Karens

[36] A slightly different emphasis is provided by many British accounts of the time. For example, 'The (British) army disappeared over the Assam border (to India) but the Hill peoples fought on—not only the Kachins but also the Chins, the Karens and the Nagas. Those Hill peoples were the rocks against which the tide of invasion by the "Invincible Japanese Army" broke. Without them, their bravery and devotion to killing Japs and making life terribly difficult for them, they, the Japanese, might well have been able, as their radio never ceased to tell us, to "march on to Delhi"' (Rt Hon Sir Reginald Dorman-Smith G.B.E., Governor of Burma, 1941–1946 in the *Foreword* to *The Battle for Naw Seng's Kingdom* by Fellowes-Gordon 1971).

against the Burmese as well as the other communities who were pushing them out of everything, and treated them fairly. The Japanese could win Karen loyalty in the same way. There was nothing more to it than that, I told him. (Maw 1968, 194)

The novel *Harp of Burma* does, however, present a vivid picture of the chaos, desperation and despondency of the Japanese Imperial Army's retreat from Burma;

> However, the tide of war had begun to turn against us and at last it was obvious to everyone that our situation was hopeless. We were reduced to fleeing from mountain to mountain through unknown territory, trying somehow to get over the eastern border range into Siam (Thailand).... One by one our trucks had broken down, so that we finally had to pull our equipment in oxcarts, or carry it on our backs. We lived by foraging everywhere we went. It was a wretched time for us, and one of great danger.... One village would send word to another about us, and hide their food. Sometimes when we put up in a village for a much-needed rest we would find that the natives had informed the enemy and that we were under attack. (Michio 1966)

Merely fiction? Perhaps. Takeyama Michio's novel makes no claims to historical accuracy; it was later made into a movie of the same name, directed by Ichikawa Kon, in 1956. The movie has become perhaps the most famous and best-loved of Japan's Second World War movies. Other records paint the same gloomy picture. One account mentions the fate of retreating Japanese civilians;

> In the wake of the Japanese defeats in Burma, a stream of bedraggled refugees began pouring across the border into Thailand. Japanese civilians in Rangoon had been left to their own devices in the face of the British advance. After ordering reservists to carry out a suicidal defense, regular army officers had left the city, some of them by plane. Non-reservist male civilians were mobilised, too, and given responsibility for evacuation of the Japanese community. One Mitsubishi employee recalled that 40 of his group of 140 had died in the retreat, and survivors reached Bangkok half-alive. (Reynolds 1994, 211)

Figure 4.21 The Ban Kat War Memorial Built over the Well Where the Remains of Japanese Soldiers Were Found

Source: Website of Hak Hakanson; http://www.lanna-ww2.com/

At the risk of repetition, the point here is that much of this retreat occurred over the 'Burma Road' to Thailand, and that villages such as Ban Sala Mae Noi lie close to the road's original track. The retreat and the road ended in Chiangmai, and it can be assumed that the bones of the Japanese dead were left where they died throughout Burma and Northern Thailand, just as Takeyama Michio's novel describes. A memorial was formally opened in June 1995 with a number of Japanese priests and elderly army veterans from Saga Prefecture in attendance. An annual ceremony is held here by the Japanese community in memory of the cessation of hostilities, attended by the Japanese Consul to Chiangmai (Figure 4.21).[37]

[37] Photographs of the event are still kept in the Ban Kat Technical School, together with lists of participants and relevant newspaper articles. A Buddhist Bell Tower was subsequently erected at the site, perhaps by the Ministry of Health and Welfare containing a large bell, the inscription of which had been penned by a member of the Imperial family.

4.8. THE CHUMPHON–MERGUI (MYEIK) ROAD

The Kra Isthmus Railway was but one project to link Burma and Thailand across the narrow peninsula. Towards the end of the war, the Japanese quickly constructed another link in the hope of providing an escape route from Burma for their defeated armies. As Allied POWs were used on its construction, the Mergui Road may explain the confusing (and inaccurate) claims of some commentators that Allied POWs had been involved in the construction of the Kra Isthmus Railway. According to Donald Smith's account in his published memoirs *And All the Trumpets*, several prisoners from the Thai-Burma Railway were used in the building of a road from Prachuap Khiri Khan (some distance north of Chumphon) on the Gulf of Siam through Tenasserim to Mergui (Myeik) on the south Burma coast. Smith was one of those prisoners.

> We did not know that the Mergui Road was merely intended as a back-door through which the broken forces of imperial Japan might yet escape the relentless fury of total war and utter annihilation. It was not wise that we should be told such things.... The Railway of Death was a supreme tragedy, cast on tremendous, heroic lines. The building of the Mergui Road in 1945 must always remain, in comparison, an intimate drama, presented by a small cast of tired hut [sic] seasoned players.... Few men came back from the Mergui Road.[38]

The road itself was a very basic affair,

> In effect, the road was little more than a sandy track through the jungle, varying in width from 15 to 20 feet. On either side ran a narrow ditch to help drain away the monsoon waters when they came.... By the end of the first week in July, the accursed road had been completed, and a Japanese lorry drove over it from Mergui to the Siamese coast.

After the road's completion, Smith's small group of prisoners were ordered to stay on 'as maintenance men, ensuring that the road we had made would not fall into disrepair during the forthcoming wet season'. Despite its interest as a rare description of

[38] This and subsequent quotations are all from Smith (1954, Chapter 4, 156–193).

the Mergui Road, Smith's account is somewhat problematic and perhaps over-dramatized. It is difficult to gauge any overall statistics from his description, but he states that he himself worked alongside Dutch and New Zealanders as well as British prisoners. He apparently found evidence to suggest that a considerable number of Australian prisoners had been similarly involved. An overall general impression from reading Smith's account is that the total number of Allied POWs may not have been very great. Although the Allied POWs and their Japanese overseers (as well as some Korean guards) are portrayed in dramatic detail, Smith's memoirs do not make any mention whatsoever of any Asian labourers. Nevertheless, his account of the Mergui Road is important for detailing some of the smaller, and now all but forgotten, Japanese military construction projects. His account of one of the camps, Maudung, is particularly vivid:

> Maudung had come to be called Death Valley. The name was well deserved. More men had died at Maudung than at any other camp on the Mergui Road. Death struck every hour of the day and night. Prisoners perished not so much from any single definite disease, but from the crushing combination of many diseases—dysentery, beri-beri, septicemia and spinal malaria. It was a camp of the walking dead. The camp stood on a little wooded promontory, from which a flight of broad earthen steps led down to the river. In many places the bamboo sleeping platforms had entirely collapsed, and men lay on the ground on a tangled bed of dusty laths and withered attap. One of the huts had become so infested with bugs and lice that it stood empty, its inhabitants preferring to lie in the open, under the shade of an adjacent banana-grove. A few men were still able to move slowly as far as the cook-house and back but the majority lay inert, staring stupidly into space with eyes which had lost both luster and interest. It was more than a man could stand to look at those human skeletons overlong.

The bulk of the labour must have been provided by Asian workers, with many of the survivors being among those dejected and forlorn individuals whom Gilchrist later found at Chumphon. This is confirmed by another account, that of Albert Edward George Raven (formerly a member of the 18th Division, Royal Corps of Signals). While Raven's account confirms Smith's description that the conditions faced by those working on the Mergui Road were far worse than those pertaining to the Death Railway, he provides some important background information. Raven was one of a party of 1,000 'light sick' POWs who were gathered from the men at Nakhon Pathom and sent to Kra Isthmus to complete the building of the Mergui Road.

> Various sections of the road had been completed by native labour. Our task was to link up the various sections and finally link up with the Mergui end. There were no natives left on the road—they had all either died or run away.... They were retreating headlong before the victorious Allied Armies and this road was to be an avenue of escape. Hence the urgency of this task and the need for its completion before the monsoon season in July. (Raven, n.d.)

Albert Raven's scant information does, however, suggest an extremely unpalatable possibility. Who were the dying 'natives' that Sir Andrew Gilchrist encountered in the Chumphon camps? The construction of the Kra Isthmus Railway through relatively flat and inhabited countryside could hardly have produced such human wrecks as described by Gilchrist, however harshly they may have been treated. Both Smith and Raven tell us there were no Asians working on the road, but Raven states that the road construction had been begun by Asian workers. Gilchrist's Chumphon 'natives' had probably been literally worked to their deaths on the Mergui Road and, when weakness and disease rendered them no longer able to engage in productive labour, they were removed from the Mergui Road project and relocated to the Chumphon base camp. Hence, the need arose to replace the 'native labour' with that of relatively healthy POWs! Needless to say, such speculation must remain highly hypothetical, for the truth and total numbers of the original Asian workforce will now never be known.

> We finished the road and took a well-earned rest waiting for the lorries to come from Kirikan (Prachuab Khiri Khan) with food, but it was too late. The monsoons broke and the top slopes of the road became a slipping, sliding quagmire through which no mechanical transport could run....

> The rest partially revived me and though the fever was still with me I began to take notice of events around me. Kirikan had changed; its hive of activity being replaced by an air of desolation. Frequent air strikes by Allied aircraft had left a train of destruction... The remainder of that journey was a haze. We passed through the old staging area of Ban Pong where so many of us had camped when we first came to Thailand. We stopped at Non Pladuk (Nong Pladuk Junction)—scene of the disastrous bombing by Allied planes early in 1945 where so many were killed. I remember being propped up on the parade ground at Nakhon Pathom. I awoke in hospital two days later. I was alive! I had beaten the combination of the Japanese and spinal malaria. The nightmare of the Mergui Road was over. (Raven, 8, 11 and 12)

REFERENCES

Ahmad, Abu Talib. 2000. 'The Malay Community and Memory of the Japanese Occupation'. In *War and Memory in Malaysia and Singapore*, edited by Patricia Lim Pui Huen, and Diana Wong. Singapore: Institute of Southeast Asian Studies.

Bangkok Post. 1990. 'Grisly Find: Mass Grave Unearthed'. *Bangkok Post*, 18 November.

Boggett, David. 2000. *Notes on the Thai Burma Railway*. Series of articles extracted from *Journal of Kyoto Seika University* from 2000 to 2006. Kyoto: Kyoto Seika University.

Brooke, Micool. 1995. *Captive of the River Kwai*. Bangkok: Merman Books.

Clarke, Hugh V. 1986. *A Life for Every Sleeper: A Pictorial Record of the Burma–Thailand Railway*. Sydney: Allen & Unwin.

Dunlop, Sir Edward. 1994. *The War Diaries of Weary Dunlop: Java and The Burma-Thailand Railway 1942–1945*. Docklands: Penguin.

Evers, Cornelis B. 1993. *Death Railway*. Bangkok: Craftsman Press.

Fellowes-Gordon, Ian. 1971. *The Battle for Naw Seng's Kingdom: General Stilwell's North Burma Campaign and Its Aftermath*. London: Leo Cooper.

Fisher, Charles A. 1979. *Three Times a Guest*. London: Cassell.

Fritsche, Carl H. n.d. *Liberators on the Kwai* (undated private pamphlet available in Kanchanaburi).

Gilchrist, Andrew. 1970. *Bangkok Top Secret*. London: Hutchinson.

Goodden, Christian. 1996. *Three Pagodas: A Journey Down the Thai-Burmese Border*. Halesworth: Jungle Books.

Hardie, Robert. 1983. *The Burma-Siam Railway: The Secret Diary of Dr. Robert Hardie, 1942–1945.* London: Quadrant Books and Imperial War Museum.

Haseman, John B. 1978. *The Thai Resistance Movement during the Second World War* (Special Report No. 17). Northern Illinois University, Center for Southeast Asian Studies.

Kametaro, Tominaga. 1987. *Chototsu Hachijunen* (*Eighty Reckless Years*). Tokyo: Aato Kopansha.

Ken, Iwai. 1978. *C56 Nampo Senjo e Iku* (*The C56 Goes to the Southern Battlefields*). Tokyo: Jiji Tsushinsha.

Khamsan. 1982. 'Kiat Tamruat Thai thi Yuthaphum Ban Pong' (The Honour of the Thai Police on the Ban Pong Battlefield). *Tamruat Samphan* (*Police Relations*) 5, no. 55: 10.

Khwanyun, Sathapon. 1991. 'A Newly Discovered World War II Graveyard in Kanchanaburi' (in Thai). *Sinlapawathanatham* (Art & Culture) 12, no. 4 (February).

Kiattisahasakul, Puengthip. 2001. *The Southern Railways in the Shadow of the Rising Sun* (in Thai). Bangkok: Chulalongkorn University Press.

Kinvig, Clifford. 1992. *River Kwai Railway: The Story of the Burma-Siam Railroad.* London: Brassey's.

Kratoska, Paul H., ed. 2006. *The Thailand–Burma Railway, 1942–1946* (Vol. VI). Abingdon: Routledge.

———. 1998. *The Japanese Occupation of Malaya, 1941–1945.* St. Leonards: Allen & Unwin.

Lomax, Eric. 1995. *The Railway Man.* New York: W. W. Norton.

Lwin, Lin Yone Thit. 1968. *Thai-Myanmar Railway: A Personal Memoir (Yodaya-Myanma Miyhta-Lan Kodwe Chwaydat Hmattan),* Translated by Daw Hmwe. Rangoon: Duwun Sarpay.

Maw, Ba. 1968. *Breakthrough in Burm: Memoirs of a Revolution, 1939-1946.* New Haven: Yale University Press.

McCormack, Gavan, and Hank Nelson, eds. 1993. *The Burma–Thailand Railway.* Chiang Mai: Silkworm Books.

Michio, Takeyama. 1996. *Harp of Burma.* Translated by Howard Hibbert. Tokyo: Tuttle. Originally published in Japanese as 'Biruma no Tattegoto' (Tokyo: Kaiseisha).

Murashima, Eiji, Nakharin Mektrairat, and Somkiat Wanthana. 1991. *The Making of Modern Thai Politics.* Tokyo: Institute of Developing Economies.

Phonsawek, Praphan. 1991. 'Thang Rotfai Khokhot Kra (The Railway at the Isthmus of Kra)'. *Sinlapawathanatham* (Art & Culture) 12, no. 8(June), Bangkok.

Ramaer, K. 1994. *The Railways of Thailand*. Bangkok: White Lotus Press.

Raven, Albert Edward George n.d. *The Mergui Road, Burma*. COFEPOW (Children and Families of Far East Prisoners of War). https://www.cofepow.org.uk/armed-forces-stories-list/the-mergui-road-burma

Reynolds, E. Bruce. 1988. General Nakamura Aketo—A Khaki Clad Diplomat in Wartime Thailand. In *Thai-Japanese Relations in Historical Perspective*, edited by Chaiwat Khamchoo, and E. Bruce Reynolds. Bangkok: Institute of Asian Studies, Chulalongkorn University.

———. 1994. *Thailand and Japan's Southern Advance, 1940–1945*. Basingstoke: Palgrave Macmillan.

Rivett, Rohan D. 1946. *Behind Bamboo: An Inside Story of the Japanese Prison Camps*. London: Angus and Robertson.

Searle, Ronald. 1986. *To the Kwai and Back: War Drawings, 1939–1945*. Boston: Atlantic Monthly Press.

Skinner, G. William. 1957. *Chinese Society in Thailand*. Ithaca, NY: Cornell University Press.

Smith, Donald. 1954. 'I Walk With the Ox'. In *And All the Trumpets*. London: Geoffrey Bles.

Takashi, Nagase. 1990. *Crosses and Tigers*. Bangkok: Post Publishing.

Toshio, Hiroike. 1971, 17 October. 'Taimen Tetsudo—Senju ni Nokeru Hashi (The Thai-Burma Railway: The Bridge Remaining on the Battlefield)'. *Yomiuri Shimbunsha* (Newspaper).

Wiriyawit, Wimon. 1997. *Free Thai: Personal Recollections and Official Documents*. Bangkok: White Lotus Press.

Wyatt, David. 1982. *Thailand: A Short History*. Chiang Mai: Silkworm Books.

Yoshikawa, Toshiharu. 1994. *Taimen Tetsudo: Kimitsu Bunsho ga Akasu Asia Taiheiyo Senso* (*The Thai-Burma Railway: The Asia Pacific War as Revealed in Secret Documents*). Tokyo: Dobunkan.

Yoshinori, Murai. 1993. 'Asian Forced Labour (Romusha) on the Burma-Thailand Railway'. In *The Burma-Thailand Railway*, edited by Gavan McCormack, and Hank Nelson, 59–67. Silkworm Books.

PART II

REGIONAL PERSPECTIVES ON THE SOUTHERN EAST–WEST ECONOMIC CORRIDORS

CHAPTER 5

MYANMAR'S PERSPECTIVE ON THAILAND–MYANMAR SOUTHERN ECONOMIC CORRIDOR IN THE CONTEXT OF ASEAN INTEGRATION

Mu Mu Theint

5.1. INTRODUCTION

The economic, geographical concept is widely used in many border countries, apart from the normal trading concept. A country cannot get the favourable location to trade with other non-neighbouring nations which are trying to develop economic integration among regions. Greater Mekong Subregion (GMS), Association of Southeast Asian Nations (ASEAN) and the Bay of Bengal Initiative for Multi-Sectoral Technical and Economic Cooperation (BIMSTEC) are examples of economic integration in the Asian region (Myint and Than 2015). A number of studies on economic integration aim to generate models (comprising market, policy and geopolitics) which are fit for the region by using single and multidisciplinary perspectives. This integration will not only expand the possible production boundaries but also promote the flow of connectivity in ASEAN nations. The key elements of ASEAN connectivity include the following: (a) physical connectivity (information and communications technology [ICT]), transportation and energy, (b) institutional connectivity (liberalization of trade, facilitation, investment, mutual recognition agreements/arrangements, procedures of cross-border and capacity-building programmes) and (c) people-to-people connectivity (culture, education and tourism; ASEAN 2011). Southeast Asia is noted as a growing, integrated, connected and dynamic region to meet the global needs. Several scholars have noted a rise in the economic success of Asia, particularly led by seven economies, namely China, India, Indonesia, Japan, Korea, Malaysia and Thailand. Many Asian and non-Asian nations have an aspiration to capitalize on their partnership with ASEAN nations to gain mutual benefits (Htun et al. 2010). Although Myanmar does not succeed as favourably as other Asian nations, the country possesses a strategic location, to connect the land bridge between ASEAN and other Asian countries, so as to have great potential as an important player in shaping the future development of the region.

Historically, Myanmar turned to its neighbours gradually as a trade partner with Thailand, India and China. After 1989, the Myanmar government has undertaken more trade liberalization and democratization policies with a series of measures to develop policies for creating connectivity (Thein 2004). Myanmar has predominantly traded with the People's Republic of China (PRC). However, the country has shifted its foreign policy towards greater engagements with India and Thailand and developed policies and directions for the Southeast Myanmar, bordering on Thailand inland (Ikumo 2010). Border trade in Southeast Myanmar has increased in the last few years due to increasing demands of Chinese consumers. Consequently, an open door policy is being implemented by Myanmar, China, India and Thailand (Asian Development Bank [ADB] 2009, 2012a). In hunting the trade openness policy, planning on economic development corridors is a key concern. The country has agreed to five economic corridors; among them, GMS countries agreed to start with Southern Economic Corridor (SEC) linking up to East–West Economic Corridor (EWEC) routes between the Indian Ocean and the Pacific Ocean in 2011 (ADB 2012b). This was the only change in the configuration of the economic corridors since the adoption of the Strategic Action Plans (Interdormitory Link, which connects the three SEC sub-corridors with EWEC).

EWEC has its western end at Dawei in Myanmar. In 1998, SEC and EWEC were launched to achieve the infrastructural benchmarks and strengthen regional cooperation among neighbouring countries that aim to be world-class business centres. Among the ASEAN connectivity, linking Thailand and Myanmar is an integral element to connect ASEAN to the Middle East and Europe. The link is important for transportation of goods and exports from ASEAN to these markets. The link comprises both road and marine routes from the north of Thailand to the southern region, which are at different stages of development. To know the current status of the routes, this chapter aims to identify the options for addressing problems/issues that are faced in the area and to analyse potential trade, investment, people and transport integration with ASEAN. Dawei, Myeik, Kawthaung from the Tanintharyi Region and Myawaddy from Kayin State are chosen in this study.

5.2. BACKGROUND OF MYANMAR ECONOMY

Myanmar is strategically located in the mainland of Southeast Asia with a land area of 676,577 sq. km. The population was estimated at 54.45 million in 2016 and more than 70 per cent of the population was living in rural areas. Myanmar is bordered by several other nations such as China, Thailand, Lao PDR, Bangladesh and India. It is placed as a trade hub between three of the most dynamic Asian economies, namely China, India and Thailand. Consequently, neighbouring and other countries can have several opportunities to expand their businesses by using abundant natural resources of the country such as arable agricultural land, natural forests, precious minerals, available fuel and natural gas, livestock and fisheries, and marine resources (Myint 2009).

Myanmar was one of Asia's leading economies in the 1960s. In later years, growth in Myanmar was inhibited by low investment, limited integration with global markets, the dominance of state-owned enterprises in key productive sectors of the economy, and recurring periods of macroeconomic instability until the late 1980s. Thereafter, the military government adopted a market-oriented economic system by initiating various economic reform measures to enhance economic growth since 1988. The participation of a wide range of private sectors was allowed by the government with a series of guidance, for example, five-year short-term plans to solve political, economic and social challenges that the economy faced (Min and Kudo, 2012). These significant efforts aiming at increasing economic activities caused stabilization between 1989 and 2000s. A new favourable business environment was created through a new Myanmar Investment Law (MIL) and Rules.[1]

In 2010, the country experienced election, which was a great turning point from military administration to a quasi-civil government bringing into a new era under the Union, Region and State Governments formed on 30 March 2011 to introduce the change of decentralized government such as system, ideology and procedures. Since opening up in 2012, Myanmar has become one of the fastest-growing economies in Southeast Asia, with an average economic growth of 7.5 per cent during the period 2012–2016. This growth is expected to continue for several years (ADB 2016a). National League for Democracy (NLD) party won the election in 2015 and took the authority to continue to develop the economy by adopting and enforcing a suitable legal and regulatory framework for both public and private sectors to achieve sustained economic growth. The current macroeconomic indicators of Myanmar economy are presented in Table 5.1.

5.3. MYANMAR'S EXTERNAL TRADE AND FOREIGN DIRECT INVESTMENT

Myanmar economy has transformed from centrally planned to a market economy since the military regime introduced several reforms including trade and investment in 1989 (Thein 2004). Private sector businesses were allowed to engage in external trade to promote export. Myanmar's foreign trade rapidly increased, but imports grew more rapidly than exports in the 1990s and 2000s. Imported goods poured into the emerging markets as consumer items, machinery and raw materials. On the other hand, exports

[1] For more details on MIL, refer to the Directorate of Investment and Company Administration (DICA) website: https://www.dica.gov.mm/

Table 5.1 Macroeconomic Indicators of Myanmar Economy

GDP	US$67.4 billion (2016)
GDP growth rate	5.9% (2016)
GDP per capita	US$1,420.50 (2016)
Inflation rate	5.43%
Exchange rate	1,345 MMK/US$
Unemployment rate	4%
Major exports	Natural gas, garments, re-export sugar, black matpe, jade, rice, green mung bean, fish, metal and ore, maize
Major imports	Petroleum products, vehicles, machinery and parts, iron and steel construction materials, iron and steel materials, raw plastics, palm oil, motor-cycles, telephone and communication accessories, pharmaceutical
Major trade partners	China, Thailand, Singapore, Japan, India, Malaysia, South Korea, Indonesia, USA, Vietnam
Export volume	US$12.0 billion (2016/2017)
Import volume	US$17.21 billion (2016/2017)

Source: Ministry of Commerce (2018).

consisted mainly of primary commodities. Among them were cash crops such as beans, pulses and sesame and marine products such as fish and prawns. One major cause for the slow growth of exports was the government's monopoly and restrictions on major export items, competitive disadvantages in term of price and quality and unfavourable terms of trade (Chantayanich 2012). By the 2000s, Myanmar's external trade sector had improved dramatically due to the rapid growth of demand for garments (high demand from many European countries) and natural gas, but the momentum was lost due to international trade sanctions in 2000. Therefore, there was a decline in garment exports, but a rise in natural gas exports from 2001 onward. Trade value increased from about US$0.40 billion in 1988–1989 to US$11.77 billion in 2009–2010, which was an increase of more than 25 times.[2] Promoting traditional exports cannot help achieve the long-term growth goals, and therefore, the country needs to encourage export of more value-added commodities so that service sector development can generate economic growth (Min and Kudo 2012).

Due to inadequate infrastructure and a closed economy, Myanmar's trade was mainly with its neighbours before 2012. China, India, Japan, Indonesia and Hong Kong were the main trading partners, of which, China was the single largest trade partner. After the country opened up and with the relaxation of the sanctions, trade geography has expanded (OFAC 2015). Today, Myanmar's major export items are oil, natural gas and other natural resources; other important export items include vegetables, fruits, wood, garments and rubber. Fuel products, vegetable oil, vehicles, tyres, pharmaceutical products, construction equipment and machinery are the major import items. Myanmar is likely to remain a raw commodity exporter. In addition, ASEAN countries are priority countries to follow ASEAN standards in terms of trade promotion and the Common Effective Preferential Tariff (CEPT) Scheme.

Myanmar and its neighbouring countries have an economic relationship in terms of trade, capital and human flow. Before 1988, the practice of a centralization system created inflexibility in doing business by causing a mismatch between demand and supply that led to the growth of the grey market (ADB Institute 2015). As Myanmar set many restrictive rules and regulations on illegal border trade, low transportation cost motivated trading across borders (Aung 2008). In this situation, the volume of border trade cannot be counted officially. The statistics published by the government on foreign trade were much understated. Data became closer to actual when border trade was legalized in the 1990s, and the magnitudes of trade volume/balance for normal and border trade are clearly stated (Jaroenwanit and Ratanasithi 2011). While normal trade is in deficit, border trade is in surplus, the overall trade balance is in deficit since a surplus of border trade was offset by deficit in normal trade as shown in Table 5.2.

[2] Data retrieved from Central Statistical Organization.

Table 5.2 Export, Import, Trade Balance and Trade Volume of Normal and Border Trade (US$ Million)

	2012–2013		2013–2014		2014–2015		2015–2016		2016–2017		2017–2018	
	Normal	**Border**	**Normal**	**Border**	**Normal**	**Border**	**Normal**	**Border**	**Normal**	**Border**	**Normal**	**Border**
Export	6,843	2,134	8,443	2,761	8,231	4,293	6,588	4,549	7,089	4,910	9,347	5,490
Import	7,830	1,239	11,933	1,827	14,139	2,494	13,973	2,605	14,344	2,867	15,673	3,012
Trade balance	–987	895	–3,490	934	–5,908	1,799	–7,385	1,944	–7,255	2,043	–6,326	2,478
Trade volume	14,673	3,373	20,375	4,588	22,370	6,787	20,561	7,154	21,433	7,777	25,019	8,502

Source: Ministry of Commerce (2018).

Myanmar has 16 official border trade points, including Muse, Lweje and Chinshwehaw bordering on China; Myawaddy, Kawthaung and Tachileik bordering on Thailand; Sittwe and Maungtaw bordering on Bangladesh; and Tamu and Rhi bordering on India. According to official data from the Ministry of Commerce, the contribution of border trade from Muse, Myeik and Myawaddy is the highest among the 16 border points as shown in Table 5.3. Border trade contributed 82 per cent of Myanmar's export and 89 per cent of import. Among the border posts with the four countries, Muse is the most dominant in total volume of border trade. The trade value between Myanmar and China accounted for 79 per cent (Muse and Yunnan posts), between Myanmar and Thailand accounted for 18 per cent (Myawaddy, Kawthaung and Myeik posts), and the rest accounted for 3 per cent in 2017–2018. There are two types of informal players in border areas. One group is the broker trading companies that take responsibility for documented trade, and the other group is smugglers who are responsible for undocumented trade. They are often referred to as carriers. The route used by the broker trading companies is called the 'upper channel' and the route used by the smugglers is called the 'lower channel'. Products that are restricted or too expensive pass through the lower channel (Aung 2008).

Concerning foreign direct investment (FDI), Myanmar government enacted foreign investment law in November 1988 to bring foreign capital into the country, with an aim to achieve greater participation of private national investment and larger foreign capital inflows. Although the government offers several incentives to allow FDI, it was not a large recipient of FDI as expected. Unclear and inconsistent policies, poor infrastructure, unstable financial market, multiple exchange rates and economic sanctions of some developed countries deterred foreign investors. Although the country has been trying for FDI, Myanmar witnessed US$1.4 billion FDI in 2012–2013, which reached to a peak of US$9.4 billion in 2015–2016 and then dropped to US$6.6 billion in 2016–2017. Top three origins of FDI for Myanmar were China (26.16%), Thailand (23.88%) and Hong Kong (15.38%) in 2017–2018.[3]

---

[3] Data retrieved from Directorate of Investment and Company Administration, Ministry of Commerce on 28 June 2018, https://www.commerce.gov.mm/

Table 5.3 Export and Import Value of Border Trade in Myanmar (2012–2013 to 2017–2018)

Sr. No.	Border Post	2012–2013		2013–2014		2014–2015		2015–2016		2016–2017		2017–2018	
		Export	Import	Export	Import	Export	Import	Export	Import	Export	Import	Export	Import
1	Muse	1,816	1,014	2,211	1,307	3,614	1,704	3,810	1,568	3,704	1,658	4,128	1,695
2	Lweje	22	11	69	7	64	9	64	13	186	16	221	13
3	Chinshwehaw	57	7	216	31	358	66	333	53	516	58	525	47
4	Kanpitetee	2	9	6	23	9	50	29	67	64	42	86	31
5	Kyaing Tong	–	–	–	–	7	5	6	7	2	2	0	2
6	Tachileik	12	28	14	59	8	94	10	65	14	67	15	76
7	Myawaddy	56	89	49	222	33	424	44	682	60	868	83	869
8	Kawthaung	30	49	39	109	36	80	46	86	69	65	141	61
9	Myeik	127	28	113	41	106	40	141	30	157	52	184	75
10	Nabulae	–	–	0	1	0	4	2	11	11	1	5	117
11	Maw Daung	–	–	0	2	0	1	0	2	2	1	5	2
12	Mese	–	–	–	–	–	–	–	–	0	0	0	1
13	Sittwe	4	0	10	6	6	0	5	1	4	0	14	1
14	Maungtaw	–	–	5	1	8	0	5	0	6	0	14	–
15	Tamu	7	2	16	10	33	13	33	13	38	10	43	3
16	Rhi	1	1	12	7	10	6	20	6	25	15	26	18
	Total	2,134	1,239	2,761	1,827	4,293	2,494	4,549	2,605	4,860	2,855	5,490	3,012

Source: Ministry of Commerce (2018).

5.4. LINKING MYANMAR–THAILAND AND ASEAN TRANSPORTATION ROUTE

The economic corridor is much more complex than a mere road connecting two cities. It involves connectivity of infrastructure, laws and regulations to trade among the border areas. Formulation and adoption of SEC and EWEC projects are not only to transform transport corridors into economic corridors but also for accessing markets, linking border region/country, creating social activities, developing factories, attracting tourism, protecting environmental activities and other aspects of the economic and social development and also for establishing interconnectivity within and outside of the areas (Brunner 2013). There is no doubt that South and Southeast Asian connectivity cannot be achieved without Myanmar since the country is strategically located. In the southern part of Myanmar, there are two corridors linking Thailand and southern Myanmar. These are the SEC and EWEC (ADB 2016b).

SEC is a part of the economic corridor approach adopted by the Mekong Subregion countries in 1998 to extend the route to Dawei (Myanmar) from Bangkok, Thai (Thailand), Koh Kong, Kampot (Cambodia), Ha Tien, Rach Gia, Ca Mau and Nam Can (Vietnam). It aims to achieve further integration of ASEAN by improving trade and connectivity. SEC comprises the sub-corridors and an inter-corridor to connect between Myanmar and Thailand, namely the southern coastal sub-corridor connect. The route of the corridor is Mekong–India Economic Corridor (MIEC) that enhanced the connectivity between Ho Chi Minh City–Phnom Penh–Bangkok–Dawei and Chennai (India) by sea route. In this route, Dawei possesses a deep sea port, which can open up a new shipping route to India, the Middle East and Europe, thus benefitting the firms in Chennai. Therefore, the development of the Dawei project in SEC is a prerequisite for the development of connectivity links with ASEAN and non-ASEAN countries. Primarily, four primary Asian highway routes are constructed; AH1 (Myawaddy–Phayagyi–Meikhtila–Mandalay–Tamu) and AH2 (Tachileik–Kentung–Meikhtila–Mandalay–Tamu) are linking India and Bangladesh with Myanmar and the rest of Southeast Asia, while AH15 and AH16 are linking Myanmar with Lao PDR, Thailand and Vietnam (Lord 2010).

Apart from Dawei, the other two main cities from Tanintharyi region, namely Myeik and Kawthaung, will be connected to the border of Thailand through the SEC. Myeik is being linked to the Prachuap Khiri Khan province, which has domestic airports and interesting features. Myeik is in a little more difficult position. The city itself does not have the potential to build an international deep sea port. However, there is potential to upgrade its temporary checkpoint to be a permanent checkpoint. Kawthaung is in the southernmost part compared to the other two cities. It is located close to Ranong province in Thailand. It has quite notable ports, which export items, such as construction materials (like cement), shipped to the southern cities in Myanmar and Yangon. Kawthaung and Ranong provinces have already obtained the status of permanent checkpoints for trading of goods between Ranong province and Myanmar (Ministry of Labour, Immigration and Population 2017; UNHCR 2014).

The EWEC stretches from Mawlamyine in Myanmar to Da Nang in Vietnam, strengthening the links between several cities of Myanmar, Thailand, Lao PDR and Vietnam: Mawlamyine–Myawaddy in Myanmar, Mae Sot–Phitsanulok–Khon Kaen–Kalasin–Mukdahan in Thailand, Savannakhet–Dansavanh in Lao PDR, and Lao Bao–Hue–Dong Ha–Da Nang in Vietnam. The corridor runs from Da Nang port in Vietnam through Lao PDR and Thailand and to the Mawlamyine port in Myanmar. It extends 1,320 km, intersecting the North-South Economic Corridor at the provinces of Tak and Phitsanulok in Thailand. Each trip takes a few hours, and traders are making the most use of it. Plans are ongoing to extend the corridor's western end from Mawlamyine to Yangon–Thilawa in Myanmar, by using Myawaddy–Kawkareik–Eindu–Hpa-An–Thaton–Kyaikto–Payagi–Bago–Yangon–Thilawa route, with a possible extension to Pathein.

5.5. ANALYSIS ON CURRENT STATUS OF SOUTHERN AND EAST–WEST ECONOMIC CORRIDORS IN MYANMAR

There are four levels of the economic corridor: level 1—transport corridor, level 2—multimodal transport corridor, level 3—logistics corridor and level 4—economic corridor (Ministry of Construction

2016). SEC and EWEC are strategically and critically important for Myanmar, Thailand, ASEAN and non-ASEAN countries. To evaluate the development, data are obtained from secondary (desk review) as well as from primary research (interview).

5.5.1. Background of the Region

Tanintharyi, formerly known as Tenasserim, covers an area of 43,344.9 sq. km with a population of 1,406,434 (CSO 2015). It is a long narrow southern part of the country, bordering the Andaman Sea to the west and the Tenasserim Hills, beyond which lies Thailand to the east. The 900-km-long Tanintharyi (Tenasserim) coastline extends from the Gulf of Mottama south to the mouth of the Pakchan River. There are many islands off the coast, with the large Mergui Archipelago in the southern and central coastal areas and the smaller Moscos Islands, off the northern shores. Dawei (Tavoy) is the capital city, but Myeik (Mergui) and Kawthaung are the other important cities. Tanintharyi is at the southern end of Myanmar with the mountainous land that limits cultivation (Myanmar Survey Research 2014). However, rubber and palm oil plantations are the main agricultural products, and businesses have their own processing plants to produce edible vegetable oil. Since the location is close to the sea, fishing is a significant industry. Several local prawn and fish farms have processing plants to supply not only to the local consumers but also for exports, mostly to Thailand. Dried fish, dried prawn, dried shrimp and Ngapi (shrimp paste) are exported from this region. In addition to fishing, birds' nests are also gathered from offshore islands. The natural resources from this region, mostly the gemstones, are very popular (e.g., pearl). It is cultured at the Pearl Island and generates income from foreign countries (Kruewan 2014). Regarding mining, Tanintharyi supplies up to two-thirds of Myanmar's tin and tungsten production. Famous mines in this region include Heinda, Hamyingyi, Kanbauk, Yawa, Kyaukmetaung, Nanthida and Yadanabon. A number of mines and plantations throughout the region are owned by foreign corporations. For example, the Yadana gas pipeline is owned by Total and Unocal, two multinational oil and gas companies.

Another significant township is Myawaddy, which has a strategic location within this transportation network between Myanmar and Thailand. Myawaddy started operating as a transit point in the late 1990s. It became the official border trade post through the signing of an Agreement with Thailand on 16 September 1998. The major export items from Myanmar to Thailand through the border are basically primary products such as natural gas, wood products, jade and gems rather than value-added products. Myanmar supplies natural gas to Thailand, but Thailand exports back LPG to the country. Loss in the additional production of value-added reduces the productivity of the country. Therefore, the government needs to encourage establishment of manufacturing and processing industries and encourage local businesses to come up with new export items. Most farmers are planting crops, rubber, sugarcane, coffee, cardamom and fruits in the border towns of the country. Myanmar's farmers have faced some considerable issues such as higher labour costs of cultivation, decreasing labour force from within or outside household members, lack of finance to use appropriate inputs and lack of advanced technology and information. As a result, Myanmar witnessed decreased yield of crops, small marginal profits for the farmers and declining productivity in farming. Nonetheless, the agriculture sector is shrinking with a large area of land lying fallow. Paddy cultivation has gradually decreased. In this situation, the government has been trying to implement new farming technology to improve its agriculture sector.

5.5.2. Trade Performance

Relationship with Thailand is very important for Myanmar and other Asian nations since Southeast Myanmar borders with Thailand as a trade hub. This relation benefits the regional development of Southeast Myanmar without creating any conflict of interest between Myanmar and Thailand. Connectivity between the two countries in terms of market, policies and geopolitics is important when economic corridors through Thailand and border towns are planned in Southeast Myanmar. Regarding the normal trade with Thailand, Myanmar has a favourable trade position since the value of export to Thailand is greater than the value of import from Thailand. The reverse effect happened in 2013–2014 for Myanmar since there was a decline in the export and increase in the import that favours Thailand's trade performance. The informal trade relation between Myanmar and Thailand exists for several decades, but after 1990, there is a formal trade and border trade. A study on the role of informal cross-border trade in Myanmar conducted by Aung (2008) explained that there are many reasons for engaging in informal trade practices, such as transportation cost is cheaper than shipping, to avoid heavy duty on imported consumer items, etc.

Trade from Thailand to Southern Myanmar from border ports such as Myawaddy, Myeik and Kawthaung represents the second largest share of Myanmar's border trade next to Muse (border with China). Myanmar has six border trade points with Thailand—Tachilek in Shan State; Myawaddy in Kayin State; and Kawthaung, Myeik, Htee Khee and Maw Daung in the Tanintharyi region. The route of trade flow between Myanmar and Thailand creates favourable advantages to Thailand to penetrate Myanmar domestic market. It is interesting how the ratio has changed in the border trade and normal trade between Myanmar and Thailand.

Of the overall trade performance between Myanmar and Thailand, the trade volume increased from US$4,514.972 million in 2011–2012 to US$5,711.19 million in 2014–2015 and then declined to US$4,288.172 million in 2016–2017. The trade balance also started to decline from US$3,132.682 million in 2011–2012 to US$116.296 million in 2016–2017 (Table 5.4). It is important to

Table 5.4 Myanmar's Trade Volume/Value with Thailand (US$ Million)

	Thailand			
Year	***Export***	***Import***	***Trade Volume***	***Trade Balance***
2011–2012	3,823.827	691.145	4,514.972	3,132.682
2012–2013	4,000.576	696.793	4,697.369	3,303.783
2013–2014	4,304.016	1,362.468	5,666.484	2,941.548
2014–2015	4,031.756	1,679.434	5,711.19	2,352.322
2015–2016	2,893.18	1,972.886	4,866.066	920.294
2016–2017	2,202.234	2,085.938	4,288.172	116.296

Source: Ministry of Commerce (2018).

know the reason for declining trade volume and balance between Thailand and Myanmar.[4] Regarding border trade in the EWEC region, Myawaddy has the highest total trade volume with Thailand as compared to Myeik and Kawthaung as shown in Table 5.5.

5.5.3. Economic Zone

The Special Economic Zone Law was enacted in 2014, and it was published in 2015. Tanintharyi's coastal position presents an opportunity for the region to build on its historical tradition as a strategic trading hub. The Myeik Industrial Zone is active in the region (Myeik), and the Maunttang Region Economic Zone is under development. Alongside its deep sea port the development of a Special Economic Zone (SEZ) is underway in Dawei. Dawei Special Economic Zone (DSEZ) is located some 300 km west of Bangkok, and it serves as a cross-border trade point for trade with Thailand. The industrial estate project and Dawei deep sea port follow the supervision of the central body for trade and transportation in the South East Asian Region. The DSEZ is already considered to be a part of SEC; it is expected to be one of the biggest deep sea ports in ASEAN, and the project is now agreed upon between the Thai and Myanmar governments (Robertson and Taung 2015). DSEZ has the potential of being the Western gateway to the Southeast Asian region to link the two Oceans—the Indian and the Pacific Oceans—and to link the two giant economies, that is, India and China. Its deep sea port will also open soon as a new gateway to the Malacca Strait from western Myanmar. DSEZ consists of five different zones as shown in Table 5.6.

The zone is a bilateral economic cooperation project owned jointly by the national governments of Thailand and Myanmar. It was initiated in 2008. In 2010, a 60-year concession was granted to Italian-Thai Development (ITD) Plc. International Trade Development, and Myanmar did a joint venture named Dawei Development Company Ltd (DDC), which is a joint venture company owned by ITD (75%) and Max Myanmar (25%). In July 2012, Max Myanmar withdrew its investment; therefore, new investment

[4] Data retrieved from the Directorate of Investment and Company Administration (DICA) website: https://www.dica.gov.mm/

Table 5.5 Myanmar–Thailand Border Trade from 2017 to 2018 (US$ Million)

	2017			2018			
Checkpoints	**Export**	**Import**	**Total**	**Export**	**Import**	**Total**	**Increase/Decrease**
Myawaddy	31.48	289.30	320.78	20.39	309.03	329.43	–8.64
Kawthaung	34.88	15.13	50.00	26.70	29.35	56.05	–6.04
Myeik	78.61	25.67	104.28	41.24	21.46	62.70	41.579

Source: Ministry of Commerce (2018).

Table 5.6 Layout of Dawei Special Economic Zone

Zones	Industry Type
A	Coal-fired power plant, steel mill, fertilizer, ship building and cargo yards and deep sea port
B	Heavy industry zone for oil and gas storage, oil refinery, gas separation plant and compound circled power plant
C	Medium and heavy industry zone; petroleum industry
D	Medium industry zone
E	Light industry zone
Public area	Commercial complex, authority center and township and district offices.

Source: Ministry of Commerce (2018).

partners are needed. Consequently, the project is currently stalled. Notwithstanding some delays, the Dawei SEZ's initial development phase was launched in 2015. In June 2016, the governments of both Myanmar and Thailand reaffirmed their commitments to pushing forward the zone's implementation. The government of Myanmar has been trying to promote the foreign investment in SEZ and has brought Dawei to foreign investors' eyesight (ADB 2016a). Myanmar has taken its first step by moving the regional office to Dawei, while Thailand was enthusiastic in opening the permanent border gate in Aumphur Banpunumron in Kanchanaburi province to make a linkage with Htee Khee border gate of Dawei. According to the Ministry of Construction, there will be an urban network and special business development activities done in DSEZ, such as developing the international airport, seaport and tourism. Investors are exempted from income tax for the first seven years of operation in the exempted zone and five years of operation in the promotion zone. If they can operate both zones, they will receive 50 per cent of income tax relief for the second year and 50 per cent relief for the third year. Customs duties for construction materials, machinery, equipment, heavy machinery and vehicles are exempted for the developers of DSEZ.

5.5.4. Myeik Industrial Zone

It has been established since 1995 with 153 registered firms. Myeik is the commercial hub of the region with an active trading port and a large population of over 280,000. In order to restructure the Myeik Industrial Zone as privately owned, a proposal for the new economic zone has been submitted to the regional government for review. The Myeik Future Development Public Company (MFDPC) requested revisions to the existing master plan and intends to start implementing the project within this year. The 1,000-acre project to the east of Myeik airport requires negotiations with local residents to compensate for their land as required in the provision of the master plan.

5.5.5. Myawaddy Industrial Zone

It is located 12 km from Myawaddy on the way to Thin Gan Nyi Naung and has been constructed since 2006 with a total area of 315 acres. The purpose of developing Myawaddy SEZ is to fill up the missing link of the EWEC, to create job opportunities for Myanmar migrants in Thailand and for ethnic nationalities and to develop the border area. For the development of the zone, Myawaddy Chamber of Commerce Industry (MCCI) has been a great support to link and assist the public-private stakeholders and to promote cross-border trade between the countries. Since early 2010, the zone has been in operation as a service of Border Trade Departments and zone warehouses. To develop the area, the government introduced the rules and regulations for the private warehouses to store commodities within the Myawaddy Trade Zone. The zone provides incentives to promote trade along the Thai-Myanmar border in the form of a duty-free zone (DFZ), which means that transportation of goods and storing the goods in the DFZ will be free from duty, but they will be charged sales tax upon the delivery of goods. Another advantage of investing in the zone is the cost of transportation, which could be reduced after the Dawei deep sea port on the Myanmar coast is developed. Currently, the development of the industries in the SEZ is still very limited, although Myawaddy exists in a significantly strategic location and is expected to finish soon.

5.5.6. Tourism

Tanintharyi region is composed of more than 800 untouched islands that have a high potential for tourism. Apart from that, virgin beaches, mountains, forests and other attractive eco-tourism sites are interesting places in the Tanintharyi region. Therefore, the government designated the pleasant southern state as the destination for the sustainable tourism project, creation of jobs and generating income. The government has an inclusive project, namely the International Trade Centre (ITC). Other advantages for the region are the efforts by the Japan International Cooperation Agency to create a tourism master plan for Tanintharyi. To implement effectively, a tourism development committee is formed for the combined working together of public and private sectors, with stakeholders from the region. There are cultural tour centres around Dawei to show the traditional way of life, arts, food and religious practices. Myeik is also a favourite place for both local and oversea travellers since it has 800 untouched islands, and it has the potential to accord highest growth in the region. Travellers ranging from lower- to upper-income levels can be targeted. Since Myeik is a busy harbour town with cottage industries, crab farming and candle-making firms have a potential to earn extra money if they are linked to the travel and tour companies. Some villages in the region have already started to develop community-based tourism. Hoteliers in the Tanintharyi region and members of private-sector travel organizations have been drawing up a master plan for developing tourism in the region, and specifically the Myeik Archipelago.

Regarding the EWEC route, there are many tourist attraction places in Mon and Kayin states. Kyaiktiyo (or Golden Rock) in Kyikehto is one of the attractions for Thai travellers (ADB 2015; Northeastern Strategic Institute, 2006). Myawaddy is an important focal point for border trade and tourism between Thailand and Myanmar, and it is just a 3-hour drive to Hpa-An from here. Although investment in the hotel business of Kayin State has been increasing, existing hotels are insufficient to provide needed customer services, and we recommend that facilities and activities have to be made more hospitable. Improvement in accommodation and transportation in Kayin State will lead to an increase in both inbound and outbound tours. In addition, boat tours, hiking tours, bike tours, rock climbing, visits to traditional villages, homestays, restaurants and handicraft businesses are likely to grow in the region. The distance between the Thai and Myanmar immigration checkpoints is only 400 m and it is easy to walk over the bridge. It is an opportunity to attract Thai travellers by providing better service to visit Myawaddy and provide service to take the travellers to other places such as Hpa-An, Yangon and other famous attractions in Yangon. One of the obstacles for hotels in the country is that accommodation in Mae Sot is cheaper than the cost of living in Myawaddy. For improving tourism, there is a need to reduce barriers between the countries and the development of the two Myawaddy-Mae Sot Friendship Bridges (UNHCR 2014).

5.5.7. Employment

Due to the development of the economic zone and tourism, there is a creation of job opportunities for local people. The majority of workers are from the agriculture, service and manufacturing sectors. Economic opportunities have also driven a significant proportion of Tanintharyi's working-age population across the border to Thailand. It is hoped that the development of the Dawei SEZ and other industrial projects would generate local jobs. There are many migrant workers coming from Tanintharyi to Thailand (ADB 2012a). The reason for their working in Thailand rather than in Myanmar is because of salary incentives. According to immigration reports, Thailand is the largest recipient of Myanmar migrants, with approximately 2 million migrants. Analysis of migration in Myanmar reveals that a major impetus for migration from Myanmar is to maximize important economic *pull* and *push* factors (Myint and Than 2015). Significant push factors are low investment, employment opportunities and low socio-economic status within the country of origin (that tend to encourage forced economic migration). The main pull factors that encourage simple economic migration through various informal channels include migration of friends and relatives and better socio-economic status of neighbouring migrants' families/households. However, the heightened socio-economic status of migrants' families (who live in the sending communities) that has been inspiring young people in sending communities to migrate may also be interpreted as a push factor (Kruewan 2014). Significant flows of cross-border migration led to the loss of the workforce for the country. Due to the high costs associated with formal channels of migration, they normally try informal ways to go and work in Thailand. During the research days, a queue of people waiting to go through the Friendship Bridge for working in Thailand was seen. Due to the incentive of a higher salary in Thailand and unwillingness to work in the farming industry, many young people have been working in Thailand. To reduce labour mobility, the country should encourage establishing more factories and industries in the border areas, which would create job opportunities, followed by the average minimum wage law.

5.6. OPPORTUNITIES AND CHALLENGES IN SOUTHERN EWEC: MYANMAR'S PERSPECTIVES

This study investigates the most significant economic and business activities in the Tanintharyi region and Kayin State, which have cross-border trade with Thailand and Myanmar, to figure out opportunities and challenges with regard to trading, transportation, tourism, employment, legal, social, environment and community. Development of the economic corridor is expected to reduce trade barriers among countries by coordinating in geo-economics and political context by promoting cross-border transportation. Working together with a shared vision of a more prosperous future drives a stronger link between nations to facilitate cross-border travel, trade and economic growth (ADB 2012c). Four cities, namely Dawei, Myeik, Kawthaung and Myawaddy from the Tanintharyi region and Kayin State are selected, each of which have different interesting characteristics. Potential impact of development on each city in Myanmar and ASEAN is the main objective of the study. The opportunities and challenges are figured from the evaluation of the current situation that is presented in the previous section. Development of SEC and EWEC favours Myanmar and ASEAN in the areas of trade, transportation, cross-border logistics, investment, tourism and employment (Staples and Qiu 2017).

First, the current and potential benefits of the economic corridor on Myanmar in terms of border trade are that the flow of goods is faster and the role of trading companies is becoming stronger, especially in Myeik, Kawthaung and Myawaddy since they are in strategic locations. Majority of the businesses are SMEs and individual traders, who have been dealing in the cross-border trade. The amount of trade volume has been increasing for both the countries. The role of businesses and trading houses is significant in facilitating cross-border trade via road and sea. To promote regional development through trade, the government implemented projects, namely the ITC and the One Stop Service, to inspect the trading cargoes. Businesses engage daily for documentation process with government bodies for transportation and for the payment of customs duties.

Second, cross-border logistics cost will significantly decrease since Myanmar exports more goods to Thailand by road. Due to the connectivity advantages, Myanmar will have access to get logistics services in Thailand. There are opportunities to link Southeast Asia with South Asia and the Middle East, Europe, and Africa via the Dawei seaport. Distance will be shortened by approximately 50 per cent in case of the use of trading routes through Dawei SEZ seaport to Vietnam, Cambodia and Thailand. The duration of shipping time too will be lessened by approximately three days for a shipment to arrive in Thailand. Transforming a good transportation infrastructure generates a very efficient distribution system and warehouse service. Myanmar insurance companies have opportunities to provide services that cover Myanmar owners of trailers and containers.

Third, regarding the payment system, there were no private banks in Myawaddy apart from a few government banks. However, currently, there are many banks in all cities for local or global payments. The most significant banks are KBZ, AYA and CB Bank, whereas the role of the government bank is on the verge of declining due to the services offered by these private banks. Regarding the payment of customs duties, businesses do not have to pay in cash instead they use the Myanmar Automated Cargo Clearance System (MACCS), which has been introduced and implemented at the border.

Fourth, SEZs in the region provide a great opportunity for boosting Myanmar economy, linking ASEAN production bases and global market networks. This strategic location is important for connecting Asia to the world. As mentioned in the earlier section, Dawei will become one of the ASEAN's next promising major centres for the world-class mega deep sea port and top-grade industrial estates. DSEZ has become a new commercial district and an international urban city after completion of the project. In the plan, income-generating businesses will be developed after completion of the project, such as first-class golf courses, hotels and entertainment sector.

Finally, hotel and tourism sector is one of the promising industries in the development of the economic corridor in Tanintharyi and Kayin. In Tanintharyi, there are 800 untouched islands, virgin beaches, natural mountain forests and attractive eco-tourism sites which can be utilized to generate regional income and create jobs. In addition, potential cultural tour centres from different segments can be developed to attract business and vacation travellers. Community-based tourism is another area to generate revenue for the region. Hoteliers in the Tanintharyi region and travel and tour organizations from the private sector have been drawing up a master plan for developing tourism in the region and a specific plan for Myeik island. Kyaiktiyo (or Golden Rock) located in Mon State, one of the main attractions for Thai travellers, is connected to the EWEC, and Hpa-An capital city of Kayin State is also just a three-hour drive from Myawaddy by car. Therefore, Myeik and Myawaddy are important focal points not only for border trade but also for tourism between Thailand and Myanmar. Due to the increasing number of travellers, there is a need to develop accommodation and transportation in the area. In this situation, there is a great potential for inbound and outbound tourism. Some cottage industries, near the Myeik harbour town, have the capacity to create community-based tours and link them with travel and tour companies to show their traditional methods of crab farming and candle-making.

Despite the opportunities for the country, there are some weaknesses in the SMEs themselves and challenges for Myanmar after the development of SEC and EWEC. In fact, trade and degree of competitiveness, changes in government policies, barriers to trade and complications in the handling process with regard to the documentation process are some examples.

First and foremost is that, trade and competition are the main challenges for the local businesses after completion of the SEC. Most exports are based on primary products such as precious minerals (jades, pearls, rubies and sapphires). The value-added products (manufactured items) are rarely exported via normal and border channels. Resource trade is conducted to achieve short-term gains at the expense of long-term sustainability. At the three border trade ports, namely Myawaddy, Myeik and Kawthaung, export to Thailand has been declining, while the import from Thailand has been increasing; this suggests a huge cross-border trade deficit for Myanmar. Myanmar is highly dependent on the manufacturing goods and construction materials coming from Thailand via border trade. Increasing local demand for Thai products is favourable for trade performance of Thailand with Myanmar since Myanmar cannot compete in products from Thailand in term of cost-effectiveness (economies of scale), price and quality. Although the SEC and EWEC projects are mapping global value chain opportunities for SMEs, these cannot be implemented due to unclear rules and regulations, inadequacies in the logistics system, lack of accessibility of information and market, and no incentives for foreign buyers to deal with the local business. There is also a lack of international competitive advantage which generates a lack of confidence to compete in the global market. Frequent changes in policies are one of the obstacles for business. It leads to higher costs such as legal and hidden costs; therefore, buyers cannot create better relationships with traders in Thailand.

Second, in the documentation process, traders and brokers face delays in licensing processes, bank transactions and inspection processes and have to pay high tax. Most businesses follow formal trade, but some deal in informal undocumented cross-border trade with neighbouring countries. In the market, formal businesses cannot compete with the informal traders with regard to price, although the product may be the same in both the cases.

Third, transportation is a physical infrastructure that is important for the flow of goods and services. The uncertainty and a lack of consensus on sustaining the quality of road links result in an inefficient flow of goods and services across borders. As discussed in the previous section, the routes of transportation in SEC and EWEC can be used by land, sea, air and rail, but they are in progress. In the case of Myawaddy, Friendship Bridge 1 is the main transportation road, but Bridge 2 is also in progress. Although cross-border trade procedures in Thailand is not complicated, but there is a lengthy wait time because of the documentation process and requirement of various documents on Myanmar's side. There is only a one-stop service centre that exists at Myawaddy. There is a time-consuming long line for checking the cargo. Another infrastructure constraint is access to electricity, which is a major challenge for administration, industrial and socio-economic development. According to the Ministry of Electric Power, Tanintharyi had an electrification rate of only 9 per cent in 2013, which meant only 9 per cent households had electricity. Lack of access to electricity is one of the barriers to the development of DSEZ, and it will be a major challenge for foreign investors.

Finally, regarding the society, environment and community, all stakeholders such as civil societies, local and national governments, businesses and investors are interested in sustainable development through regional development. Illegal logging is a well-known challenge, and it is destroying the major rivers and mangrove. This situation leads to deforestation, which can result in changes in the climate. There were also community complaints on the SEZ and Asian Highway Projects. The SEZ project has been criticized extensively for human rights abuse of local villagers because there was a lack of adequate compensation for the construction. Due to the construction and pollution, there is a significant fear of health problems, as the massive industrial complex will be a significant polluter. The Dawei Development Association (DDA) estimates that 20–36 villages housing 22,000–43,000 people will be affected by the project. The DDA called for a freeze on the SEZ in 2014 in the hope to prevent it from resuming on a large scale without violating human rights. The DDA also called for The National Human Rights Commissions of Thailand and Myanmar to conduct a full investigation on human rights abuse in the mega-project.

5.7. CONCLUSIONS AND RECOMMENDATIONS

The aim of the study was to assess the current situation in the Tanintharyi region and Kayin State by conducting primary and secondary research; to find out opportunities and challenges for the country; and to provide recommendations to improve trade flows, business performance, people-to-people contacts, employment, hotel and tourism and social and community development of the country. Overcoming the challenges and reducing some constraints can create a better economic and business environment for the region. Therefore, strategic recommendations are added in this section.

The Tanintharyi region is also strategically linked to the EWEC and is logistically important for trade between the Gulf of Thailand and the Andaman Sea. Businesses from the Tanintharyi region and Kayin State are mainly based on primary products rather than producing value-added products. Major export products are rubber, natural gas, wood products, jade and gems, and livestock and fisheries. Encouraging formal export is one of the appropriate strategies for the country, and therefore, it is required to investigate further detailed strategic plans to penetrate and to create products as per international conventions related to export control. Capacity building and training should be provided to enhance the quality of products as per international standards. The government should encourage local businesses to come up with new export items. While strengthening cooperation with neighbouring countries, immigration authorities are key authorities who are in-charge of transnational crime control. The government should promote supporting large-scale industries and small- and medium-sized industries for cost-effective product development. Implementing effective trade policies to determine how short-term gains from natural resource trade should be efficiently utilized to ensure long-term sustainability. To increase export of agricultural products, the government should encourage development and production of good quality seeds of both existing and new crop varieties and should improve agricultural techniques and introduce efficient water harvesting systems along with good irrigation facilities. The government also needs to provide loans to SMEs and farmers to buy machinery and sell value-added goods back to Thailand. This will create diversification in export items, which till now are based only on exports of natural resources.

In order to improve trade facilitation, the government needs to simplify import/export and customs procedures, eliminate the licensing system, cooperate with finance authorities for faster processing of financial transactions, providing trade credits, etc. Emphasis should be on the signing of bilateral, and if possible, multilateral trade agreements with as many countries as possible. The government should consider dissemination processes to get agreements from stakeholders. Enactment of clear guidelines for the legal framework is also important. In the trading system, the third party should be made to participate legally. Research on illegal cross-border activities and the control of such activities should be encouraged. Payment of cross-border trade through the conventional trade method is preferred, and the banking system at border areas should be made efficient through online payments, where banks need to focus more on efficient trade facilitation.

Regarding socio-economic development, the government should provide educational programmes and increase investment in human resources within the country. Improvement in electricity infrastructure should also be made. Households from Dewei, Myeik and Kawthaung have access to electricity, but Myawaddy and Kawkareik are getting electricity generated by the private sector. More employment opportunities should be created in the country, and reduction in labour migration to Thailand should be controlled. Enforcement of laws and regulations related to environmental protection is needed to reduce resource usage. Legal framework for environmental protection should be in place.

In terms of land policy, land grabbing and commercial investment in the 1970s and 1980s drove a large-scale displacement of people. Access to land remains a complex and pertinent issue in Tanintharyi even today. This is also evident from the high number of land disputes being led by some township administrations. The government enacted the Farmland, Vacant, Fallow and Virgin Lands Management Law on 30 March 2012. Although the laws are enacted, the government should assist land right programmes. Apart from this, other rights-based programmes that should be carried out by the government are human rights, human trafficking and property rights. Local farmers need assistance to obtain or access official land ownership. Community development programmes, community empowerment and integration with various livelihood security programmes are also necessary to introduce integrated land-use practices, ensure sustainable food security, create a proper balance in the ecosystem, and conduct agricultural practices in both lowland and upland areas.

Promoting SEZs for the country is necessary to facilitate a good business infrastructure. According to the SEZ registration list, there is a limited number of official registrations in Dawei, Myeik and Myawaddy. Government encouragement is needed to engage a private firm to develop and manage the SEZ, but the state must be an active player to improve transport, electricity, water, telecommunications, waste disposal and other infrastructure required for linking the SEZ to the global economy. The Dawei Industrial Estate is planned for both medium-sized and light industries and for the development of a fully integrated industrial complex. For the SEZ development in Dawei, there should be a balance between policy, funding and construction of the area. To achieve the competitive advantage for Dawei location in creating gateway by connecting Mekong Subregion countries, it is a great opportunity to penetrate the global exporting markets such as India, the Middle East, Africa and Europe. Hence, meeting the global standards is important for Myanmar businesses in order to grab those opportunities. Another obstacle in the development of the SEZ is that a significant number of both large and small industrial firms operate outside of the industrial zones. Therefore, government should force businesses to move into the SEZ. The motivation for cross-border investment is also one of the driving forces to develop the SEZ. Regarding the social and environmental issues, the government needs to facilitate sustainable development and welfare of the society. Legal and environmental laws have to be enacted and implemented.

From the policy perspective aimed at transforming the SEC and EWEC into economic corridors, it would be more fruitful to concentrate on how aspects linked to the political, institutional and regulatory environment have affected efficiency and effectiveness of stakeholders from different industries who have significant operations in Dawei, Myeik, Kawthaung and Myawaddy ports. This study presents a number of conclusions in terms of the transformation of the SEC and EWEC from transport corridors to economic corridors. The main ports such as Dawei, Myeik, Kawthaung, Myawaddy and Kawkareik will have potential benefits as well as challenges from the development of the SEC and EWEC. Among the ports, Dawei is targeted as an export-oriented port, and there is a potential to transform it as the major connectivity point between mainland Southeast Asia and South Asia. Thailand–Myanmar ASEAN integration could be enhanced with physical infrastructure development and effective institutional arrangement. Building enhanced regional connectivity requires not only the development of infrastructure but also the development of new strategies and institutions and more effective implementation of existing and future initiatives.

In conclusion, SEC and EWEC connectivity projects are strategically important for Myanmar since Dawei, Myeik, Kawthaung and Myawaddy are trading hubs. These projects will be beneficial for Myanmar, Thailand, India, ASEAN countries and Asia as a whole. Although there are many challenges for Myanmar, it is better to respond to the opportunities offered by geographical and natural advantages in order to have competitive advantages through the global market chain. Therefore, the economic integration depends on guidelines or policy frameworks and strong political desire to set and agree on a common and shared vision to integrate the economies. Business collaborations between the two countries will increase opportunities for trade and investment in the region. Since hotels and tourism, energy, fishery and construction are dominant sectors in the region and because southern part of Myanmar is linked to the six provinces in Thailand, namely, Kanchanaburi, Phetchaburi, Ratchaburi, Chumphon, Prachuap Khiri Khan and Ranong, there is a huge market for trade and investment between Myanmar and Thailand.

REFERENCES

Asian Development Bank (ADB). 2012a. *India: East–West Project*. ADB.

———. 2012b. *Initial Assessment of Road Transport Infrastructure and Transport Logistics for Trade Facilities in the GMS Countries*. Manila: ADB.

———. 2012c. *Myanmar in Transition: Challenges and Opportunities*. Mandaluyong: ADB.

———. 2015. *Asian Development Bank in Myanmar: Support for Kayin State and Mon State*. Yangon: ADB.

———. 2016a. *Greater Mekong Subregion Regional Investment Framework Implementation Plan: Mid Term Review and Revised Regional Investment Framework Implementation Plan 2020*. Chiang Rai: ADB.

———. 2016b. *Review on Configuration of the Greater Mekong Subregion Economic Corridor*. Mandaluyong: ADB.

ADB Institute. 2015. *Connecting South Asia and Southeast Asia*. Tokyo: ADB Institute.

ASEAN. 2011. *Master Plan of ASEAN Connectivity*. Jakarta: ASEAN Secretariat.

Aung, W. 2008. 'Myanmar Informal Trade with Neighbouring GMS Countries'. *Regional Policy Dialogue on Trade Facilitation Policy Gap Analysis on Cross Border Transport Agreement, Mekong Institute*. Khon Kaen: Khon Kaen University.

Brunner, Hans-Peter. 2013. 'What Is Economic Corridor Development and What Can It Achieve in Asia's Subregions'. *Working Paper Series on Regional Economic Integration, No. 117*. ADB.

Chantayanich, S. 2012. 'Myanmar Migrants to Thailand and Implications to Myanmar Development'. *Policy Review on Myanmar Economy, 07*. Bangkok Research Centre.

CSO. 2015. *Myanmar Statistical Year Book*. Central Statistical Organization. https://www.csostat.gov.mm

Florento, Hector, and Maria Isabela Corpuz. 2014. 'Myanmar: The Key Link between South Asia and Southeast Asia'. *ADBI Working Paper Series, Paper No. 506*. Tokyo: Asian Development Bank Institute.

Htun, K. M., N. N. Lwin, T. H. Naing, and K. Tun. 2010. 'ASEAN–India Connectivity: A Myanmar Perspective'. In *ASEAN–India Connectivity: The Comprehensive Asia Development Plan, Phase II*, edited by F. Kimura and S. Umezaki. Jakarta: ERIA Research Project Report.

Ikumo, I. 2010. 'Economic Impact of the Economic Corridor Development in Mekong Region'. In *The Investment Climate of*

Major Cities in CLMV Countries (Vol. 4), edited by M. Ishida. Bangkok: Bangkok Research Centre, IDE-JETRO.

Jaroenwanit, P., and S. Ratanasithi. 2011. 'Barriers to Border Trade along the East–West Economic Corridor: The Case of Thailand-the Lao PDR Trade on the Border of Mukdaban Province'. *GMSARN International Journal* 5: 201–210.

Kruewan, M. 2014. *Thailand Development Policy for Neighbouring Countries: Dawei Development Project Case Study*. Bangkok: Ministry of Finance.

Lord, M. J. 2010. 'Impact of the EWEC on Development in Border Provinces: Case Study of Savannakhet Province in Lao PDR'. *Development Study of the East–West Economic Corridor Greater Mekong Subregion*. Manila: Asian Development Bank.

Min, A., and T. Kudo. 2012. 'Newly Emerging Industrial Development Nodes in Myanmar: Ports, Roads, Industrial Zones along Economic Corridors'. In *Emerging Economic Corridors in the Mekong Region*, BRC Research Report No. 8, edited by M. Ishida. Bangkok: Bangkok Research Centre, IDE-JETRO.

Ministry of Commerce. 2018. *Directorate of Investment and Company Administration* (Department of Trade, Producer), 28 June. https://www.commerce.gov.mm/

Ministry of Construction. 2016. *Preparatory Survey for the Project for Strengthening Connectivity of Internal Highway in Mekong Final Report Phase II Survey Report*. JICA of Oriented Consultant Global.

Ministry of Labour, Immigration and Population. 2017. *Myanmar Population and Housing Census: Thanintharyi Region, Dawei District, Dawei Township Report*. Myanmar: Ministry of Labour, Immigration and Population.

Myanmar Survey Research. 2014. *The State of Local Governance: Trends in Thanintharyi*. Yangon: UNDP.

Myint, A., and M. Than. 2015. *East West Corridor and Myanmar*. ASEAN.

Myint, U. 2009. 'Myanmar Economy: A Comparative View'. *Asian Paper*, 1 December. Stockholm: Institute for Security and Development Policy.

Northeastern Strategic Institute. 2006. *Strategy for Trading, Investment and Tourism along East West Economic Corridor (EWEC)*. Northeastern Strategic Institute.

OFAC. 2015. 'Burma Sanction Programme'. https://www.treasury.gov/ofac202/622-2490

Robertson, B., and M. S. Taung. 2015. *Industrial Zone in Myanmar Diagnostic Review and Policy Recommendation*. Friedrich Naumann Foundation for Freedom.

Staples, Andrew, and Pamela Qiu. 2017. 'Building Myanmar: Bringing the Infrastructure Gap'. *Economist Corporate Network (ECN) Report*. Yangon: Baker McKenzie.

Thein, M. 2004. *Economic Development of Myanmar*. Yangon: ISEAS, Yusof Ishak Institute.

UNHCR. 2014. *Thanintharyi Profile*. UNHCR South-East Myanmar Information Management Unit.

CHAPTER 6

THAILAND–MYANMAR EAST–WEST CORRIDOR

An Indian Perspective

Prabir De

6.1. INTRODUCTION

Over the last two decades, India has steadily engaged with the extended neighbours on the east through a series of regional and sub-regional forums and initiatives. Both Myanmar and Thailand have been playing the role of connectors, connecting India and South Asia with Southeast and East Asia.

In the last 25 years, India and Southeast Asian countries have made important strides towards deepening regional integration. Connectivity has gained most of the attention, since it has played a catalytic role in integrating India with countries in the east. However, a lot more can be done in the areas of trade, investment, agriculture, public health and people-to-people linkages, to mention a few. We present some of the connectivity projects which have strong relevance to the Thailand–Myanmar East–West Corridor.

Corridors are often characterized by good features—non-rivalry and non-excludability—though their extent could vary across services.[1] For instance, a corridor can be national (e.g.,

[1] Refer to Rimmer (2014) for a detailed discussion on corridors in the Asia-Pacific region.

Leipzig–Frankfurt Corridor, Tokyo–Osaka Corridor), regional (e.g., Greater Mekong Subregion [GMS] or Central Asia Regional Economic Cooperation Program[CAREC] corridors) or even international (e.g., undersea telecommunication cables or energy pipelines), thereby connecting a country or countries across the region. Corridor-based infrastructure development received worldwide attention when the GMS countries jointly decided to promote an economic corridor for the improvement and expansion of economic opportunities by linking cities and towns with urban centres.[2] A corridor helps to strengthen industrial (or services) agglomeration over time through the establishment of industrial zones (or Special Economic Zones [SEZs]) and facilitates cluster-type development of enterprises.

India's trade with Southeast and East Asia has increased considerably over the past two decades or so. To facilitate the trade, India's connectivity, although at present at an initial stage of development, may appear as a great facilitator for global integration in the coming years. Connectivity development, both physical and digital connectivity, across Asia and also with other regions may pick up pace, and there are high prospects for value chains. Improving the quality of trade—a new phase of trade facilitation—is expected to happen across the world.

Connectivity improvement in Myanmar is essential for stronger connectivity between South and Southeast Asia and East Asia. In Southeast Asia, Thailand's connectivity with Myanmar is expected to provide cost-effective and efficient logistic services to promote trade and development, not only within Southeast Asia but also between India and Southeast Asia.

In particular, India's relation with Southeast Asia is firmly embedded in culture, commerce and connectivity in the backdrop of the 'Act East' Policy (AEP). India's connectivity projects with Southeast Asia have been perused in three ways: first, physical connectivity projects; second, soft infrastructure to make the physical connectivity smooth and functional; and third, financing schemes to implement the connectivity projects as well as generate new

[2] A detailed discussion is available at several seminal publications of Asian Development Bank (ADB 2014).

investments. Thailand's connectivity with Myanmar is, therefore, likely to supplement India's connectivity effort and strengthen the India–Association of Southeast Asian Nations (ASEAN) physical linkages in multifaceted ways.

6.2. INDIA'S OWN CONNECTIVITY PROJECTS WITH SOUTHEAST ASIA

The ASEAN–India Plan of Action (POA) (2021–2025) has mandated the following:

> 69. Work closely to promote physical connectivity in the region by completing the missing links between South and Southeast Asia, including, but not limited to, expediting the completion of relevant sections of the India-Myanmar-Thailand trilateral highway and supporting steps to build an economic corridor along it and its extension to Cambodia, Lao PDR, and Viet Nam; and encouraging private sector participation in the development of roads and railways and relevant logistics networks.

India has taken several initiatives to upgrade and develop national infrastructure facilities by launching several flagship projects such as Sagarmala, Bharatmala and the Golden Quadrilateral that would ensure time-bound creation of world-class infrastructure in the country. India's connectivity projects with Southeast Asia are primarily India–Myanmar–Thailand Trilateral Highway (TH); extension of TH to Cambodia, Lao PDR and Vietnam (CLV); and the Kaladan Multimodal Transit Transport Project, which are presently at different stages of implementation.

Table 6.1 presents the ongoing connectivity projects between India and Mekong countries. Road connectivity covers the TH and its extension to CLV; Kaladan Multimodal Transit Transport Project; Rih–Tiddim Road; and bus services between Imphal in Manipur and Mandalay in Myanmar. In particular, the ongoing connectivity project of the TH between India, Myanmar and Thailand and the proposed extension of the TH towards CLV will enable an increased exchange of goods, services, and the movement of people between India and ASEAN. Connecting India's northeastearn region (NER) with Southeast Asia would contribute

Table 6.1 Status of Connectivity Project in MGC

	Project Details	Connecting Countries	Status	Remarks
Road connectivity	Trilateral Highway (TH)	India, Myanmar, Thailand	Ongoing	Construction of a 1,360 km highway connecting Moreh in Manipur to Mae Sot in Thailand through Myanmar.
	Tamu–Kalewa–Kalemyo Road	India and Myanmar	Ongoing	The project commenced on 28 May 2018 and is expected to be completed by 2022. Part of the TH Project.
	Imphal–Moreh Highway	India and Myanmar	Ongoing	The length of the road is 110 km. The project has three phases. The first phase is under the tendering process. The second phase is undergoing construction. For the third phase, loan has not yet been sanctioned.
	Extension of Trilateral Highway	All Mekong-Ganga Cooperation (MGC) Countries	Proposed	The ASEAN–India POA (2021–2025).
	Kaladan Multimodal Transit Transport Project	India and Myanmar	Ongoing	Road Component—Ongoing.
	Imphal–Mandalay Bus Service	India and Myanmar	Ongoing	Ongoing—Repairing work of about 70 bridges on the Yargi–Kalewa route. MoU was signed between Yangon-based Shwemandalar Express and Imphal-based Seven Sisters Holiday on 14 February 2020 for the commencement of a bus service by April 2020.

Rail connectivity	India Side–Jiribam to Moreh; Myanmar Side–Tamu to Kalay	India and Myanmar	Proposed	Rail India Technical and Economic Service (RITES) limited conducted a study to link from Jiribam in Manipur to Mandalay in Myanmar (885.4 km).
	Delhi–Hanoi Railway Link	India–Myanmar–Thailand–Vietnam	Proposed	Although railways are in service on major parts of these routes, there are about 238 km of missing links that have to be built in Myanmar in order to enable a Delhi–Hanoi railway operation.
Air connectivity	India–Bangkok	India and Thailand	Functioning	Thailand: Bangkok India: Covers 12 major Indian Cities
	India–Yangon India–Mandalay	India and Myanmar	Functioning	Myanmar: Yangon and Mandalay India: Covers three cities: Delhi, Kolkata and Guha Proposed route for Imphal.
	India–Ho Chi Minh	India and Vietnam	Functioning	Covers three cities. Delhi is routed through via Kolkata.
Maritime connectivity	Mekong–India Economic Corridor	Myanmar, Thailand, Cambodia Vietnam and India	Proposed	Construction of SEZ is ongoing. Construction of the Dawei deep sea port has not yet started.
	Kaladan Multimodal Transit Transport Project	India and Myanmar	Completed	Connecting Kolkata Port and Sittwe Port.

Source: Author's own based on various sources.

to higher trade and investment, strengthen regional value chains (RVCs), create jobs and increase people-to-people contact, and the NER would further strengthen the relationship with Myanmar for enhancing ASEAN–India connectivity.

The TH project involves construction of a 1,360 km highway connecting Moreh in Manipur to Mae Sot in Thailand through Myanmar. The TH is presently under construction and likely to be completed by 2023. The Tamu–Kalewa–Kalemyo road, or the India–Myanmar Friendship Road, as part of the TH, was inaugurated in 2001. India has undertaken upgrading and repairing of the 70 bridges on the highway, and this is expected to be completed soon.

Economic Research Institute for ASEAN and East Asia (ERIA) has recently completed a study on extension of the TH to CLV (ERIA 2020). According to ERIA, except for one small section between Xieng Kok and Luang Namtha via Muang Sing in Lao PDR, all sections of the suggested northern route are already designated as parts of the Asian Development Bank (ADB), United Nations Economic and Social Commission for Asia and the Pacific (UNESCAP) and Master Plan on ASEAN Connectivity (MPAC) 2025 transport corridor projects (ERIA 2020). All sections of the southern route of the eastward extension overlap with the East–West Economic Corridor (EWEC), North–South Economic Corridor and the Southern Economic Corridor of ADB. The development of TH's eastward extension, therefore, requires close cooperation with international projects executed by ASEAN, ADB, Asian Infrastructure Investment Bank (AIIB), UNESCAP and the World Bank.

At the same time, the Trilateral Motor Vehicle Agreement (T-MVA) is being negotiated. This Agreement will allow vehicles and passengers to move seamlessly for regional and international trade transportation purposes along the TH. The T-MVA shall provide a series of procedures that would facilitate the movement of cargo and passengers along the corridors, such as operating procedures (OP) for vehicles, customs procedures and facilitation measures. The T-MVA will also provide transit and transportation rights and obligations through Annexes and Protocols. This Agreement will have a critical role in realizing seamless movement of passengers and personal and cargo vehicles along the TH.

Without the T-MVA, the TH will be non-operational. However, the reality is that progress in the negotiation of the MVA between India, Myanmar and Thailand for the TH has been slow.

Another important cross-border connectivity project is the Mekong–India Economic Corridor (MIEC), which involves integrating four Mekong countries, namely, Myanmar, Thailand, Cambodia and Vietnam, with India. It aims to connect Ho Chi Minh City (Vietnam) with Dawei (Myanmar) via Bangkok (Thailand), Phnom Penh (Cambodia) and Chennai (India). The major part of the necessary investment is for the development of a port at Dawei and SEZ. This corridor, when completed, is expected to augment trade between Southeast Asia and India by reducing the travel distance and removing the supply-side bottlenecks.

6.2.1. Kaladan Multimodal Transit Transport Project

One of the objectives of the Kaladan Multimodal Transit Transport Project is to provide access from the Bay of Bengal to the landlocked NER of India, particularly the Mizoram state. The components of this project include the following: (a) construction of an integrated port and inland water transport (IWT) terminal at Sittwe with dredging; (b) development of a navigational channel along the Kaladan River from Sittwe to Paletwa (158 km); (c) construction of an IWT–highway trans-shipment terminal at Paletwa; (d) construction of six IWT barges (each of 300 tonne capacity) for the transportation of cargo between Sittwe and Paletwa; and (e) building a double-lane highway (109 km) from Paletwa to the India–Myanmar border (Zorinouri) in Mizoram.

Framework Agreement and two protocols (Protocol on Transit Transport and Protocol on Maintenance) were signed by India and Myanmar on 2 April 2008. Construction of integrated port with IWT jetty at Sittwe is substantially completed. Construction work of the IWT terminal at Paletwa has been started in April 2013. The Border to NH 54 (Lawngtlai) road on the Indian side in Mizoram is in progress under the Ministry of Road Transport and Highways, Government of India.

The road contract of the 109 km road from Zorinpui on the India–Myanmar border to Paletwa in Myanmar has been awarded. The project is likely to be completed soon.

6.2.2. Mekong–India Economic Corridor

Another important cross-border connectivity project is the MIEC, which involves integrating four Mekong countries, that is, Myanmar, Thailand, Cambodia and Vietnam, with India. It will connect Ho Chi Minh City (Vietnam) with Dawei (Myanmar) via Bangkok (Thailand), Phnom Penh (Cambodia) and Chennai (India). The major part of the necessary investment is for the development of a port at Dawei and SEZ. While the construction of SEZ has been ongoing for quite some time, the construction of the Dawei deep sea port is not yet started. The emphasis of the corridor has been on expanding the manufacturing base as well as trade with the rest of the world, and particularly between ASEAN and India. It may enable ASEAN economies and India to integrate further and collectively emerge as a globally competitive economic bloc.[3]

Establishing rail connectivity with Myanmar would be crucial, both in terms of increasing bilateral trade and improving people-to-people contacts. Rail links will significantly reduce journey times, especially for long distance cargoes and passengers. The study for a rail link from Jiribam in Manipur to Mandalay in Myanmar was conducted by Rail India Technical and Economic Service (RITES) limited in 2005. According to the study, the total length of rail line from Jiribam to Mandalay is 885.4 km, out of which the length of the Jiribam–Imphal–Moreh route is 219 km, and the length of the Tamu–Kalay route is 127.4 km. This rail project is part of the southern corridor of the Trans-Asian Railway network. On completion of the Jiribam–Imphal–Moreh route, there could be possibilities for (a) the India–Myanmar–Thailand–Malaysia–Singapore rail link and (b) the India–Myanmar–Thailand–Hanoi rail link.

Table 6.2 presents tourists flows between India and Mekong countries. India has several flights with Thailand all through the week. Bangkok is connected with major tier-I and tier-II cities in India by direct flights. Air connectivity between India and Myanmar

[3] To finance the construction of a 132 km connecting road from the Thailand–Myanmar border to the Dawei deep sea port, the Government of Myanmar has agreed to borrow Baht 4.5 billion from the Government of Thailand (refer, *Bangkok Post* dated 16 February 2017).

is the only mode of transportation for religious tourism (e.g., Buddhist circuits) and medical tourism. For instance, people from Myanmar are interested to visit Bodh Gaya. Kolkata to Yangon and New Delhi to Yangon via Gaya are the only direct air routes between the two countries. Imphal and Mandalay are likely to be connected by air. There are direct flights between Kolkata and Ho Chi Minh City and between Kolkata and Hanoi, which have started operating since 2019 (now temporarily closed due to the COVID-19 pandemic). However, India is yet to be connected with Cambodia and Lao PDR by air. Outflow of tourists from India has been more than inflow. Indian tourists fly mostly to Thailand, Vietnam and Myanmar, whereas inflow of tourists is from Thailand and Myanmar. Most of the tourists from the MGC countries come to India to visit Buddhist circuits.

Missing rail and road links in Myanmar obstruct the overland connectivity between India and Southeast Asia. Therefore, the average road conditions and the railway system inside Myanmar need to be improved and upgraded. Extension of the TH to Mekong countries, direct air links, completion of ongoing connectivity projects and maritime links with Cambodia and Vietnam are some of the projects that will take the cooperation between India and Mekong countries to a new plateau. A better coordination mechanism between Mekong countries and India would be helpful in building cross-border connectivity.

Myanmar has set up cross-border fibre optic networks with many of its neighbouring countries including India. The first cross-border fibre optic link between India and Myanmar was set up in February 2009, running from Moreh in Manipur to Mandalay in Myanmar, for a distance of 500 km. The 640-km-long link passes through Tamu, Kampatwa, Kyi Gone, Shwebo, Monywa and Sagaing. The fibre optic link is a high-speed broadband link for voice and data transmission.[4] Besides, India has also offered over US$1 billion Special Fund to Cambodia, Lao PDR, Myanmar, Vietnam (CLMV) countries to promote projects that support physical and digital connectivity and a Project Development Fund (PDF) with a corpus of US$77 million to develop manufacturing

[4] Refer to https://www.globaltimes.com

Table 6.2 Tourist Flow between India and Mekong Countries

Country	ASEAN Tourists Arrival in India			Indian Tourists Arrival in ASEAN		
	2011	2018	CAGR (%)	2011	2018	CAGR (%)
Cambodia	0	0		15,240	65,882	23.26
Lao PDR	0	0		3,227	4,864	6.04
Myanmar	25,043	75,773	17.14	12,318	102,702	35.39
Thailand	92,404	166,293	8.76	916,787	1,596,772	8.25
Vietnam	9,809	31,427	18.1	16,520	132,371	34.62
MGC	127,256	273,493	11.5493	947,572	1,902,591	10.47083
ASEAN	521,755	887,088	7.88	2,711,316	4,670,574	8.08
Total	24.38999	30.83042		34.94879	40.7357	

Source: Department of Tourism, India and ASEAN Secretariat.

Note: CAGR is Compound annual growth rate.

hubs in CLMV countries, which can be used to strengthen digital connectivity between India and the Mekong sub-region. India has established IT centres in Myanmar: India-Myanmar Centre for Enhancement of IT Skills (IMCEITS) and Centre of Information & Communication Technology Training (CICTT) in Yangon. Nonetheless, there is ample scope to promote digital connectivity between India and Mekong countries, particularly in the areas of Industrial Revolution 4.0.

6.3. MYANMAR–THAILAND CONNECTIVITY PROJECTS: REGIONAL COOPERATION IMPLICATIONS

The following economic and transport corridors are being investigated to strengthen bilateral (between Thailand and Myanmar) and regional (India–ASEAN or Bay of Bengal Initiative for Multi-Sectoral Technical and Economic Cooperation [BIMSTEC]) connectivity.

- Eastern economic corridor from Thailand to Myanmar
- Singkhon/Prachuap border crossing to Myeik
- Ranong to Victoria Point

Connectivity projects between Myanmar and Thailand are unique regional cooperation initiatives in terms of geographical contiguity and access to the ocean. The aforesaid envisaged projects are directly connecting Thailand and Myanmar with the Bay of Bengal community. These corridor projects have far-reaching implications in terms of trade, connectivity and regional integration. Our objective would be to accelerate economic growth and social progress in the 'Bay of Bengal region' through joint endeavours and to cooperate more effectively in joint efforts that are supportive of and complementary to national development plans of the countries. As shown in Figure 6.1, the connectivity projects have the potential to convert the Bay of Bengal into a 'Development Triangle'. The Bay of Bengal countries are at different levels of development with different income levels. There are three developing countries (India, Sri Lanka, and Thailand) and four Least Developed Countries

Figure 6.1 Development Triangle

Source: The author.

(LDCs; Bangladesh, Bhutan, Nepal and Myanmar). Given such a structural variation, regional integration may generate high hope, particularly among LDCs and smaller economies. Therefore, in view of new connectivity projects in the region, the scope for further cooperation is very high.

Moreover, with zero inter-state political or border dispute on a continuous basis in the Bay of Bengal, countries are motivated to speed up the integration process, both within and across the region. The corridors as envisaged by Thailand will lead to generating growth through trade and investment. Due to cross-regional free trade agreements (FTAs) between some of the Bay of Bengal countries, these corridors may be transformed into an effective alternative for the Bay of Bengal countries to connect with the world.

6.3.1. Tourism Cooperation

Tourism may witness a quantum jump in view of the improvement in connectivity between Thailand and Myanmar. The connectivity between Southern Myanmar and Thailand has high potential to promote tourism in the Bay of Bengal, particularly in the Andaman Sea. This also offers high investment opportunities for cruise terminals in the Andaman Ocean belt.

Port Blair shall be connected with Ranong and Phuket by direct flights. Port Blair has an international airport. While the Port Blair airport does not have adequate resources for night landing facilities of aircrafts, allowing international flights to operate from Port Blair can facilitate tourism. Besides, some of the popular tourist places such as Penang and Langkawi in Malaysia and Sabang in Indonesia can also be connected with Port Blair through cruise and air linkages.

Visa facilitation in the form of a regional arrangement should be promoted. India's e-Visa along with Thailand's visa on arrival experiences may be shared with the region. Bay of Bengal countries may consider introducing Schengen-type visa for tourists, business people and health patients in the region. This is very much possible since most of the countries in the Bay of Bengal offer either e-visa or on-arrival visa.

6.3.2. Short Sea Shipping and Development of Ports

To handle the increased ocean cargoes, particularly between ASEAN and India, we need to improve the efficiency of existing ports in the eastern coast of India as well as develop existing ports as hub ports in the Bay of Bengal. It would provide opportunities for private investments in ports and shipping. Short sea shipping in the Bay of Bengal shall be promoted with relaxed cabotage rules and in line with India–Bangladesh coastal shipping agreement. New shipping routes may emerge between India (Chennai, Vizag and Kolkata) and Myanmar and Thailand. Countries in the Bay of Bengal need to advance the multi-modal physical connectivity (air, rail, roads and waterways) and agree to a Coastal Shipping Agreement in the Bay of Bengal.[5] Greater port connectivity between Colombo and Ranong or between Colombo and Dawei would be required to strengthen the port and shipping networks. Besides, we need to design port and shipping plans to connect Port Blair,

---

[5] BIMSTEC Coastal Shipping Agreement (BCSA) is presently being negotiated by the member countries. The BCSA is proposed to deal with cargo ships and applicable up to 20 NM. The first Working Group Meeting of the BCSA was held from 28 to 29 November 2017 at New Delhi. Member countries have agreed to complete the negotiations of BCSA at the earliest.

Ranong, Kolkata, Haldia, Chennai, Vizag, Dhamra, Dawei, Klang, Singapore, Colombo, etc.

6.3.3. Development of Special Economic Zones

Development of SEZs in Dawei, Myeik, Ranong, Sabang and the east and southern coast of India would trigger investments in the Bay of Bengal region. SEZs would generate additional economic activities, promote trade and investment, develop infrastructure and generate employment opportunities.

6.3.4. Promoting Trade

Connectivity improvement, particularly ocean linkages, would eventually generate new trade. The Bay of Bengal countries have substantially high untapped trade potential,[6] a large part of which has remained unrealized due to barriers to trade and structural differences in the economies, among which some are policy barriers such as tariff and non-tariff measures (NTM) and exchange rate volatility, whereas some of the barriers are related to the environment such as remoteness and low connectivity, inadequate banking and financial instruments, and unfavourable business environment (De 2016). Therefore, such enormous untapped potential can be unlocked if member countries take effective measures to reduce the barriers to trade.

Although there have been some improvements, the cost and time to trade within the Bay of Bengal countries are still relatively high. Tariffs do not appear to be the major barrier to trade. It is the non-tariff issues that are holding back the growth of trade. The regional integration arrangements in the Bay of Bengal have done little to break barriers between the countries so far (FICCI 2018). Breaking existing trade barriers is, therefore, needed, and the countries need to shoulder shared responsibilities.

---

[6] BIMSTEC has a trade potential of US$760 billion against the current intra-regional trade of US$40.5 billion. Trade volume refers to the year 2016, sourced from Direction of Trade Statistics Yearbook (DOTS), International Monetary Fund (IMF) and the trade potential is sourced from ITC's Trade Map. Refer, De (2016) for the country-wise potential trade for the year 2016.

FTA in the Bay of Bengal may certainly activate the production links between the countries, which would ultimately generate RVCs and thereby more regional trade in the circle. Regional FTA coupled with trade facilitation would generate higher value addition to the economies at a time when all the Bay of Bengal countries have ratified the WTO Trade Facilitation Agreement in 2017. Therefore, to unlock the untapped trade potential, member countries should look at the possibilities of finalizing negotiations for a comprehensive FTA, introduce state-of-the-art trade facilitation measures, undertake measures to harmonize NTMs, establish region-wide physical and digital connectivity and strengthen energy linkages. These measures will help jump-start economic integration in the BIMSTEC.

6.3.5. Strengthening Value Chains

The Bay of Bengal countries such as Bangladesh, India, Thailand, Myanmar, Malaysia and Indonesia need to link themselves through production networks and develop regional and global value chains, both in goods and services. RVCs should be looked at as building blocks for global value chains. The creation of RVCs will depend on a host of factors. One such factor lies in the ability of firms to capitalize on existing resources and opportunities. For example, countries having access to the Bay of Bengal are also home to several agricultural and horticultural resources. Developing more agricultural value chains across the Bay of Bengal countries could be the key to unlock the vast business potential.

6.3.6. Investment Cooperation

Investment cooperation should be accorded high importance and priority to strengthen intra-regional investment in the Bay of Bengal. India's economic reforms, in the last three years, have resulted in higher foreign direct investment (FDI) flows, which have created opportunities for Thailand and Malaysia. There is, however, a wide variation in the pace of investment reform(s) in the region. In order to achieve increased FDI, BIMSTEC countries should further reinforce their macro-economic environments towards liberalizing and harmonizing the investment regimes. Investment facilitation should be an upfront priority to build the needed infrastructure in the Bay of Bengal. Investment facilitation can be achieved either through the agreements on services and investment or through common regional investment measures. The Bay of Bengal countries should take initiatives to make the arbitration proceedings faster and should move towards the convergence of intellectual property rights (IPR) policy.

6.3.7. Promoting Open Sky

Improved air connectivity is an important catalyst for the promotion of tourism and trade services. The Bay of Bengal countries should facilitate air connectivity, particularly to link India's NER and the Andaman Islands with Myanmar, Thailand, Malaysia, Singapore and Indonesia. The Bay of Bengal countries may consider extending Second Freedom Right to each other's airlines and promote an Open Sky in air cargo. To start with, Bangkok Airways or Thai Smile or Indigo or Air Asia may resume flights between Port Blair and Phuket or between Port Blair and Bangkok.

6.3.8. Dealing with Non-traditional Security Threats

Security is indivisible, whether it is the security of undersea cables for communication in the Bay of Bengal region or the persisting challenges of terrorism and transnational crimes. The Bay of Bengal countries face severe security threats like smuggling, human trafficking, fake currency, drugs and piracy. These countries need deeper regional cooperation for strengthening security in the Bay of Bengal region, particularly, to stop smuggling, human trafficking, fake currency and drugs. There are several agreements on non-traditional security areas signed in 2014, but they are yet to be fully operational. The Bay of Bengal countries should also strengthen the maritime security through greater cooperation among coastguards and navies for constant vigilance, exchange of information, search and rescue, Humanitarian Assistance and Disaster Relief (HADR), etc.

6.3.9. Disaster Management and Emergency Response

Disaster risks and vulnerabilities have no national boundaries. Any major disaster like a tsunami can have a devastating effect beyond borders. Most of the Bay of Bengal countries have been experiencing climatic and natural disasters. Several studies have also demonstrated that disasters particularly affect the poorest and most marginalized people, thereby widening social inequalities and harming economic growth. Therefore, ignoring disaster risk and allowing the risk to accumulate would have an undermining effect on its own future potential for social and economic development. In this regard, several countries have now focused their priorities on disaster risk reduction to overcome the potential losses and preserve the critical resources for development. It is essential to underscore the importance of cooperation in disaster management and emergency response. India has endorsed the Sendai Framework and developed National Disaster Management Plan (NDMP) 2016 consistent with globally accepted best practices. India hosted the First Annual BIMSTEC Disaster Management Exercise during 10–13 October 2017 in New Delhi.

We need an early warning system for the Bay of Bengal region as well as technical support for the disaster management force. To better prepare for disaster management, countries have decided to set up a Disaster Management Centre to provide training, capacity building and share country-specific experience in building disaster resilience. India has established the Tsunami Early Warning System for the Indian Ocean Rim Countries. Its National Disaster Response Force has been deployed in other affected countries for response operations.

6.4. CONCLUDING REMARKS

Greater connectivity between the Bay of Bengal countries can yield numerous benefits. Larger markets can bring about economies of scale in production and enhance competitiveness. Integration of markets can facilitate the movement of production networks and attract more foreign investments along with the benefits of knowledge and technology transfer and opportunities to connect to regional and global supply chains. We have to design strong implementation mechanisms to ensure that effective coordination takes place among various agencies. Such cooperation has the potential to absorb large investments in infrastructure and industry. Expanding trade is one of the many manifestations of growing economic integration. The Bay of Bengal countries have to identify the connectivity projects, which would trigger the trade and investment. India and Thailand should work more closely for physical and digital connectivity and develop industrial zones or SEZs, logistics and customs systems. These are essential for improving country's the competitiveness of India, Myanmar and Thailand, while addressing the global challenges.

REFERENCES

AIC-RIS. 2021. *ASEAN-India Development and Cooperation Report 2021*. New Delhi: ASEAN-India Centre—Research and Information System for Developing Countries.

Asian Development Bank (ADB). 2014. *Economic Corridor Development for Inclusive Asian Regional Integration: Modeling Approach to Economic Corridors*. Manila: ADB

De, Prabir. 2014. 'India's Emerging Connectivity with Southeast Asia and East Asia: Progress and Prospects'. *ADBI Working Paper 507*. Tokyo: Asian Development Bank Institute

De, Prabir. 2016. "India: Building Connectivity under the Act East Policy", in M.G. Plummer et al. (eds.) Connecting Asia: Infrastructure for Integrating South and Southeast Asia, Cheltenham: Edward Elgar

De, Prabir. 2018. *Twenty Years of BIMSTEC: Promoting Regional Cooperation and Integration in the Bay of Bengal Region*. Dhaka: BIMSTEC Secretariat.

ERIA. 2020. The India-Myanmar-Thailand Trilateral Highway and Its Possible Eastward Extension to Lao PDR, Cambodia and Vietnam: Challenges and Opportunities. Jakarta: Economic Research Institute for ASEAN and East Asia (ERIA).

FICCI. 2018. *Reinvigorating BIMSTEC: An Industry Vision for the Next Decade*. New Delhi: FICCI.

Rimmer, P. J. 2014. *Asian-Pacific Rim Logistics: Global Context and Local Policies*. Cheltenham: Edward Elgar

PART III

THE REGION IN FOCUS

CHAPTER 7

MYEIK

Trade and Investment Trends, Challenges and Opportunities

Piti Srisangnam

7.1. INTRODUCTION

Myeik, formerly Mergui or 'Beik' as the locals call their hometown, is the largest city in the Tanintharyi region in Myanmar, located between Dawei (the capital city of the region) in the north and Kawthaung (the southernmost part of the country) in the south. Myeik is located at the centre of the Mergui Archipelago annexe to the Andaman Sea with more than 800 islands. As of the 2014 census, the population was 693,087 (UNFPA 2015).

The Tanintharyi region is administratively divided into 10 townships covering 3 districts: Dawei District, Kawthaung District and Myeik District. Myeik District itself has four townships and one sub-township: Myeik Township, Kyunsu Township (Mergui Archipelago), Palaw Township, Palauk Sub-township and Tanintharyi Township which has an international cross-border checkpoint with Thailand's Singkhon Pass or Maw Daung Pass on the Myanmar side. The border passes on both sides are not yet upgraded to permanent checkpoints (Map 7.1).

This chapter is divided into three parts: general information on Myeik economy, production sectors and business opportunities, and challenges and policy recommendations.

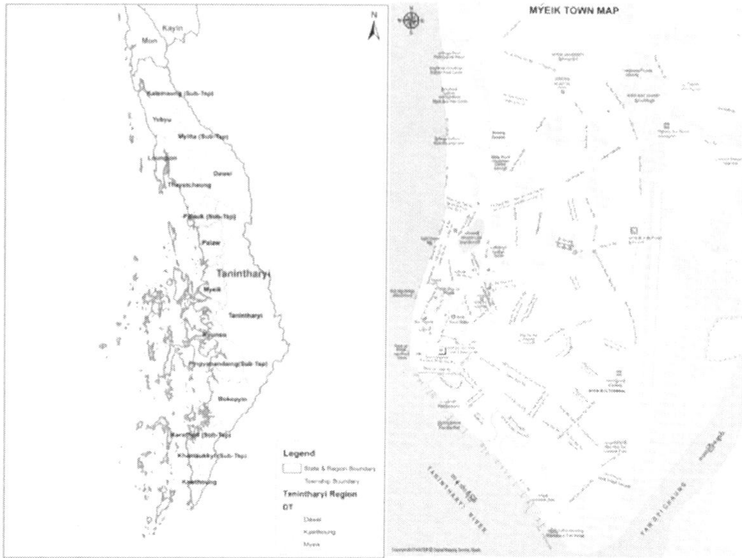

Map 7.1 Tanintharyi Region, Showing the Townships

Source: Myanmar Census 2014: Myeik Township Report; https://www.merguidolphin.com/en_US/myeik-map/

Disclaimer: This figure has been redrawn by the author/s and is not to scale. It does not represent any authentic national or international boundaries and is used for illustrative purposes only.

7.2. MYEIK ECONOMY

7.2.1. Population and Labour Force

According to the 2014 census, the total population of Myeik District was 693,087 people with 21.8 per cent urban population (151,315 people). The median age of Myeik individuals is 24.5 years. The population density of Myeik Township in 2014 was 201 people per sq. km, and the average household size was five persons per household. This is slightly more than the country's average of 4.4 persons living in each household (Table 7.1).

The percentage of the productive working population aged 15–64 years in Myeik Township is 63.5 per cent, whereas the percentage of children (aged 14 years and below) combined with the percentage of the elderly (aged 65 years and older) is lesser than the percentage of the working-age group population.

Table 7.1 Population Census of Myeik District

Name	Status	Total Population (29 March 2014)
Myeik	District	693,087
Kyunsu	Township	171,753
Myeik	Township	284,489
Palaw	Township	129,992
Tanintharyi	Township	106,853
Myanmar	Republic	51,486,253

Labour Force (Aged 15–64)	Both Sexes (%)	Male (%)	Female (%)
Labour force participation rate	63.5	85.0	40.1
Unemployment rate	4.9	4.4	5.8
Employment-to-population ratio	59.0	81.3	37.7

Source: Department of Population, Ministry of Labour, Immigration and Population (2017).

Lower percentage of children and elderly reduces the dependency of these age groups on the working age population. However, the birth rate in Myeik Township has been declining in the last 10 years. The population has significantly declined in the age group 15–19 onwards. Compared to the national level, there is a lower percentage of working-age group population aged 15–64 in Myeik Township. Starting from population aged 40–44, there are fewer males than females in all age groups. The age-specific fertility rate in Myeik Township is the highest among women aged 25–29 years. For women aged 15–49 years, the average total fertility rate is 2.8 children per woman, slightly higher than the total fertility rate of 2.5 at the national level (Figure 7.1).

School attendance in Myeik Township drops after the age of 13 years for both males and females. The literacy rate of population aged 15 years and older in Myeik Township is 96.4 per

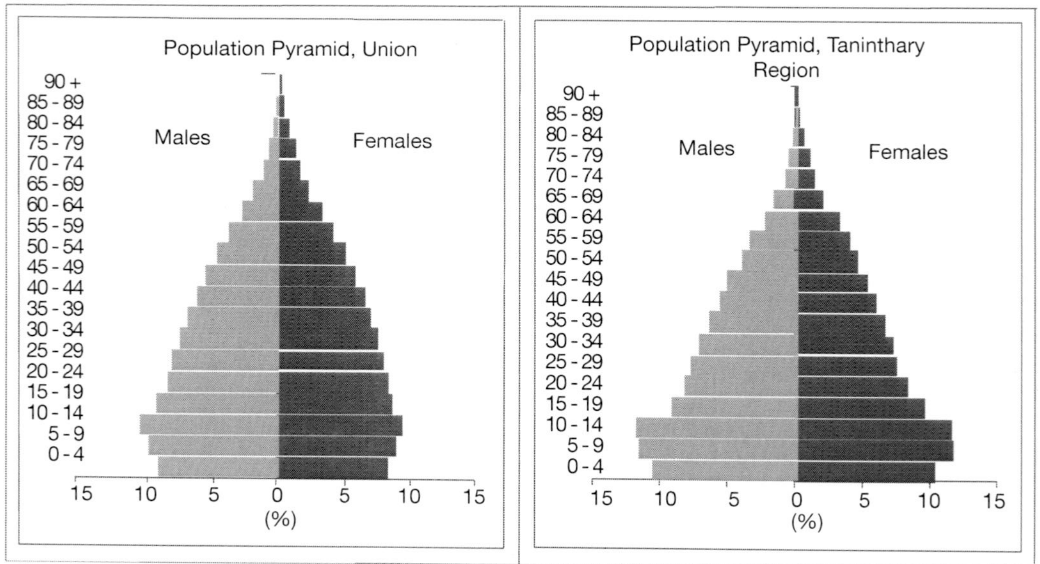

Figure 7.1 (Continued)

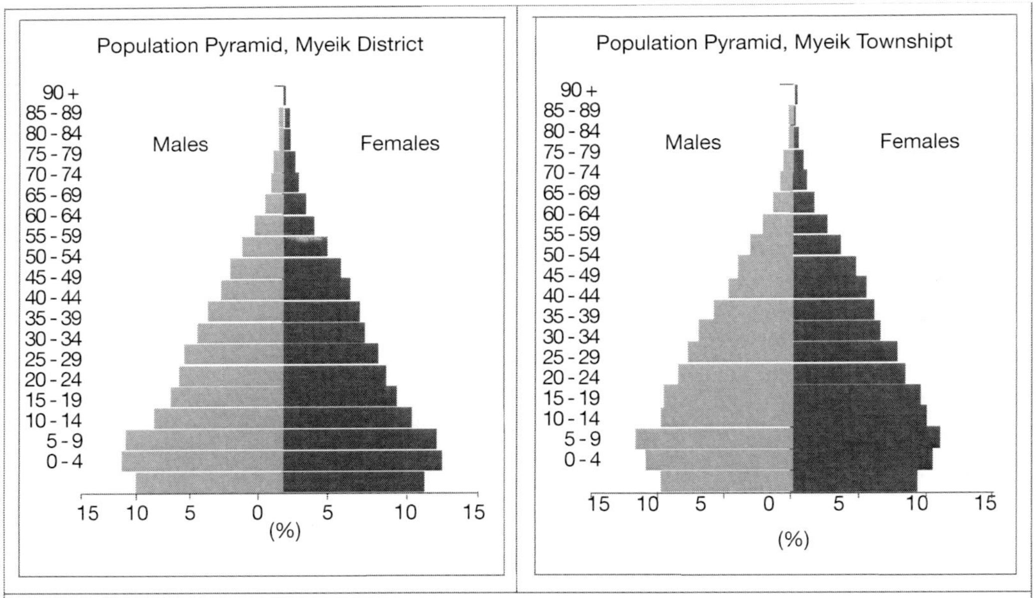

Figure 7.1 Population Pyramid (Union, Tanintharyi Region, Myeik District and Myeik Township)

Source: Department of Population, Ministry of Labour, Immigration and Population (2017).

cent. It is higher than the literacy rate in the Tanintharyi region (92.8%) and the Union (89.5%). The female and male literacy rate is 95.4 per cent and 97.5 per cent respectively. The literacy rate in youth aged 15–24 years is 98.1 per cent, with the rates being 98.1 per cent and 98.2 per cent for females and males respectively.

In Myeik Township, skilled agricultural, forestry and fishery workers were the largest group of employed persons aged 15–64 years with 28.6 per cent, followed by services and sales workers with 19.7 per cent. Analysis according to gender shows that 36.7 per cent of males are skilled agricultural, forestry and fishery workers and 39.6 per cent of females are services and sales workers. In the Tanintharyi region, 43.7 per cent are skilled agricultural, forestry and fishery workers and 14.1 per cent are services and sales workers (Figure 7.2).

7.2.2. Logistics and Transportation

- **By road:** Myeik is approximately 460 km from Bangkok, 180 km from Singkhon checkpoint, Prachuap Khiri Khan province and 266 km from Dawei. From Yangon's Aung Mingalar bus station, there are 4–5 buses starting daily at 5 AM, and they charge Myanmar Kyat (MMK)20,000. Foreigners are now allowed to travel to Dawei. The bus from Myeik to Dawei takes about 7–8 hours and costs about MMK8,000. There is also a mini-van service for MMK10,000 and it takes about 6 hours. A local bus is available between Myeik and Kawthaung. Alternatively, there are vans for MMK25,000.
- **By air:** The flight time from Yangon to Myeik is 1 hour and 25 minutes. The flight time table is shown in Table 7.2.

7.3. PRODUCTION SECTORS AND BUSINESS OPPORTUNITIES

7.3.1. Agriculture and Fishery

Agriculture and fishery are significant industries and sources of livelihood in the Tanintharyi region. Four major projects in the Tanintharyi region were introduced at the Invest Myanmar

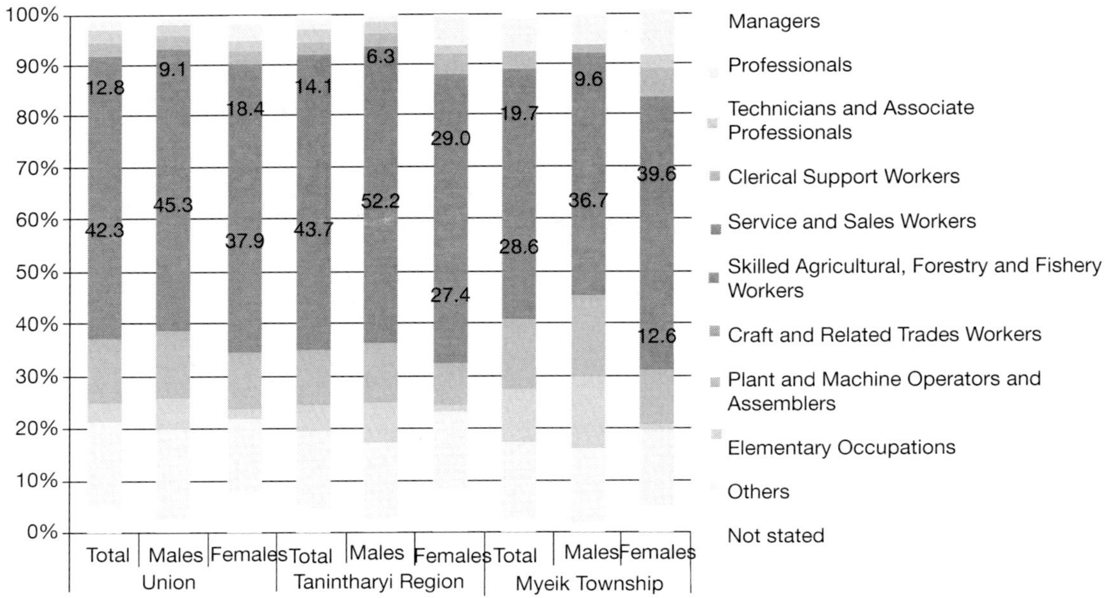

Figure 7.2 Percentage of Employed Persons

Source: Department of Population, Ministry of Labour, Immigration and Population (2017).

Table 7.2 Flight Time from Yangon to Myeik and from Myeik to Yangon

Flights from Yangon to Myeik											
6:30 AM	→	7:35 AM	Myanmar National Airlines 303	S	M	T	—	T	—	S	RGN-MGZ
6:30 AM	→	8:05 AM	Myanmar National Airlines 303	—	—	—	W	—	F	—	RGN-MGZ
6:45 AM	→	8:20 AM	Myanmar National Airlines 335	S	—	—	W	—	F	—	RGN-MGZ
7:00 AM	→	8:35 AM	MAI 4118	S	—	T	—	T	—	S	RGN-MGZ
7:00 AM	→	8:35 AM	Air KBZ 336	S	—	T	—	T	—	S	RGN-MGZ
7:15 AM	→	8:50 AM	Myanmar National Airlines 337	—	—	—	—	—	—	S	RGN-MGZ
Flights from Myeik to Yangon											
8:05 AM	→	9:10 AM	Myanmar National Airlines 304	S	M	T	—	T	—	S	MGZ-RGN
8:25 AM	→	10:00 AM	Myanmar National Airlines 304	—	—	—	W	—	F	—	MGZ-RGN
8:50 AM	→	10:25 AM	MAI 4119	S	—	T	—	T	—	S	MGZ-RGN
8:50 AM	→	10:25 AM	Air KBZ 337	S	—	T	—	T	—	S	MGZ-RGN
11:10 AM	→	12:45 PM	Myanmar National Airlines 336	S	—	—	W	—	F	—	MGZ-RGN

Source: Data collected by the author.

Summit held by the Myanmar government in Nay Pyi Taw in January 2019. The showcased projects included the construction of the Sin Phyu Pyinn Wholesale Fish Market in Dawei; the Made in Myanmar Sustainable Rubber Products project in Dawei, Myeik and Kawthaung; development of the Sepho River Side Hotel and Villa, along with a Sepho commercial zone and fresh market; and development of saltwater shrimp farming in Kawthaung.

7.3.1.1. Natural Rubber

The Tanintharyi region is a major rubber-producing area in Myanmar, representing 20 per cent of rubber farming market in the country. The cost of labour and materials for establishing a rubber plantation in Tanintharyi was generally lower than that in Thailand (Vagneron et al. 2017). The total output of rubber from Tanintharyi ranked number two in Myanmar after that in Mon State (Table 7.3). However, the weakness of rubber producers in these areas is low productivity because of the low quality of

Table 7.3 Rubber Production by State and Region in 2015/2016

State/Region	Planted Area (acres)	Productive Area (acres)	Yield (lb/acre)	Production (metric tons)
Mon	491,100	317,448	730.11	105,130
Tanintharyi	343,052	128,396	565.60	32,941
Kayin	266,820	139,138	732.55	46,233
Shan	183,394	44,306	460.69	9,258
Bago	116,693	48,993	682.15	15,159
Kachin	78,950	2,039	523.52	484
Yangon	43,415	10,276	420.90	1,962
Rakhine	35,522	2,433	523.95	578
Ayeyarwady	35,274	842	681.46	260
Others	13,208	407	457.66	84
Total	1,607,428	694,278	673.47	212,089

Source: Land Management and Statistics Department, Vagneron (2017).

planting material and saplings. Moreover, small farmers still lack skills. There are poor extension services. Also, because of the lack of capital, small farmers cannot access credit. Also, there is no rubber processing industry yet in the region. Thus, the linkages with Prachuap Khiri Khan and the Southern provinces of Thailand will strengthen.

7.3.1.2. Crude Palm Oil

Myanmar's 30-year National Development Plan drafted and launched in 1999 positions the Tanintharyi region to become an 'Oil Bowl of Myanmar' (Win 2016). Land reserved for oil palm plantations has increased rapidly in Myanmar, particularly in the southern Tanintharyi region. Following the 2012 ceasefire agreement between the Myanmar government and the Karen National Union (KNU), many former conflict zones became attractive for both local and foreign investment. Between 2011 and 2016, no less than 1.9 million acres were reportedly granted to oil palm companies. However, only a small share of the land has actually been developed into plantations, while parts of the remaining concession areas seem to be used for timber logging (Environmental Investigation Agency 2018). The largest oil palm concession issued by the Myanmar government was granted to Myanmar Auto Corporation (MAC) in the Tanintharyi region. The concession covers 133,600 acres. However, this oil palm plantation has caused conflicts with customary users over land grabbing, environmental change and deforestation (*Myanmar Business Today* 2018).

Cultivation technology has not been developed much; as a result, palm oil production is approximately 15 tonnes per *rai*, and almost all of it is sold in the form of crude palm oil that has not yet been developed to add value. Most of the produce is sold and transported to Yangon (Pittungnapoo 2016). Therefore, if there is better connectivity and trade facilitations between Myeik and Prachuap Khiri Khan, investment in oil palm plantations and exports to Thailand may be another trade and investment opportunity for the Thai entrepreneurs. PTT Green Energy (PTTGE) has invested in this region since 2014 with a 4,000 hectare oil palm plantation.

7.3.1.3. Pearls

Pearls are famous local products of the Mergui Archipelago. The islands of the Mergui Archipelago are the ideal cultivating place for the best-quality pearls since the environment is pristine clean. The local pearls, both white and golden, are produced by the local water oyster *Pinctada maxima*. The cultured pearls of this area have become popular and high valued due to their quality. The golden pearls from the Mergui Archipelago present a unique colour and large size and are widely recognized as the best in the world. Myanmar produced a total of 687,000 pearls in 2017–2018, showing a 10 per cent increase in number in 3 years (Chan 2019).

Since the 1800s, Myanmar's South Sea has been prominently known for natural golden pearls collected by the nomadic people, known as sea gypsies, who dive to the ocean floor for collecting natural pearls around the 800 islands of the Myeik Archipelago. It is renowned for its beautiful pearls. The technology of pearl oyster farming was introduced into Myanmar around 1954, and now cultured pearls are widely produced. At present, there are several pearl farms of both domestic and international pearl culture companies along the group of islands in the Mergui Archipelago, such as Nino Company and Tasaki Shingu Company from Japan; Andaman Pearl Company from Thailand; and Ocean Pearl, which is a local company. There is also a Myanmar–Australia joint venture known as Myanmar Atlantic at Ross Island; Nino Company operates at Kamar Island and Andaman Pearl Company at Bentick Island. Tasaki, which pioneered pearl production in Myanmar, is based on Letsutaw Island. In Myeik, most pearls are collected near the town of Boatpyin known as Pearl Island, which is called by locals as Phoe Maung Saung Island.

7.3.1.4. Birds' Nest

In Myanmar, birds' nests can be found only in two areas, that is, the Mergui Archipelago and the group of islands in the Ayeyarwady region. However, birds' nests from Myeik are considered to be higher quality and hence are more expensive. These nests are built by swiftlets to lay eggs and nurture their little chicks. The nest is actually the solidified saliva of the birds. After the chicks are grown and strong enough to take care of themselves, the whole family of swiftlets no longer needs the nest and abandons it. These abandoned nests are collected by people as they believe that the birds' nest is a supplement with high nutritional value. Edible birds' nests are sold at prices up to several thousands of US dollars per kilogram, depending on type and grading of the nest. Chinese traditional practitioners believe that birds' nests promote good health, especially for the skin (Htike 2019). Myeik has two kinds of birds' nests, that is, island and house birds' nests. The island ones are collected from the island ahead of Myeik Township. An island birds' nest is usually three times more expensive than the house birds' nest and is believed to be of better quality. A Mali Island's nest is the highest rated birds' nest in the Mergui Archipelago (Htike 2019).

7.3.1.5. Fisheries

According to the 2014 Census data, more than 28.6 per cent of the people in Myeik are engaged in agriculture, forestry and fisheries (see Figure 7.2). According to the study by Witiya Pittungnapoo and her team in 2016, there are more than 100,000 fishermen working in the Mergui Archipelago. There are about 8,000 fishing boats, of which most boats (around 5000) are used for catching squids.

The fishing potential of a medium-sized fishing boat is around 1,000 tonnes per boat per day. In this area, fishermen can catch fish for 9 months in a year, except for the monsoon season between July and September. It is estimated that 80 per cent of the seafood is exported to Thailand. The annual fishing capacity is approximately 280,000 tonnes (Pittungnapoo 2016).

From the survey trip in 2018, the research team found that seafood ingredients are very abundant in the local market in Myeik. There are many seafood items that are considered premium and popular among Thai consumers, such as lobster, sea urchin, mantis shrimp, and soft shell crab, which are available at selling prices that are about 2–5 times lower than the price at which they are sold in Thailand.

For Myanmar people, 'Ngapi' or shrimp paste from Myeik is very well known and considered the best since it is tastier and saltier than those from other regions. Even in Yangon and Mandalay, the best and most expensive Ngapi sold in the local markets are always claimed to be from Myeik.

Fresh seafood raw materials from Myeik are transported from the Mergui Archipelago through Kawthaung to either Satun or Ranong province. They are then transported to the seafood processing areas of Thailand in Samut Songkhram Province and Samut Sakhon Province. The processing plants are around 850 km from the sea, and at present, it takes more than 30–34 hours to transport seafood products from the sea to the processing plants and sometimes up to 40–57 hours during the monsoon season. The Myanmar government and Thai importers would like very much to move the transportation and trade bases to the Prachuap Khiri Khan Province via the Singkhon Border Pass. This new route will reduce the transportation time to 6.5–8 hours and cover a distance of only 480 km (Nurak 2015; Pittanapo, Phanakarn, and Phongcharoen 2016; Rattanaset 2017).

In 2017, Myanmar exported Thailand Baht (THB) 3.345 billion (US$104.19 million) fisheries and seafood products to Thailand, of which more than 80 per cent came from the Tanintharyi region (Myeik, Mergui Archipelago) via the Port of Ranong. However, Myeik's fisheries industry, which is linked to the processed seafood industry in Thailand, has not yet been fully utilized. Although Myeik has a rich source of raw materials with high-quality seafood, the logistics system has not yet been developed fully. The crossing point from Myanmar to Thailand is also not yet ready. These two factors result in longer transportation time. For seafood, the duration of transport is a major drawback because for every minute of delay, the freshness and quality of the raw materials are reduced. According to the survey by Witiya and her team in 2016, the current situation and a better option for the logistics system between Myeik in Myanmar and Mahachai, Samut Sakhon in Thailand is summarized in Table 7.4.

7.3.2. Tourism

The charm of Myeik is that it is a new city that overlays the heart of the old city. There is a mixture of old and new culture. The old city is a place of worship with Buddhist temples, Hindu temples,

Table 7.4 Logistics Option for Seafood Transportation from Myeik to Samut Sakhon

Beginning and Ending points of Transportations	Mode of Transportation	Distance (km)	Duration (hours)
Transport seafood from Myeik by boat to Ranong and then to Mahachai, Samut Sakhon by truck			
Myeik-Ranong	Fishing Boat	300	20–22 hours in dry season 30–45 hours in monsoon season
Ranong-Mahachai	Truck	550	10–12 hours 12–15 hours that includes the driver's resting time as required by the traffic law
Total		850	30–57 hours
Transport seafood from Myeik by truck to Prachuap Khiri Khan via Singkhon Border Pass and to Mahachai, Samut Sakhon by truck			
Myeik-Singkhon Border Pass	Truck	200	3–4 hours
Singkhon Border Pass-Mahachai	Truck	280	3.5–4 hours
Total		480	6.5–8 hours
Transport seafood from Myeik by truck to Prachuap Khiri Khan via Singkhon Border Pass when the road is fully upgraded and then to Mahachai, Samut Sakhon by truck			
Myeik-Singkhon Border Pass	Truck	200	2.5–3 hours
Singkhon Border Pass-Mahachai	Truck	280	3.5–4 hours
Total		480	6–7 hours

Source: Adapted from Witiya (2016).

Chinese shrines, Islamic mosques and Christian churches, and it also has many old colonial-style buildings that were built since the British colonial era. One important Buddhist pagoda is Thein Daw Gyi. The pagoda is located on a hill in the city centre. It attracts both local and foreign tourists and is also famous for the sunset view.

According to 2018 data, the Tanintharyi region has 1,437 hotel rooms, and it welcomed 134,000 tourists during January–November of 2017. In addition, the local government has approved nine islands from a total of 800 islands in the Mergui Archipelago for foreign investments (Business Information Center 2018). The community-based tourism schemes have been launched by the regional government covering Dawei, Myeik and Kawthaung townships. In 2018, both foreign and local tourists were allowed to visit the pearl farms in the Myeik Archipelago. According to the Tanintharyi office of the Directorate of Investment and Company Administration (DICA), 12 hotel projects were implemented by local and foreign investors in the region. These hotel businesses are currently run by foreign investors from Thailand, New Zealand and France (Lwin 2019).

In the Andaman Sea on the eastern side of the Indian Ocean, there are more than 800 islands that are part of the Mergui Archipelago. As most of the islands are untouched and natural, Myeik has the potential to develop eco-tourism. Our research team explored some of these beautiful unexplored islands:

- **Marcus or Lay Kyun or Harris Island:** The main attraction of this island is viewing the mesmerizing sunrise and sunset. There is a walking trail linking the front and the back of the island. Travellers can walk through the rocks when the tides are low and enjoy the boat ride direct from one beach to the other beach when the tide is high. The seawater is transparently turquoise. There is an electric generator on the island. There are bungalows and tents with food services for overnight stay for visitors. At present, it is the only island on which the government allows foreigners to stay overnight (Nyein 2019).

- **Thamee Hla Island:** The shoreline has more ocean rocks than sand, but the location of this island is exceptional for snorkelling. The small waterfall that flows directly from the rocks into the beach makes the island charming and attracts local fishermen for freshwater fishing.
- **Drakes Island or Daung Kyun Island or Done Nyaung Mine Island:** This is the island where the original sea people tribe 'Mawken' ('Morgan' in Thai) reside now in the village called 'Done Nyaung Hmine'. Travellers can learn about the traditions and habits of the sea people, which amazingly never changed much in decades. They are friendly and more than happy to be photographed. On the island, there are also some grocery stores, food stalls and homestays for travellers who would like to learn more about the way of life of Mawkens. Mawken or Morgan or Moken are Austronesian people of the Mergui Archipelago on both Myanmar side and Thailand side. Most of the 2,000–3,000 Moken lead a semi-nomadic hunter–gatherer lifestyle heavily based on the sea, though this is increasingly under threat now.
- **Pahtaw Pahtet Island:** This island is famous for the enormous reclining Buddha image 'Thein Daw Gyi'.
- **Par Pank or Smart Island:** There are only six pebble beaches (shingle beach) among the 800 islands of the Mergui Archipelago, and Smart Island has the longest pebble beach. Smart Island has a pebble beach on the eastern side that is connected to the white sandy beach on the western side of the island by a 5-minute walk through a jungle trail. On the centre of the trail is located a shelter for an overnight stay; however, overnight stay on Smart Island is not yet officially allowed by the Myanmar government. At the time when our research team visited the island (2018), there was no electricity generator installed on the island.
- **Done Waterfall Island:** As the name suggests, this island has a lovely natural 15-metre waterfall that falls into the ocean from the top. One can easily climb to the top of waterfall and jump into and feel refreshed by bathing in its crystal clear cool pools.

7.3.3. Energy and Mining Sectors

Mining is a significant industry in the Tanintharyi region. Coal, tin, tungsten and iron are the major minerals mined in this region, and up to two-thirds of the country's tin and tungsten requirements are supplied from this region (UNHCR 2014, 11). The conflict area in Karen State possess many valuable that were targeted by foreign investors willing to take advantage of new ceasefire agreements with ethnic armed groups whose territories contain vast mineral wealth. (Vagneron et al. 2017). According to TNI (2013, cited in Vagneron et al 2017), the major mines and the main products of each mine are as follows:

- Heinda: Tin-tungsten deposit
- Hamyingyi: Hydrothermal quartz vein and greisen-type tungsten-tin deposit
- Kanbauk: Hydrothermal quartz vein-type tin-tungsten deposit
- Yawa: Tin-tungsten deposit
- Kyaukmetaung: Tin-tungsten deposit
- Nanthida: Tin-tungsten deposit
- Theindaw, Myeik District, Tanintharyi Region, Myanmar: Alluvial tin mining area
- Yadanabon: Tin-tungsten deposit (primary and alluvial cassiterite)

There is a shortage of energy and electricity in the region. The National Power Grid has not arrived yet in the Tanintharyi regions of Dawei, Myeik and Kawthaung. The price of electricity in Yangon is less than 2 baht per unit, whereas it costs 7–8 baht per unit in Myeik and Kawthaung. A group of scholars from Myeik University, in an interaction in 2018, said that, given the situation of high demand for energy in Myanmar, building the coal power plant in Myeik is also another business opportunity with full support from the local governments. The local governments can approve a special tax privilege for investment projects worth up to US$5 million and electricity projects that are less than 30 MW capacity (Global Thailand 2018).

7.4. CHALLENGES AND POLICIES RECOMMENDATIONS

7.4.1. Challenges and Policies Recommendations for the Government

7.4.1.1. Upgrading the Singkhon–Maw Daung Pass to the International Permanent Border Crossing Point with Local Government and Local Collaboration

The Tanintharyi Region Chambers of Commerce and Industry (TCCI) has formed a focus group with the provincial authorities, businesspeople and scholars on both Myanmar and Thailand sides. The research conducted by the focus group revealed that there is a need for pushing forward the plan to upgrade the Singkhon Pass to a permanent border crossing point to support both economic growth and tourism. Between 2014 and 2018, the Department of Public Works and Town and Country Planning (DPT) has received a budget of more than 240 million THB from the Thai government for the construction of the border crossing office building to facilitate the immigration process. Upgrading of the Singkhon Pass will further stimulate trade and investment along the Thailand–Myanmar border.

To make this proposal a reality, the still un-demarcated borderline is the main stumbling block, although both Thai and Myanmar authorities have surveyed the area. The research team would like to propose a solution to this problem. There is a need to establish a Joint Development Agreement (JDA) model to upgrade the Singkhon–Maw Daung Pass. The Maw Daung Pass international cross-border checkpoint on Thailand's side has been developed since 2014. The Singkhon Pass has also been upgraded to a Temporary Border Pass since 2015.

The narrow definition of JDA mainly focuses on gas and oil exploration and utilization. Most of them are temporary arrangements, but there is a legal platform such as the United Nations Convention on the Law of the Sea (UNCLOS) Article 74.3, Article 83.3 and Article 142 to support boundaries. From this platform, we can assume the broader definition and learn from the achievements in the past, for example, JDA in addition to a boundary line between Australia and Papua New Guinea and between China and Vietnam; JDA in the absence of a boundary line, such as for Australia–Indonesia, Cambodia–Thailand, Cambodia–Vietnam, Malaysia–Thailand, Malaysia–Vietnam, and Joint Fishing Zone in East Asia.

The provisions of JDA and the common interest issues between Thailand and Myanmar, which can be set as a starting point for sustainable border management, are presented in Figure 7.3.

7.4.1.2. Physical Connectivity: Hardware Connectivity to connect Prachuap Khiri Khan and the Tanintharyi Region

It is in the common interest of both the countries to connect Prachuap Khiri Khan and the Tanintharyi region to serve as a distribution and logistics centre linking the two peninsulas between the Gulf of Thailand and the Andaman Sea. The Prachuap Khiri Khan province can be positioned as a hub for connecting raw materials from the eastern side of Thailand to the Myeik town on the Andaman coast of Myanmar and further connecting to the Bay of Bengal countries, especially to the biggest market of India.

To make this happen, there is a need for the development of transportation infrastructures, such as the two seaports of the Prachuap Khiri Khan province: Bang Saphan Pier and Khlong Wan Docks. Currently, Bang Saphan Pier can handle 100,000 deadweight tonnage (DWT). Both these development projects are needed to support future business expansion in the area.

With the upgrading of these infrastructures and upgrading of the border crossing point (see Maps 7.2 and 7.3), this new route will be able to transport fisheries and seafood products worth THB 3.345 billion (US$104.19 million) from Myeik to Samut Sakhon and will reduce transportation time to just 6.5–8 hours with a distance of only 480 km (see Section 7.2.1 for more details).

Development of air transportation infrastructures, such as the development of Wing 5 Air Force Airfield in Prachuap Khiri Khan for commercial use or the development of Hua Hin Airport, and allowing low-cost airlines to operate with lower transaction from Hua Hin, Prachuap Khiri Khan to Myeik, Dawei and Yangon are important physical connectivity infrastructures that are needed

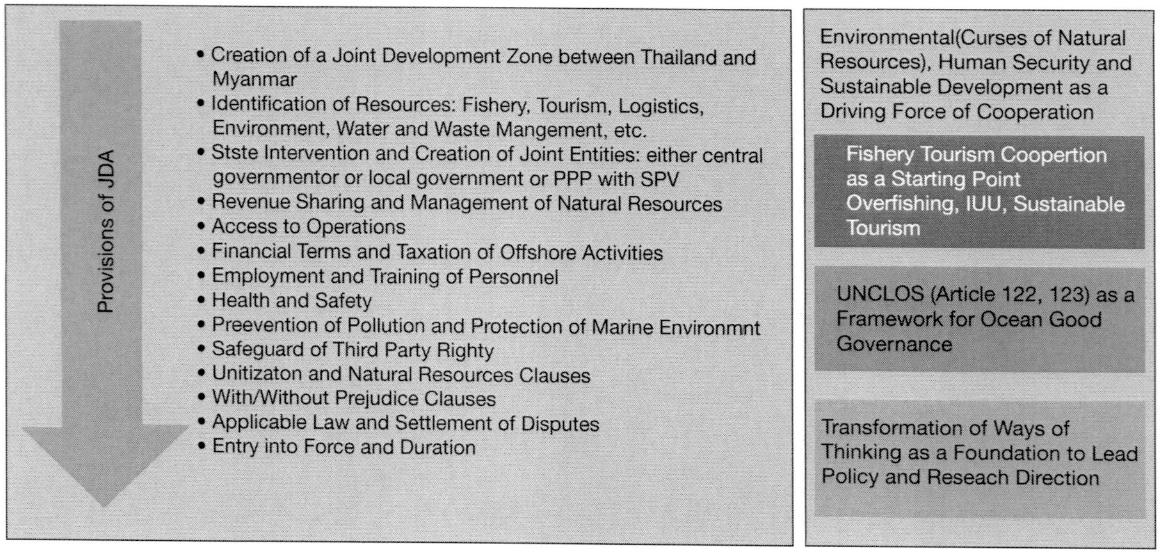

Figure 7.3 Provisions of the JDA to Upgrade the Singkhon–Maw Daung Pass to an International Permanent Border Crossing Point

Source: Network of ASEAN-China Academic Institutes (NACAI) and Shanghai Forum 2018.

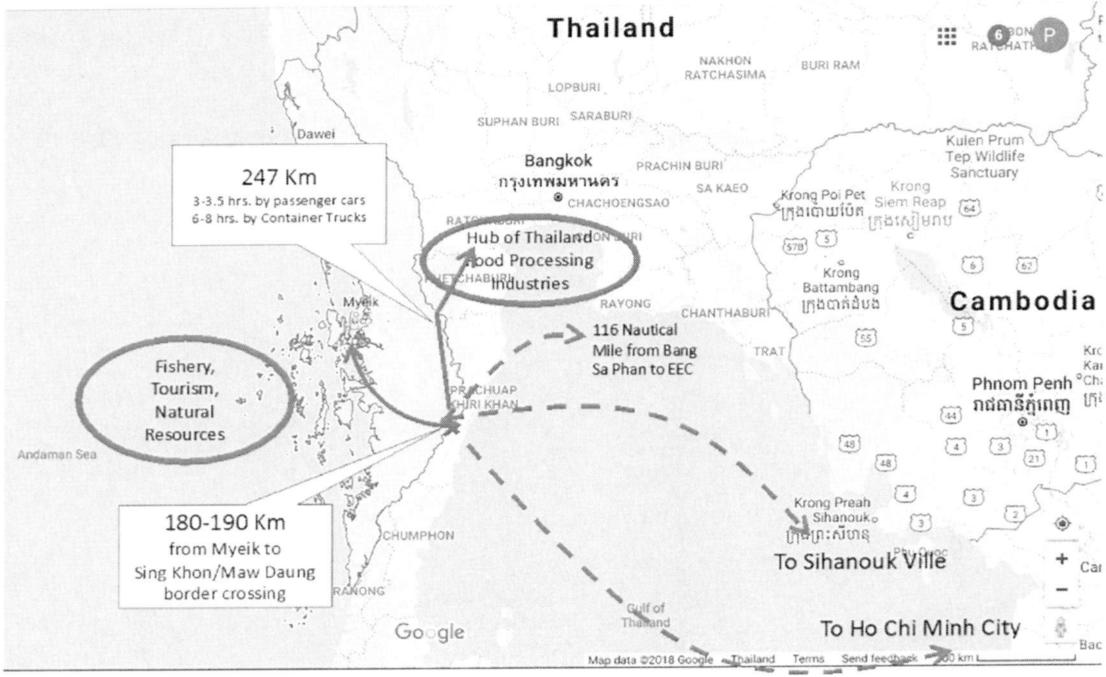

Map 7.2 New Trade Route from Myeik to Samut Sakhon with Upgrading to Singkhon Pass

Source: The author.

Disclaimer: This figure has been redrawn by the author/s and is not to scale. It does not represent any authentic national or international boundaries and is used for illustrative purposes only.

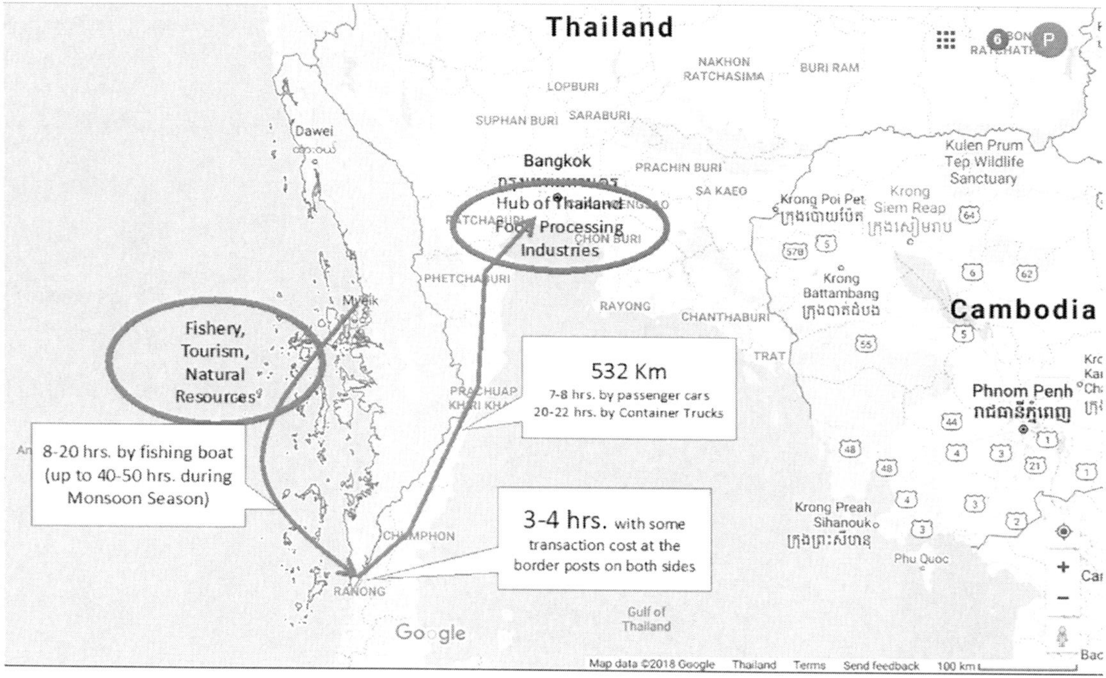

Map 7.3 New Trade Route from Andaman Sea of Indian Ocean to the Mainland Association of Southeast Asian Nations (ASEAN) Major Seaport

Source: The author.

Disclaimer: This figure has been redrawn by the author/s and is not to scale. It does not represent any authentic national or international boundaries and is used for illustrative purposes only.

to connect the two neighbouring countries to optimize their business opportunities.

This physical connectivity is very important since the Tanintharyi region is an important source of raw materials, including palm oil, rubber, agricultural products and fishery products for Thailand. On the other side of the border, Myanmar consumers would also like to import consumer products, machinery, construction materials, seeds, fertilizers, machinery and chemicals for agriculture from Thailand. Thailand still depends on Myeik as a source of raw materials and labour and as a tourist destination. It is also an area that many Thai investors are interested in investing in. These complete supply chains will complement and upgrade the well-being of people on both sides of the border.

Last but not the least, when Prachuap Khiri Khan will be more economically developed and expanded compared to the current stage, it may face water shortages. Although Prachuap Kiri Khan is a province with heavy rainfall, the water from the steep Tanaosri Mountains flows into the sea quickly because the short and steep distance between the mountainous region do not have enough space for soil to absorb the rainwater. The narrowest part of Thailand is located in this province, and the distance is only 11 km. Fortunately, when crossing the Tanaosri Mountains, there is another flat area of almost 200 km to Myeik, and in this flat area, there are still many big branches of the basin of the Tanaosri/Tanintharyi River that has lot of water and has a mouth that is more than 2 km wide. This is an enormous amount of water nearest to the Prachuap Khiri Khan province (Srisangnam 2018).

7.4.1.3. Institutional (Software) Connectivity

Apart from the physical or hardware connectivity such as road, border point and seaports mentioned in the preceding context, to unlock the untapped potentials of international trade and investment, there is a need for utilization of trading agreements, cancellation of the non-tariff measures and full implementation of trade facilitations (TFs). Exchange rate volatilities as well as the lack of banking and financial services in the areas also pose big challenges for trade and investment.

Seamless institution/software connectivity, especially on TFs (such as customs clearance procedure, immigration procedure, and standard and commencement), and the creation of more appropriate business environment are most required to unlock the potential.

7.4.2. Challenges and Policy Recommendations for Private Sectors

7.4.2.1. Need to Have a Business Plan and Know about Consumer Behaviour in Each Market

There is a need to plan business and learn more about consumer behaviour in each market, including preparations and contingency plans for a variety of situations that may occur. This could be in the form of manuals that will enable to act step by step in the face of any unexpected incident. A stress test must be taken, and a contingency plan must be implemented in the form of a manual for middle management to follow when facing a crisis. Tests must be conducted in several mock situations such as internal uncertainty, closure of cross-border points and border checkpoints, power line instability and problematic rates of exchange or money transfer.

There is a need to think of all possible worst-case scenarios when investing. One needs to think carefully and be prepared for each situation. The manual can be a handy tool in an unexpected situation. Investors can react in haste in unexpected situations and may invest more money to redeem the situation. Unfortunately, the outcome is often tragic.

Consumers in each of the states (Chin, Kachin, Kayah, Kayin, Mon, Rakhine and Shan) and the seven regions with a majority of Burmese people (i.e., Ayeyarwady, Bago, Magway, Mandalay, Sagaing, Tanintharyi and Yangon) have different tastes and lifestyles. The preferences may go well in some countries but may fare differently in others. There is a need to understand these differences.

7.4.2.2. It Is Necessary to Have Local Business Allies

Local business allies are essential, especially when it comes to rules and regulations. Businessmen also need to foster a good relationship with the central and local governments. For instance, in Myanmar, the position of public administrators is changed on the basis of transfers, for example, the director of one government office in one township may have to migrate to other township assigned by the central government in Yangon when migration season arrives. This rule applies to all levels, even to a university professor. Laws and financial auditing systems in Myanmar are different from those which are familiar to Thai businesspeople. The local people, on the other hand, have a good idea of all these rules and regulations. Thus, having a local alliance is important. A local governor can sometimes exercise certain special powers that can affect investment in a very interesting way. Working with local people depends a lot on mutual trust. It is essential that no advantage be taken of investment partners.

7.4.2.3. Study Logistics and Communication Routes

Businesspeople need to study communication routes, including transportation systems, conditions of the facilities and logistics. There is also a need to have all the information about new and emerging routes and systems, especially those that will turn several townships into marine and/or road transportation hubs.

7.4.2.4. Have Cash Reserves and Working Capital

To do business in Myanmar where the financial system is not yet fully developed like in Thailand, businesspeople need to have good financial stability with enough cash reserves and working capital. The markets in Myanmar are still small, despite rapid growth, and may take some time before any substantial returns of investment are seen. Businesspeople need to have liquidity allocations for at least 6–8 months at hand, in case of an emergency. For certain manufacturing and service sectors, some commercial banks require a substantial amount of paid-up capital on the part of business operators.

7.4.2.5. Study the Payment System and Foreign Exchange Transactions

Businesspeople need to carefully study the foreign exchange system, including international payment channels. There exist more than one foreign exchange rates in Myanmar. In some areas of Myanmar, some business firms use their own currency alongside USD and THB. According to business operators and financial service providers, an informal financial transaction banking system will continue for some time yet. Currently, some banks in Thailand have been authorized to open branches in Myanmar. However, international financial transactions still depend on local infrastructure which has not yet been fully developed. The advent of ASEAN and financial liberalization has led to a free flow of capital. The THB will play an even more important role in border trade.

7.4.2.6. Study Business Environment

Myanmar is still beset with basic infrastructure problems, especially power shortage, instable power supply and high rates of power bill, issues in water supply and very high rates of building rent and land lease. In most of the provinces in Myanmar (except downtown Yangon and downtown Mandalay), electricity distribution is not stable, leading to power shortage, and the electric power bill is rather high. Businesspeople need to study all this before making an investment.

7.4.2.7. Study Laws, Rules and Regulations

It is crucial to study and understand thoroughly the laws, rules and regulations on trade, investment and investment promotion, especially the tax system and laws about the environment and labour welfare at the central and local government levels. We find that in some states, the local government that comes under the control of the ethnic minority may have different ways of law enforcement from those of the central government. In Myanmar, whose economic system used to be socialist for the past 60 years, certain rules and regulations on trade and investment may be different from those normally encountered by Thai businesses. It is, therefore, very helpful to have local business alliance to help with the understanding of the concerned laws, rules and regulations.

7.4.2.8. Need for Skill Development of Workers

Investors must pay attention to the issue of labour in terms of the amount, quality and work culture. Workers need to have their skills further developed and intensively trained. Some workers do not want to be bossed around. They prefer to work with employers who speak nicely. Sometimes, the problem is about the shortage of workers with management skills, especially at the middle management level, thus making it necessary to deploy middle managers from Thailand or in certain cases to entrust the management to local business alliances to whom Thai business owners need to send instructions, or they need to manage the business as a whole from Thailand. At any rate, Thai entrepreneurs need to adjust their attitude towards foreign workers. They must bear in mind that workers in almost every country are intelligent but have not been exposed to the Western way of working.

7.4.2.9. Cultivate Good Community Relations. Prudent and Sustainable Investment Policy Is a Must

Corporate social responsibility (CSR) is a company's participation in the community in which it operates. CSR has been an important strategy of big corporations throughout the world. Even in emerging countries like Myanmar, companies have been assisting communities that suffer hardship, as was the case when Cyclone Nargis hit the country in 2008. Community relations involve interactions with local people in the community in which the company is located and with other existing Thai companies. Good relationships will make it easier to exchange information on various issues that help promote businesses.

The approach could make use of a variety of business models. For instance, the 3Cs Model of Kenichi Ohmae focuses on the knowledge of one's own 'corporation', 'customers' and 'competitors'. In the case of Thailand's neighbouring countries, one may have to add another 'C', that is, community.

Myanmar society is Buddhist-based, similar to the Thai rural community. Therefore, it does not involve much cost to send the company's representative to participate in the religious ceremonies of the community or to develop temples, schools, roads or village water sources. On the other hand, the involvement will expand the customer base and attract more workforce to work for the company, thus strengthening its sustainability alongside the community existence.

Businesses also need to keep in mind that while doing business they have to take care of the community and the environment of the area. In case they fail to do so, they may face penalties and may face cancellation of business licenses. One classic example of a Thai investor who invested in this area and caused negative effects on the local environment is the case of Heinda tin mine.

In 1999, the Thai-owned company Myanmar Pongpipat Company Limited (MPC) was granted a concession to operate the mine together with the state-owned company No. 2 Mining Enterprise (ME2) under a production sharing contract in which the product-sharing ratio was 65 per cent for MPC and 35 per cent for ME2. Heinda mine is among one of the oldest and largest tin mines in the northern part of the Great Tenasserim River Basin in the Tanintharyi region of Myanmar. The mine is located near Myitta town, about 45 km northeast of Dawei city. The tin mine covered a concession area of 2,097 acres. Around 10 villages are located close to the Heinda mine, including the Myaung Pyo village, which is the most adversely affected by the mining operations.

In 2008, heavy rainfall hit the mine causing wastewater and sediments to be washed down and accumulated into the water sources used by thousands of households for domestic purposes and consumption. In 2012, the worst flooding incidents resulted in damages to 27 houses and villagers' crops. The Myaung Pyo River, the most important source of drinking water for the villagers, was contaminated with high toxicity levels of lead and arsenic, which caused significant health impacts on the local villagers.

7.4.2.10. Learn about External Factors beyond Control

There are a variety of external factors which, though not business-related, could affect the business existence. These include environmental problems, natural disasters, internal political stability, political temperatures and international relations. These considerations all warrant the attention of businesspeople. So, Thai entrepreneurs need to keep up with the local and international news and prepare contingency plans in case of any unfortunate incidents that may happen.

REFERENCES

Chan, Aye. 2019. *The Gold Rush—Myanmar's Golden Pearls*. Yagon: Myanmar Insider.

Department of Population, Ministry of Labour, Immigration and Population. 2017. 'The 2014 Myanmar Population and Housing Census'. *Myeik Township Report*. https://themimu.info/sites/themimu.info/files/documents/TspProfiles_Census_Myeik_2014_ENG.pdf

Environmental Investigation Agency. 2018. *Myanmar Palm Oil Concessions Trample on Communities, Act as a Cover for Extracting Timber*, 20 March. https://eia-international.org/myanmar-palm-oil-concessions-trample-on-communities/

Global Thailand. 2018. *Dawei-Myeik, the Future Economic City of Thai Investors in Myanmar* (in Thai). https://globthailand.com/myanmar_0028/

Htike, Naw. 2019. 'Precious Bird's Nest'. *Mingalabar Magazine*, no. 19 (July–December).

Lwin, Nan. 2019. 'Myanmar to Host Forum to Lure Foreign Investment in Deep South'. *The Irrawaddy*, 14 August. https://www.irrawaddy.com/news/burma/myanmar-host-forum-lure-foreign-investment-deep-south.html

Myanmar Business Today. 2018. 'Govt Plans to Take Back Approved 5 Palm Oil Plantation Projects'. Online News, 2 April. https://www.ejatlas.org/conflict/mac-oil-palm-plantation-tanintharyi-region-myanmar. updated 22 Jan 2019.

Nurak, Siriporn. 2015. *Myeik … Tourist Spots, Trade Opportunities New Investment* (in Thai). ASEAN Information Center, Public Relations Department, 18 June. http://www.aseanthai.net/ewt_news.php?nid=3501&filename=index

Nyein, Nyein. 2019. 'A Close-Up Look at Mergui Archipelago's Nascent Eco-Tourism Industry'. *The Irrawady*, 11 January. https://www.irrawaddy.com/travel/close-look-mergui-archipelagos-nascent-eco-tourism-industry.html

Pittanapo, Vitiya, Bunsapan Phanakarn, and Phupong Phongcharoen. 2016. *Industrial Potential Study Project along the Border in the Myeik Route, Republic of the Union of Myanmar—Dan Singkhon, Prachuap Khirikhan Province* (in Thai). National Research Council of Thailand (NRCT) and Thailand Research Fund (TRF).

Rattanaset, Walaiporn. 2017. 'Research Project to Propose Promote and Develop of Dan Singkorn on Trade Investment and Tourism in Prachuap Kiri Khan Province'. *Ratchaphruek Journal* 15(2): 72–82.

Srisangnam, Piti. 2018. *Myeik-Prachuap Khiri Khan, a Parallel City for Development Partners* (in Thai). http://www.thansettakij.com/content/263550

UNFPA. 2015. *2014 Population and Housing Census of Myanmar—Data Sheet*. Department of Population. https://myanmar.unfpa.org/en/publications/2014-population-and-housing-census-myanmar-data-sheet

UNHCR. 2014. *Tanintharyi Region Profile*. Yangon: UNHCR South-East Myanmar Information Management Unit.

Vagneron, I., B. Chambon, Nay Myo Aung, and Saw Min Aung. 2017. *Rubber Production in Tanintharyi Region*. Yangon: WWF.

Win, Aye Nyein. 2016. 'Palm Oil Drive Under Review in Tanintharyi'. *Myanmar Times*, 11 July. https://www.mmtimes.com/business/21301-palm-oil-drive-under-review-in-tanintharyi.html

Witiya Pittungnapoo, 2016. The Study on Feasibility Industrial in Myeik Republic of the Union of Myanmar—Sing Khon Checkpoint Prachuapkhirikhan. (in Thai). Research Project No. RDG5650028 Thailand Research Fund (TRF). https://elibrary.trf.or.th/project_content.asp?PJID=RDG5650028

CHAPTER 8

THE THAILAND–MYANMAR SOUTHERN EAST–WEST CORRIDOR

Land, Sea, Air Links and Considerations for Improving Logistics

Wiwat Sutiwipakorn

8.1. INTRODUCTION

Over the past few decades, there have been numerous visions and master plans around the Thailand–Southern Myanmar border, but none have been spot on. Some of these are on the global scale, such as China's Belt and Road Initiative (BRI), which is conceived by the Chinese government and involves the Silk Road Economic Belt overland and the 21st Maritime Silk Road over the ocean from Asia and Southeast Asia to East Africa and Western Europe. Although somewhat stalled at present, the Southern East–West Corridor (SEWC), a touch under the BRI's maritime path, might generate benefits in the long run.

Another notable plan is the Master Plan for ASEAN Connectivity (MPAC) with a vision to achieve a seamless, comprehensive, connected and integrated Association of Southeast Asian Nations (ASEAN) that will promote competitiveness, inclusiveness and a great sense of community through physical, institutional and people-to-people links. Seamless logistics is one of the five main strategies of MPAC, which also includes sustainable infrastructure, digital innovation, regulatory excellence and people mobility. Development of SEWC as mentioned in this chapter would be well within this plan.

Within ASEAN lies the Greater Mekong Subregion (GMS) and the Indonesia–Malaysia–Thailand Growth Triangle (IMT-GT) Subregional Cooperation. The former involves China, Cambodia, Lao PDR, Vietnam, Myanmar and Thailand; the latter, as its name implies, concerns Indonesia, Malaysia and Thailand. The GMS programme, with the main support from the Asian Development Bank (ADB), implements high-priority sub-regional projects in a wide range of sectors. The IMT-GT, currently working under Vision 2036 and 2017–2021 Implementation Blueprint, conducts and executes several connectivity activities. However, the SEWC finds itself somehow within a huge void between the two eminent organizations and needs to make its presence relevant in the foreseeable future.

Transportation overview, physical connectivity and logistics are presented in this chapter to address the potential of the SEWC and some of its missing links that should be considered.

Currently, the transport sector in Myanmar (approximate population 54 million, land size 676,578 sq. km) is lagging considerably behind Thailand (approximate population 68 million, land size 513,120 sq. km).

8.1.1. Road Transport

Myanmar's number of vehicles per 1,000 people in 2011 was 38 (KPMG 2013), while that of Thailand was 432 (Ministry of Transport 2018). In 2017, the same for Myanmar was 120 (CEIC 2019), indicating an accelerated economic growth. The road length in Myanmar was then 150,816 km (22% of which was paved), whereas that in Thailand in 2018 was reported as 461,000 km, of which nearly all was paved. These stark contrasts occur throughout, inclusive of the Tanintharyi region.

8.1.2. Rail Transport

Approximately 6,200 km of the route length under 'Myanma' [sic] Railways (MR) annually serves some 70 million passengers and 4 million tonnes of freight (Myanma Railways n.d.). In contrast, the State Railway of Thailand (SRT) operates over 4,000 km of rail track serving annually 45 million passengers and 11 million tonnes of freight (Siam Shipping 2022). At a glance, it could be deduced that travellers/commuters in Myanmar, in general, rely on train services more than those in Thailand, but the scenario is reversed with regard to freight. Southern Myanmar, which is adjacent to the west and south of Thailand, is exceptional since the terrain at places is treacherous, and Tanintharyi is sparsely populated (<1.5 million population); hence, rail services in this region are lacking or short in comparison to the rest of Myanmar.

8.1.3. Maritime Transport

Myanmar's nine main ports are presently located along the western and southern coasts of the country. International cargo traffic has grown at the rate of 10 per cent annually, but 90 per cent of it is handled by the Yangon Port.[1] Port infrastructure development elsewhere is therefore having immense potential, especially in Special Economic Zones (SEZs) such as the Dawei SEZ. Domestic ports south of Dawei are the Myeik Port and the Kawthaung Port in the Tanintharyi region. Similarly, Thailand sits on a high geo-strategic location with ports on both the Andaman Sea and the Gulf of Thailand. Intermodal transport across the peninsula is thus of great importance and can benefit both countries and further entities in ASEAN and beyond. Notable Thai ports in this region are the Ranong Port (one of the five ports run by the Port Authority of Thailand [PAT] on the Andaman coast and the PPC [Prachuap Pier Co. Ltd.] belonging to Sahaviriya Steel Industries PCL [SSI])[2] situated south of Prachuap Khiri Khan (hereafter referred as Prachuap) on the gulf side.

8.1.4. Air Transport

Myanmar at present has 30+ operational airports (out of its 69 existing airports), of which three of them are international (Yangon, Mandalay and Nay Pyi Taw). More international airports are in the plan, and those in the Tanintharyi region are regarded as having high

[1] Thai Business Information Center. https://www.thaibizmyanmar.com

[2] See https://www.ssi-steel.com/en/ssifamily/domestic/prachuap-port-co-ltd/

potential as international airports.[3] Notable airports in the SEWC in the Tanintharyi region are the Dawei, Myeik and Kawthaung Airports. In Southern Thailand, Ranong Airport on the Andaman coast opposite Kawthaung and Chumphon Airport and Surat Thani Airport on the gulf side, are more relevant to the SEWC. Details of some of these airports and services are presented in later sections.

8.2. PHYSICAL CONNECTIVITY

8.2.1. Land Connection

This section discusses road and rail linkages in Southern Myanmar, particularly the Thailand–Myanmar network connections in the SEWC (Map 8.1).

8.2.1.1. Road Linkage

Southern Myanmar road connections to the Tanintharyi region from Mawlamyine to Kawthaung and between the Tanintharyi region and Thailand are outlined here.

1. **Roads within Southern Myanmar**

   Based on a logistics capacity assessment on Myanmar logistics infrastructure done in 2016,[4] the present connecting roads between the main settlements within Southern Myanmar, from north to south, are discussed in three sections:

   a. **Mawlamyine–Mudon–Ye–Dawei**

      This 316 km northernmost section is part of the ASEAN Highway (AH 112). It was mostly a secondary road suitable as a supply route. Being a 90 per cent all-weather road, it took 7.5–8 hours to traverse its length. The part in Mon State could be travelled at 50–80 kph (kilometres per hour), but the gravel-and-dirt road close to the border of Tanintharyi is hilly, and the average speed would usually drop to 40 kph. After approximately 50 km from the Tanintharyi border, the roadwork rendered a maximum speed of 20–30 kph. Along

[3] See https://www.thaibizmyanmar.com

[4] 'Myanmar Road Network', http://dlca.logcluster.org/display/public/DLCA/2.3+Myanmar+Road+Network;jsessionid=D0533F9D5A50948879E1499C41FFFFB2

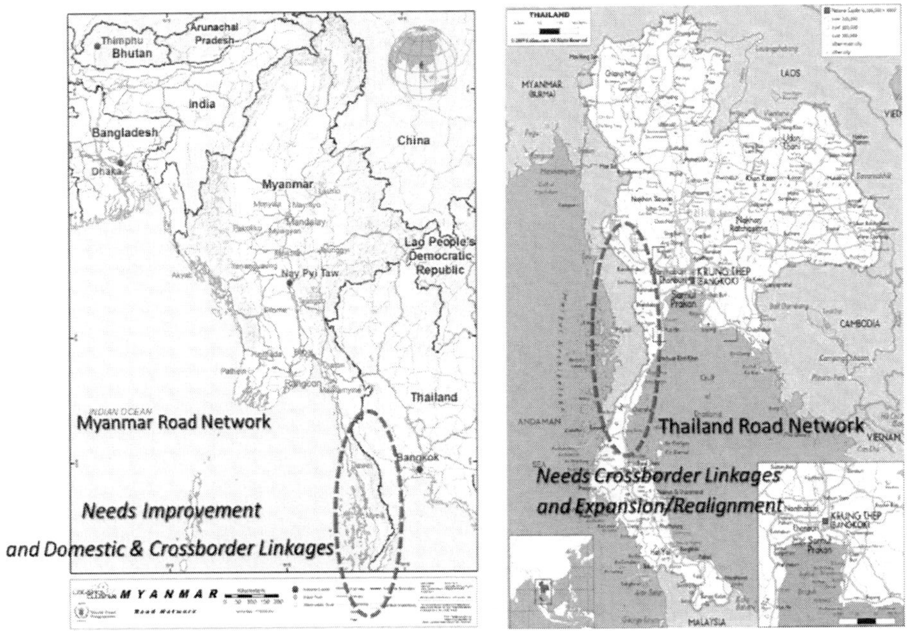

Map 8.1 Overview of SEWC's Transport Connectivity

Source: Sutiwipakorn (2018).

Disclaimer: This figure has been redrawn by the author/s and is not to scale. It does not represent any authentic national or international boundaries and is used for illustrative purposes only.

this section, road widening works from one to two lanes were the norm. Altogether, in 2015, there were 19 narrow single-lane, steel-and-wood bridges, where vehicles must wait to pass each other. However, it was not a big issue since there was not much traffic then and even now.

b. **Dawei–Thayetchaung–Palaw–Myeik**

This 260 km mid-section is also a part of AH 112. It was also a secondary road suitable as a supply route, with an attainable average speed of 30 kph since there were widening works, both on-going and planned, along a 90 km winding rough dirt/gravel section, plus a 170 km patched, bumpy single-lane tarmac road section with potholes. The time to traverse this whole length was 8 hours. Altogether, there were 46 single-lane bridges and five toll gates. The purpose of toll gates for such a road in such conditions remains a riddle to the author.

c. **Myeik–Tanintharyi–Bokpyin–Kayathuyi–Kawthaung**

The road surface on this 441 km AH 112 secondary road section, also suitable as a supply route, is composed of 37 per cent tarmac and 63 per cent gravel road sections. It was relatively better maintained than that from Dawei to Myeik, with an attainable normal average speed of 40 kph. The lengthy traverse length dictated that it would normally take up to 11 hours to get through the whole section via settlements along the route. In this section, there were 59 single lane bridges, but no toll gates.

2. **Roads between Southern Myanmar and Thailand**

There are at present two main routes linking Southern Myanmar and Thailand: one between Dawei and Kanchanaburi, and the other between Myeik and Prachuap. Currently, these routes are mostly undergoing construction and/or restoration at different stages. The characteristics of the two main connecting roads are outlined as follows:

a. **Dawei–Kanchanaburi via Phu Nam Ron**

The 138 km Dawei–Phu Nam Ron road link is part of Myanmar's 196 sq. km Dawei SEZ (DSEZ) development. The contract between the Myanmar Government and Italian-Thai Development PCL (ITD) was signed in 2010, but interest has since waned, and the project has been scaled back and turned into a government-to-government project between Myanmar, Thailand, and Japan (Thabchumpon and Middleton 2017). In 2013, ITD opened the route between Dawei and Htee Khee/ Phu Nam Ron as a narrow two-lane access road without shoulders to transport materials for the construction of the DSEZ. Though far from satisfactory, the road has somewhat activated movement of people and revitalized the local economy (Kudo 2017). In contrast to the condition of the Myanmar access road, the asphaltic two-lane road section, with at-grade paved shoulders, between Phu Nam Ron and Kanchanaburi in Thailand is ready for travel, just like many other Thai provincial roads towards the border (Map 8.2).

b. Myeik–Prachuap Khiri Khan via Dan Singkhon

The province of Prachuap is situated at the narrowest section of Thailand between the Gulf of Thailand and the Andaman Sea on the Kra Isthmus.

This Myeik–Prachuap connection consists of an approximate 180 km road section between Myeik and the Special Temporary Checkpoint of Dan Singkhon opposite the Myanmar border town of Maw Daung, plus some 25 km road length between Dan Singkhon and the Prachuap Central Business District (CBD) (Figure 8.1).

As of February 2018, the road surface conditions between Myeik and the Special Temporary Checkpoint of Dan Singkhon, from the actual team field survey, were as follows:

Concrete pavement	22 km (13%)
Bituminous surface treatment	80 km (45%)
Dilapidated single surface treatment	20 km (11%)
Dirt road	25 km (14%)
Under construction/rehabilitation	30 km (17%)

The 25 km road link between Dan Singkhon and the Prachuap CBD involves a 15 km road of the Department of Rural Road (DRR), mainly via Route PK 1039, and a section of the Department of

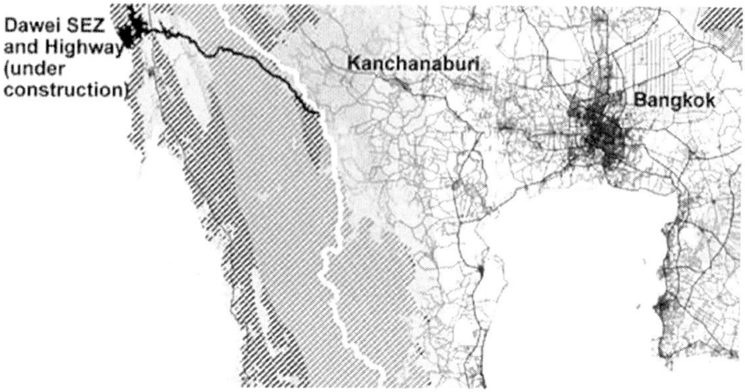

(a) Broad Route Overview

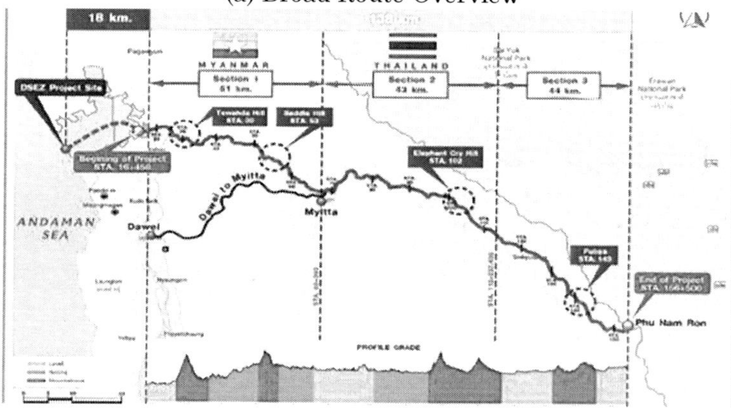

(b) The Route

(c) Myanmar-side Construction

Map 8.2 (Continued)

(d) Phu Nam Ron Border Road

Map 8.2 The Dawei–Phu Nam Ron Project

Sources: (a) http://www.wwf.or.th/en/newsroom/?uNewsID=325792#; (b) http://www.thaibizmyanmar.com/th/news/detail.php?ID=2487; (c) https://www.bangkokpost.com/business/321105/itd-seeks-joint-ventures-in-dawei#group=nogroup&photo=0; (d) https://upload.wikimedia.org/wikipedia/commons/8/81/Phu_Nam_Ron-control54.JPG

Disclaimer: This figure has been redrawn by the author/s and is not to scale. It does not represent any authentic national or international boundaries and is used for illustrative purposes only.

Figure 8.1 Dan Singkhon Special Temporary Checkpoint

Source: Sutiwipakorn (2018).

Highway (DOH) Route No. 4. The latter is part of the four-lane asphaltic concrete (AC) road AH 2 with a depressed median, while the former is a two-lane AC road at present, generally with at-grade 1.5 m paved shoulders, except near the checkpoint where four lanes are the main feature. This DRR road has recently underwent a feasibility study (FS) for upgrading, and a design has been proposed to reconstruct it into a six-lane divided, grade-separated highway in anticipation of the forthcoming connection between the two countries. In addition to the road upgrade as planned, a 240 million Thailand baht (THB) custom house is currently being built at Dan Singkhon by the Thai Public Works Department (PWD).

8.2.1.2. Rail Linkage

As stated earlier, the terrain in Southern Myanmar is rough at places, and Tanintharyi is sparsely populated. Hence, rail services have been lacking in this region as compared to the rest of the country. Rail length from Mawlamyine down to Ye and further down to Dawei is only approximately 370 km, but, at present, it takes up to 16 hours for the journey (an average of less than 25 kph). It is so slow that it had been dubbed as 'the slowest train in Myanmar' (Sheena 2016). Nonetheless, the strategic importance of the area is being increasingly noted, and line extension, including linkages with Thailand, is gaining importance due to increasing concerns.

Of the 4,000 km track in Thailand, nearly a quarter of the length lies in the southern peninsular region. However, these tracks are almost exclusively close to the eastern coast along the Gulf of Thailand. Line connections between the existing tracks on the Gulf side to the Andaman coast are being studied, starting with the Chumphon–Ranong Line, to be subsequently detailed (Map 8.3).

8.2.1.2.1. Southern Myanmar Rail

The metre-gauge Tanintharyi Line, operated by MR, runs from Mawlamyine (approximately 310 km north of Dawei) to Dawei. The track running south from Ye, halfway between Mawlamyine and Dawei, is reported to be treacherous. There are no service freight trains from Mawlamyine to Dawei due to the adverse terrain, and hence, there are no needs for cargo depot, warehouses and freight handling equipment at stations along the route (Japan International Freight Forwarders Association [JIFFA] 2012).

The line from Mawlamyine to Ye is one of the existing tracks, whereas that from Ye down to Dawei is relatively new (ADB 2016). A project in the pipeline to upgrade the 507 km Bago–Mawlamyine–Ye–Dawei railway is being considered with external

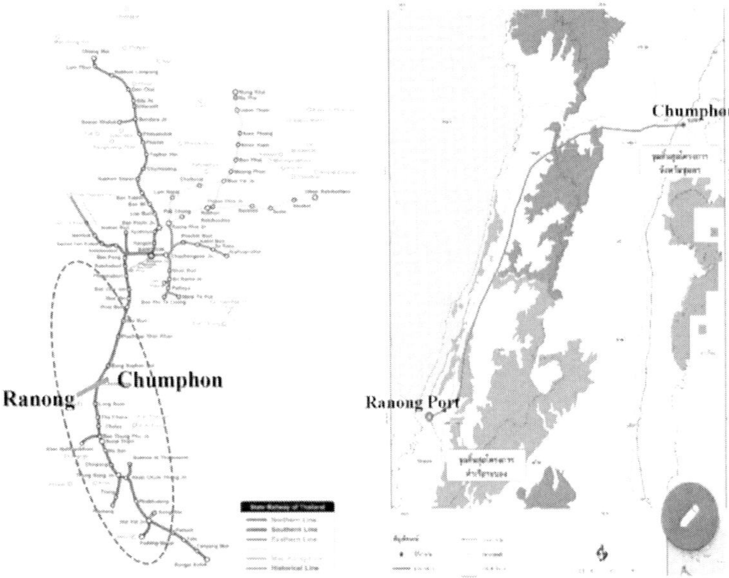

Map 8.3 Chumphon–Ranong Line

Source: Sutiwipakorn (2018).

Disclaimer: This figure has been redrawn by the author/s and is not to scale. It does not represent any authentic national or international boundaries and is used for illustrative purposes only.

assistance from the ADB at an investment of US$100 million since the Dawei deep sea port project and the Dawei–Kanchanaburi rail line project would be linked with this line for container movement (Myanma Railways 2015).

Presently, the rail line extending towards Myeik terminates some 30 km south of Dawei at the Thayetchaung Station, and the rest of the 212 km rail distance is currently under construction. It appears, however, that the actual construction could take some time.

Rail links between Thailand and Myanmar are either in the process of being considered for resurrection (such as the 110 km Thanbyuzayat–Three Pagodas Pass in Myanmar to connect with the 153 km Three Pagodas Pass–Nam Tok in Kanchanaburi, Thailand) or in the planning stages (such as the Dawei–Phu Nam Ron Line).

8.2.1.2.2. Southern Thai Rail

Historically, in June 1943, during the Second World War, Imperial Japan started building a 90 km Kra Isthmus Railway between Chumphon and La-Un (a district some 30 km north of the Ranong CBD). The rail line, laid mostly alongside DOH No. 4 between Chumphon and Ranong, involved seven stations and 31 bridges. Constructed using old rails and materials transported from Kelantan, Malaysia, it was completed in November 1943 by around 25,000 Chinese, Malay and Tamil Indian workers, mostly prisoners-of-war, but its 11-month operation was ended by Allied bombings. Abandoned and scrapped in 1945, the focus was switched to the Thai-Burma Line[5] with the construction of the legendary bridge over the river Kwai. At present, an antiquated locomotive is still on display at La-Un. Signage and information at the site are, however, in a sorry state. Nevertheless, vivid details of the event and its development, together with many other related stories, can be seen in 'Development of the Thai-Burma Border Areas in the Second World War', penned by D. Boggett, Professor Emeritus of Kyoto Seika University.

In 2014, the SRT released a study on the Chumphon–Ranong Spur. Sixth on the list of 21 proposed spur lines, its design speed was 160 kph, fenced and grade-separated, where rail crossings encounter surrounding roads. Its 116 km length would have nine stations (1 major, 1 medium and 7 minor). At an estimated investment of 18,748 million THB (approximately US$580 million), the economic internal rate of return (EIRR) was 12.71 per cent and the financial internal rate of return (FIRR) was 0.36 per cent. The anticipated number of daily passengers in 2037 is 8,700 and 1.42 million tonnes for freight.

In February 2018, the final report of another feasibility study (FS) was presented. The FS on Economics, Engineering and Environment on the Chumphon–Ranong rail connection was conducted by the Office of Transport and Traffic Policy and Planning (OTP) and had reportedly been submitted to the Ministry of Transport (MOT) for acknowledgement towards initiation of an Environmental Impact Assessment (EIA) by SRT.

[5] See https://en.wikipedia.org/wiki/Kra_Isthmus_Railway

Vital characteristics of the rail line reported are as follows: 103 km in length, mostly alongside DOH No. 4 between Chumphon and Ranong Port, plus a 5 km spur into Ranong township; single track; 9 stations; approximately 6,000 passengers in the first year of operation and 12,000 in year 30; approximately 33,000 TEUs (Twenty-foot Equivalent Unit) freight during the first year, and 85,000 TEUs by year 30; project cost 45,300 million THB (approximately US$1,400 million); EIRR 12.20 per cent.

As mentioned earlier, all currently operating Thai rails are in the east coast of the southern peninsular region. The metre-gauge single rail tracks from Nakhon Pathom to Hua Hin (165 km), from Hua Hin to Prachuap (90 km) and from Prachuap to Chumphon (167 km) are being expanded to double track in Phase I (2016–2020). In Phase II, the routes from Chumphon to Surat Thani (168 km), from Surat Thani to Hat Yai Junction and Songkhla (321 km) and from Hat Yai Junction to Padang Besar at the Thai-Malaysian border (45 km) are simultaneously in the pipeline (State Railway of Thailand 2017).

8.2.2. Maritime Connection

Situated strategically on the Andaman coast (Myanmar), the two countries could certainly garner more effectiveness and efficiency in maritime and maritime-overland intermodal transport in this SEWC region and beyond (Map 8.4).

8.2.2.1. Relevant Ports on the Myanmar Coast

At present, there are nine ports under the Myanmar Port Authority (MPA): Yangon Port (for both export and import); Sittwe, Pathein, Mawlamyine and Myeik (for export); and Kyaukpyu, Thandwe, Dawei and Kawthaung (for domestic shipping).[6] However, Dawei Port is currently being developed into a deep sea port (though progress is slow, if not stalled), while Kyaukpyu Port is being considered to be developed into a deep sea port and a tanker port. According to facts and figures reported by MPA in 2016, the import was more than export (approximately 25,000 metric tonne import

[6] Myanmar Port Authority, http://www.mpa.gov.mm/port-myanmar

(a) Myanmar Coastline

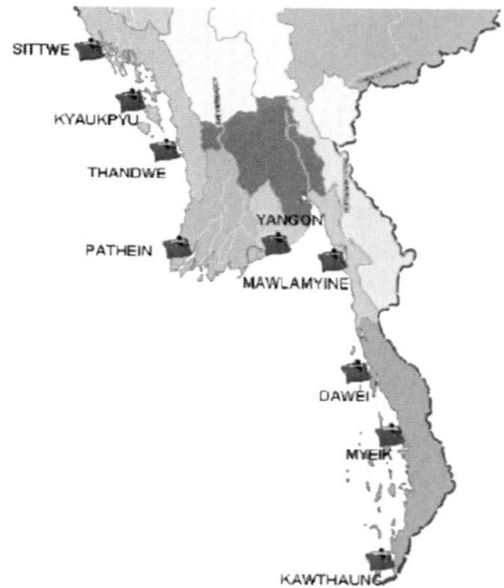

(b) The Nine Main Myanmar ports

Map 8.4 Myanmar Port Network

Sources: (a) https://dlca.logcluster.org/display/public/dlca/2.1+myanmar+port+assessment

Disclaimer: This figure has been redrawn by the author/s and is not to scale. It does not represent any authentic national or international boundaries and is used for illustrative purposes only.

as compared to 10,000 metric tonne export), approximately 60 per cent of which was containerized.[7]

The three ports in the Tanintharyi region are further outlined here: Dawei, Myeik and Kawthaung.

1. **Dawei Deep Sea Port**

   The Dawei deep sea port project is part of the DSEZ project, which was initially conceived as a joint venture between the Myanmar Government and the Thai Government, with ITD as the contractor for the construction of the port, its facilities and the transboundary access road. The three-phase project consist of a First Phase (2008–2010), a Second Phase (2011–2013), and a Third Phase (2013 onward).[8] As noted earlier, it has encountered major obstacles, and the progress is currently very slow. The port has been designed to accommodate 25,000 deadweight tonnage (DWT) general cargo vessels, 200 TEU container vessels, and 3,000 DW tankers.

2. **Myeik Port**

   At present, the Myeik Port is accessible for vessels of 73 m length overall (LOA) maximum with 2–4.5 m draft. There are 4 jetties: 1 concrete and 3 steel pontoons.[9]

3. **Kawthaung Port**

   At present, the Kawthaung Port is accessible for vessels of maximum 76 m LOA with 2–4 m draft. The port has 3 jetties: 1 concrete and 2 steel pontoons.[10]

8.2.2.2. Relevant Ports on the Southern Thai Coasts

8.2.2.2.1. Ranong Port

As stated earlier, Ranong Port is one of five ports under the PAT. The others are as follows: Bangkok; Laem Chabang (in Chonburi

[7] 'Tannitharyi Region: Facts and Figures', Myanmar Port Authority, http://www.mpa.gov.mm/facts-figures/tannitharyi-region

[8] Myanmar Port Authority.

[9] 'Myeik Port: Facts and Figures', http://www.mpa.gov.mm/facts-figures/myeik-port, and 'Myanmar Port of Tanintharyi, Myeik', http://dlca.logcluster.org/display/public/DLCA/2.1.9+Myanmar+Port+of+Tanintharyi%2C+Myeik;jsessionid=A898F0BEBD2A51F74817C5D7566F7E17

[10] 'Kawthaung Port: Facts and Figures', http://www.mpa.gov.mm/facts-figures/kawthaung-port

Province on the Eastern Seaboard); Chiang Saen and Chiang Khong (in Chiang Rai province in the north of Thailand).

The port was established in 2003 with an aim to be the main Andaman port linking South Asia, Africa and Europe. It occupies a land size of 315 rais (approximately 50 hectares). Maritime vessels, however, have to navigate through the 120 m wide, 28 km long, 8 m deep channel (at lowest tide), and hence, its second phase since 2006 could only accommodate up to only 12,000 DWT vessels (Port Authority of Thailand 2017). Presently, it is mostly a supply transportation base for offshore petroleum exploration and production equipment.

In 2016, the reported global maritime container throughput was approximately 200 million TEUs, and the five PAT ports had garnered only a 4.5 per cent share. Regarding maritime traffic, there were some 9,400 vessel calls for the five ports, with a total cargo of 93.4 million tonnes. However, only 350 (3.72%) vessel calls were made at Ranong Port with merely 0.2 million tonnes of freight. Nevertheless, the number of vessel calls at Ranong is increasing at the rate of 10 per cent from earlier years. The port is trying to present itself as an intermodal transportation network linking the port of Yangon to the port of Bangkok. It has been estimated that linking the maritime route from Yangon with Ranong plus an overland transportation to Laem Chabang could reduce the usual 15- to 20-day voyage via the Strait of Malacca and the Gulf of Thailand to 4–7 days by employing the earlier mentioned intermodal option.

8.2.2.2.2. Private Ports at Ranong

It is interesting to note here that there are a number of private piers along the Ranong coast just south of Ranong Port. A few of them facilitate boat travel across the Kraburi River mouth to established tourist hotels and destinations in Myanmar, such as the Grand Andaman Club Pier to and from Ko Son—a 70-year leased island just south of Kawthaung to an influential entrepreneur (Sa-nga Kangwan, fondly known locally as Ko Fook). Others serve as transportation termini for shipping of construction materials, particularly Portland cement of the Siam Cement Group

(SCG) and Siam City Cement (SCC), to construction sites or silos at various destinations in Myanmar or as fish piers to unload and auction marine catches gathered off the fertile coast in the vicinity of Myeik. In this regard, another well-known Thai working for his chain company of Kit Paisan is Adisak Rujiwattanakul, locally known as Ko Tong.

8.2.2.2.2.1. Prachuap Pier Co, Ltd (PPC) at Bang Saphan

PPC is a subsidiary of SSI PCL. It is a private deep sea port on the coast of the Gulf of Thailand situated approximately halfway between the CBDs of Prachuap and Chumphon Province (approximately 90 km each way). Raw materials that are unloaded here are processed as finished iron and steel products at the nearby SSI plants at Mae Ramphueng sub-district, Bang Saphan district and then are uploaded and shipped out. The port also provides services and facilities for many other vessels.

Logistically, the port could be considered to serve as an alternative intermodal maritime connection terminal for goods transport, either from Prachuap or from Ranong via Chumphon. At present, the Company has four piers (A, B, C and D) to accommodate vessels of different sizes and dimensions. Table 8.1 summarizes some of these details (also see Figure 8.2).

8.2.3. Air Connection

Air transport in Myanmar is currently regulated by the Department of Civil Aviation (DCA). In Thailand, the two main bodies of authority overseeing air transportation are the Department of Airport (DOA) under the MOT and the Airports of Thailand PCL (AOT).

In the SEWC's area of interest, some relevant information on the airports in both countries in the region as well as some other selected ones in Southern Thailand, for the sake of comparison at a glance, are tabulated in Table 8.2. In general, these airports feature asphaltic pavement, except Ranong Airport and Dawei Airport, which are of concrete. Runway lengths for Ranong, Dawei, and Kawthaung are around 2,000 ± 100 m, whereas that of Myeik is

Table 8.1 PPC Piers of Different Depth and Dimension and Limitation for Vessel

Pier	*Capacity*	*Water Depth (m)*	*Occupied Width (m)*	*Occupied Length (m)*
A	2 vessels, each not more than 100,000 DWT	15	25	450
B	2 vessels, each not more than 20,000 DWT	12	25	245
C	1 vessel of not more than 110,000 DWT	14	50	450
D	4 vessels, each not more than 2,200 DWT	8	50	250

Source: http://www.ppc.co.th/index.php/th/service/service

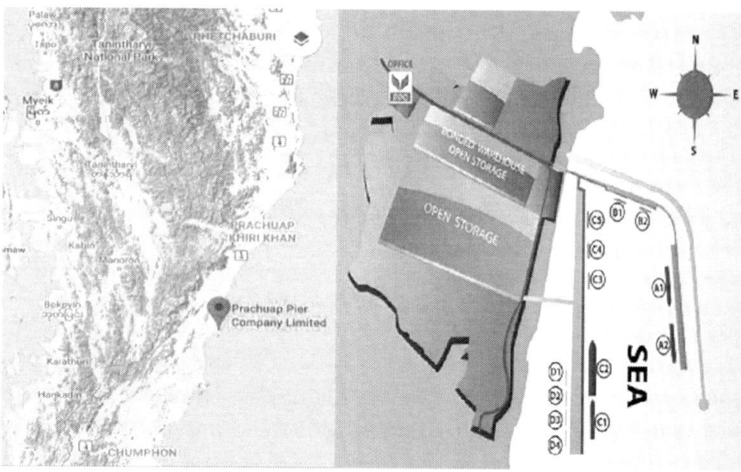

Figure 8.2 Location and Port Area of PPC

Source: PPC.

Disclaimer: This figure has been redrawn by the author/s and is not to scale. It does not represent any authentic national or international boundaries and is used for illustrative purposes only.

approximately 2,700 m and is more ready for future extension to 3,000 m or longer to accommodate larger aircrafts.

Table 8.2 Runway Dimension, Surface Type, Traffic and Affiliation of Selected Airports

Airport	*Runway Length (m)*	*Runway Surface*	*Flights per Year (Approx.)*	*Affiliation*
Dawei	2,135* × 30	Concrete	1,872**	DCA
Myeik	2,681 × 55	Asphalt	1,456**	DCA
Kawthaung	1,829 × 46	Asphalt	1,768**	DCA
Ranong Airport	2,000 × 45	Concrete	1,500	DOA MOT
Chumphon	2,100 × 45	Asphalt	3,150	DOA MOT
Surat Thani	3,000 × 45	Asphalt	17,000	DOA MOT
Trang	2,100 × 45	Asphalt	5,200	DOA MOT
Hat Yai International	3,050 × 45	Asphalt	27,000	AOT PCL
Krabi International	3,002 × 45	Asphalt	28,000	DOA MOT
Phuket International	3,000 × 45	Asphalt	80,000	AOT PCL

Source: Data collected from http://www.airports-worldwide.com

Notes: *Some other sources publish a length of 3,150 m; **estimated from the number of weekly flights. AOT PCL, Airports of Thailand Public Company Limited (Thailand); DCA, Department of Civil Aviation (Myanmar); DOA MOT, Department of Airport, Ministry of Transport (Thailand).

8.2.3.1. Flights at Dawei, Myeik and Kawthaung Airports

Inbound weekly flights into Dawei, Myeik and Kawthaung (July 2018), are compiled and presented in Table 8.3. In general, there are 14–18 inbound flights per week in each of the three SEWC airports in Myanmar. Outbound flights should be of similar numbers accordingly, and hence, it could be estimated that the yearly flights are about 1,500–1,900 for each airport—comparable to that at the Ranong Airport in Thailand (to be detailed in the next section). Notable is the only international flight, scheduled twice weekly between Myeik and Bangkok (Don Mueang), which is operated by NewGen Airlines (a Bangkok-based company) that commenced its scheduled operation in February 2018.[11] Unfortunately, the

[11] Unfortunately, New Gen Airways suspended all flight operations in August 2019, and two months after that the airline ceased all operations.

Table 8.3 Inbound Weekly Flights into Dawei, Myeik and Kawthaung Airports by Airlines

Inbound Flights		*By Airline*						
Weekly To	*From*	*MNA*	*FMIA*	*MYP*	*GMA*	*NGA*	*Sub Total*	*Total*
Dawei (TVY)	RGN	2	6	3	–	–	11	
	MNU	–	1	–	–	–	1	
	MGZ	1	–	–	–	–	1	
	KAW	5	–	–	–	–	5	
								18
Myeik (MGZ)	RGN	7	–	–	–	–	7	
	TVY	1	–	–	–	–	1	
	VBP	–	–	1	–	–	1	
	KAW	3	–	–	–	–	3	
	DMK	–	–	–	–	2	2	
								14
Kawthaung (KAW)	RGN	–	–	–	4	–	4	
	MNU	1	–	–	–	–	1	
	TVY	2	6	–	–	–	8	
	MGZ	4	–	–	–	–	4	
								17

Source: Data collected from http://www.airports-worldwide.com

Notes: DMK, Don Mueang Bangkok; FMIA, First Myanmar Investment Airlines; GMA, Golden Myanmar Airlines; MNA, Myanmar National Airlines; MNU, Mawlamyine; MYP, Mann Yadanarpon Airlines; NGA, NewGen Airlines (International); RGN, Yangon; VBP, Bokpyin.

number of passengers and the amount of freight carried could not be compiled as yet.

8.2.3.2. Flights at Ranong Airport

Prior to 16 February 2018, when Air Asia started to operate a domestic mid-day return flight daily between Bangkok Don Mueang

Airport and Ranong Airport, Nok Air was the sole airline operating two return flights daily between the destinations (one in the early morning and one in the late afternoon) plus one extra return flight during mid-week.

The total number of flights during the past few years, before the introduction of Air Asia, was roughly stable at 1,500 per year, but the number of passengers has been growing from around 65,000 per year in 2014 to 104,000 in 2016. Goods freight carried onboard totalled roughly 10,000 kg in 2016.

Introduction of a bigger plane by Air Asia, plus increasing popularity of the province's attractions, as well as the greater prospect to travel across the border to Kawthaung and its many pristine archipelagos, such as Cocks Comb Island (The Heart Island) and Nyaung Oo Phee Island, will certainly add a lot more to these figures in the years to come.

8.3. MISSING LINKS

The foregoing discussion indicates that there are certain missing links in SEWC that could be engaged, some voids that could be filled, and some existing features that could be improved. The following proposed logistics infrastructure should be further investigated earnestly for their possibility and feasibility.

8.3.1. Road

Road linkages in SEWC are presently either lacking or need major speedy rehabilitation.

North of the Corridor, the two-lane road linking Dawei in Myanmar and the Thai border town of Phu Nam Ron in Kanchanaburi was reportedly still being rehabilitated and reconstructed (Mori, Nishida and Fujisawa 2017); similarly, the route in the middle section between Myeik in Myanmar and Dan Singkhon in Prachuap, Thailand, was being reconstructed. The ongoing construction and rehabilitation must be earnestly encouraged and supported to be fully realized. On the Thai side, the two-lane routes approaching either to Phu Nam Ron or Dan Singkhon are well paved. The road in Prachuap is under the process to be widened into a 15 km grade-separated six-lane highway to the border.

A new 240 million THB customs facility is also being built at Dan Singkhon in anticipation of a collaborated agreement for a permanent checkpoint opening there soon (Figure 8.3).

South of the corridor, the watery gap between Kawthaung in Myanmar and the province of Ranong in Thailand is presently quite well ploughed by vessels across the 5 km wide Kraburi River estuary. Nevertheless, to further facilitate international travel between Ranong and Kawthaung, a third Thai-Myanmar friendship bridge at a suitable crossing point, somewhere upstream of

(a) Dawei–Phu Nam Ron Road

(b) Myeik–Dan Singkhon Road

Figure 8.3 Roads in Southern Myanmar Linking Towns at the Thai Border

Sources: (a) https://www.straitstimes.com/asia/se-asia/myanmar-thailand-road-cuts-through-last-wilderness; (b) Picture clicked by the author during the field survey in February 2018.

the Kraburi River beyond the Ranong Port, should be contemplated and studied for feasibility and EIA at a later stage, similar to the Satun–Perlis Road Bridge in the process of construction, further south at the Thai-Malaysian border that has recently been blessed to a large degree by the IMT-GT leaders.

8.3.2. Rail

Rail linkages in SEWC are lagging behind road linkages and/or need timely rehabilitation/construction for connection within and between both countries.

The 110 km Thanbyuzayat—Three Pagodas Pass rail link in Myanmar and the 153 km Three Pagodas Pass–Nam Tok in Thailand should not be unceremoniously thrown out. Though economically it was not viable, as reported in the study conducted by Korea International Cooperation Agency (KOICA) during 2005–2007, the past decade has seen some tremendous increase in economic activities in Myanmar, and the region should be given another opportunity for reconsideration.

Rail travel down south from Ye to Dawei is said to be uncomfortable and very time-consuming, but it should be considered for improvement along with the Bago–Dawei Line. This must be encouraged.

The 95 km spur line from Dawei toward Nam Tok has also been of interest to the Thai people with enthusiastic Japanese backing.[12] The lack of progress on the DSEZ has somewhat stalled the MR resolution, and the priority has shifted to the construction of new routes elsewhere.[13] However, this rail link may prove to be a good alternative to the much longer Thanbyuzayat–Three Pagodas Pass–Nam Tok connection.

Besides the main road link via National Highway No.8, Dawei ought to be better connected to Myeik through speedy realization of the Dawei–Myeik railway line (especially for freight and passengers) and even to Kawthaung at the southernmost tip of Myanmar in the long run. Currently, the 212 km length between Thayetchaung station, 30 km south of Dawei, and Myeik, is

[12] See https://en.wikipedia.org/wiki/Tanintharyi_Line

[13] See http://www.nationmultimedia.com/detail/Economy/30339168

reportedly in progress. Hopefully, it can be completed sooner than later to bolster and support the road connection between Myeik and Dan Singkhon at Prachuap. The situation would be better if the Myeik–Dan Singkhon rail line could be realized.

In Thailand, the 103 plus 5 km Chumphon–Ranong line is in the process of being resurrected and adjusted through an FS and soon through an EIA, and hopefully, the actual implementation will take place within the next few years.

To take it even further, south of pristine Ranong lies the touristic province of Phang Nga some 230 km away, and a further 80 km is another touristic province of Krabi. If the line could be extended down to these provinces and then 135 km further to Kantang Station in Trang Province, it would complete an ideal loop to the railway line spanning provinces along the gulf coast. An idea of this Andaman Rail Line to the province of Satun which borders with the State of Perlis, Malaysia, has recently been floated within the IMT-GT working groups, especially by the provincial chambers of commerce.

8.3.3. Maritime

Internationally, Ranong Port has visualized itself to connect with BIMSTEC (Bay of Bengal Initiative for Multi-Sectoral Technical Cooperation) with an aim 'to be the main port for marine cargo transport in the Andaman coast, linking trade routes with countries in South Asia, Middle East, Europe and Africa'.[14] However, the lengthy 28 km, narrow (120 m), and shallow (8 m at lowest tide) channel remains its main shortcoming and has to be improved to handle larger vessels plying its entrance.

It is strongly recommended that linkages with other ports and facilities should be sought domestically. Facing the southwesterly monsoon in the second half of each year, ship calls at the port are more frequent in the first half, at an average of only one call a day at present. Ranong Port should therefore consider collaboration with its nearby ports on domestic linkage such as Na Kluer Port at Kantang in Trang Province as well as with nearby international connections with destinations near shore in Myanmar, such as the

[14] http://www.rnp.port.co.th/eng/dataset1/data3.html

Kawthaung, Myeik and Dawei ports, when these are developed to have greater capacity. The port should also not rule out IMT-GT destinations, particularly with ports in Indonesia. Ranong is one of the 14 Southern Thailand provinces in the IMT-GT sub-region in conjunction with 10 provinces in Sumatra and 8 states in Malaysia.

On the intermodal role for transportation from ports on the Andaman side with ports on the gulf side across the Kra Isthmus via roads and rails (if and when available) envisioned enthusiastically by the Ranong Port, the port should also eye other alternative private ports besides PAT's own ports of Bangkok and Laem Chabang, such the PPC Port at Bang Saphan.

8.3.4. Air

At present, air connectivity in the SEWC region is restricted to a few Thai domestic flights from Bangkok to Ranong and Myanmar domestic flights plying the Dawei, Myeik and Kawthaung routes. An exception is the infantile stage of international flight between Bangkok and Myeik.

Besides considerations for using larger planes to accommodate the rapidly increasing number of passengers attracted to Ranong, based on recent records, and greater interests by tourists to explore some of the newly opened 800+ islands in the Andaman Sea in Southern Myanmar, a few more air linkages with other towns and cities should be investigated. One of these is the Southern Thailand domestic route between Hat Yai and Ranong. Hat Yai International Airport is the fourth largest airport in Thailand, in terms of the number of patrons, and is in the process of a major expansion to cater for increasing activities in the IMT-GT sub-region. The Hat Yai air link to Ranong should be a good start to facilitate travel from Southern Thailand and neighbouring Malaysia and Indonesia, a sub-region of some 600+ million population, to the SEWC area.

Another link, either as an alternative or as an addition, is the Krabi–Ranong route. Krabi is currently the third largest airport in Thailand in terms of patronage, and it is one of the favourite destinations for an entirely different group of travellers (the Westerners and the Chinese). Hence, the link should complement well the Hat Yai route for these travellers seeking bonus pleasure to Ranong and its neighbouring attractions in South Myanmar.

For international links, it is envisaged at this stage that the Bangkok–Myeik air link could be sustained. A link between Myeik and one of the Southern Thailand destinations could be the next step.

8.4. RECOMMENDATIONS

From all the earlier discussions, it is recommended that the two governments and the responsible agencies should speed up or consider/reconsider these processes/options to enable timely development in the SEWC region.

8.4.1. Roads

Presently on-going: These should be completed at the earliest to fulfil their functions.

- The Dawei–Phu Nam Ron Road, presently a narrow two-lane, partially sealed access road.
- The Dan Singkhon–Myeik Road, presently a two-lane, partially sealed road.

Widening, realignment and reconstruction: These should be realized or planned.

- The Prachuap–Dan Singkhon Road, presently a two-lane asphaltic rural road, to be upgraded to be a six-lane highway as studied.
- The Chumphon–Ranong Road, presently a winding two-lane Highway No. 4 section.
- The Ranong–PhangNga–Krabi Road, presently a winding two-lane Highway No.4 section.

Long-term planning: This should be considered for an FS.

- The Ranong–Kawthaung Friendship Bridge

Facility and formality: These should be completed and/or sorted out.

- The Dan Singkhon ICQS (Immigration, Custom, Quarantine and Security) Building Complex, currently being constructed.
- Realization of an actual permanent checkpoint at Dan Singkhon, presently still under certain conflicting security terms.
- Efficient and effective implementation of border agreements, such as ACTS (ASEAN Customs Transit System), AFAFGIT (ASEAN Framework Agreement on the Facilitation of Goods in Transit), AFAFIST (ASEAN Framework Agreement on the Facilitation of Inter-State Transport), AGVCBP (ASEAN Goods Vehicle Cross-Border Permit) and CBTP (Cross Border Transport of Passengers).

8.4.2. Rails

Presently on-going: This should be completed at the earliest to fulfil its functions.

- The Dawei–Myeik Line, presently being constructed between Thayetchaung 30 km south of Dawei and Myeik.

Construction/reconstruction: These should be realized or planned:

- The Mawlamyine–Ye–Dawei Line, to be rehabilitated down from Bago.
- The Dawei–Nam Tok Line, to be further studied.
- The Thanbyuzayat–Three Pagodas Pass–Nam Tok Line, to be resurrected.
- The Chumphon–Ranong Line, to be pursued after FS.

Long-term planning: These should be considered for further FS:

- The Myeik–Dan Singkhon–Prachuap Line.
- The Myeik–Kawthaung Line.
- The Ranong–PhangNga Line, in Phase I.
- The PhangNga–Krabi–Kantang Line, in Phase II.
- The Kantang–Satun Line, in Phase III.

Facility and formality: These should be completed and/or sorted out.

- Establishment of permanent checkpoints at relevant borders between the two countries, if and when the cross-border railway lines are realized.
- Efficient and effective implementation of border agreements, such as ACTS, AFAFGIT, AFAFIST and CBTP.

8.4.3. Maritime

Establishment: these should be initiated as follows:

- Roll-On, Roll-Off (RO-RO) Facility between Ranong and Kawthaung, where a friendship bridge is being considered.
- Ranong Marina for cruise ships to complement that at Krabi, together with the one at Samui Island under IMT-GT's Physical Connectivity Projects (PCP).
- Intermodal Transport Procedure utilizing private port facility to supplement operations where appropriate.

Long-term planning: these should be considered:

- Equipping and Expansion of Ranong Port, especially when relevant rail and road projects are actually on-going.
- After the Dawei Port, Myeik Port needs be considered to accommodate larger international vessels for goods and products.
- Ranong–Subang Connection within Economic Corridor 5 (EC5) of IMT-GT.

8.4.4. Air

Presently on-going:

- Deployment of larger carriers to accommodate more passengers.
- The initiated international direct flight, which needs to be supported and sustained.

Short- and medium-term planning: these should be considered:

- Hat Yai–Ranong Direct Flight
- Krabi–Ranong Direct Flight

Long-term planning:

- Hat Yai–Myeik Direct Flight
- Krabi–Myeik Direct Flight

8.4.5. Other Connectivity

Besides land (road and rail), maritime and air physical connectivity, electricity grid connectivity and water supply connectivity are recommended to be further investigated.

8.5. CONCLUSION

Now that ASEAN has just passed its 50-year mark (established in 1967), and the IMT-GT has completed 25 years (established in 1993), this might be an auspicious time for the so far neglected region to be recognized for better connectivity and prosperity (Figure 8.4).

This chapter assessed the present situation in this SEWC and found that the area is in dire need of development. It has very high potential, but somehow it has been overlooked so far.

Better road and rail connections will greatly enhance travel and land use and will help facilitate intermodal transport for maritime transportation. For Thailand, high speed train and double track are looming, but for Myanmar, a few good tracks and a good network would probably be sufficient in the early stage. Air connection needs to be sustained and expanded, and cross-border obstacles and protocols need to be sorted out.

Lastly, all these have to be conducted with the environment in mind, since an ill-conceived and/or a badly implemented project would most probably create more woes than wonders.

(a) Pristine Scene at the Southern Border Estuary Dividing Thailand (left) and Myanmar (right)

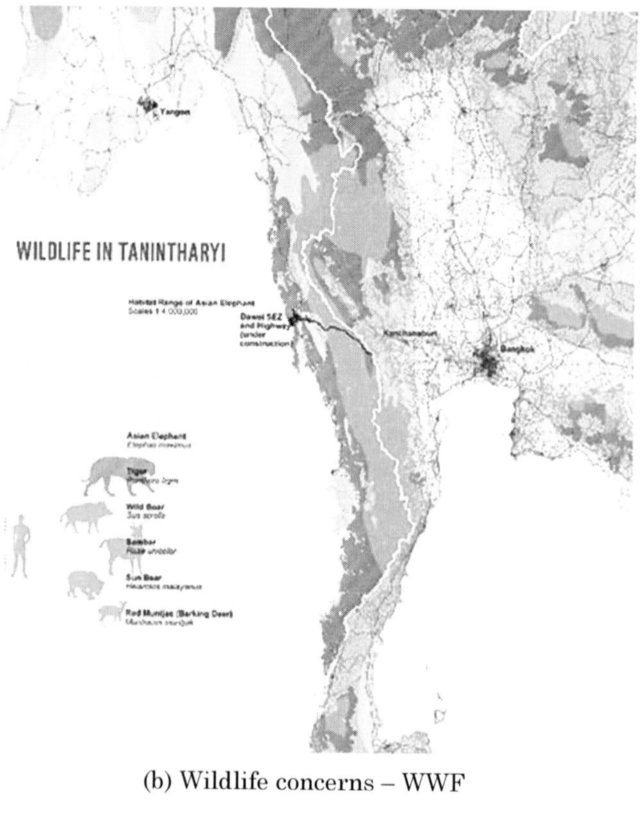

(b) Wildlife concerns – WWF

Figure 8.4 Environment Concerns

Sources: (a) From actual field survey in February 2018; (b) http://www.wwf.or.th/en/newsroom/?uNewsID=325792#

REFERENCES

Asian Development Bank (ADB). 2016. *Myanmar Transport Sector Policy Note: Railways*. Mandaluyong: ADB.

CEIC. 2019. 'Myanmar Motor Vehicle Registration'. CEIC. https://www.ceicdata.com/en/myanmar/motor-vehicle-statistics/motor-vehicle-registered

Japan International Freight Forwarders Association (JIFFA). 2012. *ASEAN Logistics Survey, Vol. 5*. Myanmar: JIFFA.

KPMG. 2013. *Infrastructure in Myanmar*. Myanmar: KPMG.

Kudo, T. 2017. 'Reconsidering the Dawei Development: Road, Border Gate, and Peace', Chapter 11. In *Comprehensive Development Strategy to Meet TPP*, edited by Daisuke Hiratsuka, 205–212. Bangkok: Bangkok Research Center.

Ministry of Transport. 2018. 'Infrastructure Development Plan to Elevate Logistics Efficiency and International Freight Transport' (in Thai). *Presentation by the Minister of Transport on the 23rd AGM,* 4 April, Bangkok.

Mori, Nobuyuki, Yoshiki Nishida, and Takafumi Fujisawa, eds. 2017. *2016 Progress Survey Report of Infrastructure Projects in CADP 2.0*. ERIA Research Project Report 2016, No. 01, p. 16. Economic Research Institute for ASEAN and East Asia. https://www.eria.org/RPR_FY2016_01.pdf

Myanma Railways. 2015. *Developing a Myanma's Rail Network That Meet Demand*. Yangon: Myanmar Railways.

———. n.d. *Challenges and Opportunities in the Railway Subsector in Myanmar*. Yangon: Myanma Railways.

Port Authority of Thailand. 2017. *Continuous Improvement towards Excellence*. Annual Report 2016 (in Thai). Bangkok: Port Authority of Thailand and Ranong Port.

Sheena. 2016. 'The Slowest Train in Myanmar: Dawei to Mawlamyine'. *Myanmar, Transportation & Border Crossings*. DIY Travel HQ. https://diytravelhq.com/dawei-mawlamyine-train/

Siam Shipping. 2022. 'Thailand's Transport Infrastructure Development'. https://siam-shipping.com/thailands-transport-infrastructure-development-strategy-2015-2022/

State Railway of Thailand. 2017. 'Progress of T.A.R. in Thailand'. In *5th Meeting of the Working Group on the Trans-Asian Railway Network*, 13–14 June, Busan, Republic of Korea. Bangkok: State Railway of Thailand.

Sutiwipakorn, Wiwat. 2018. Presentation at the Conference on Thailand-Myanmar Southern East West Corridors: Linkages and Considerations of Improving Logistics, Bangkok, Thailand, 1 June. ASEAN Studies Center, Chulalongkorn University, Bangkok, Thailand. Unpublished.

Thabchumpon, N., and C. Middleton. 2017. *Redressing Transboundary Environmental Injustice at the Dawei Special Economic Zone and Road-link Project*. Bangkok: Faculty of Political Science, Chulalongkorn University.

CHAPTER 9

SECTORAL ANALYSIS

Fishery and Tourism

Charit Tingsabadh Suthiphand Chirathivat and Buddhagarn Rutchatorn

9.1. INTRODUCTION

This chapter reviews data on two important sectors that are considered to be highly promising for the development to the Southern East–West Corridor.

9.2. FISHERY SECTOR

9.2.1. Overview of Myanmar Fishery

Production of the fishery sector from the 1960s to the mid-2010s is shown in Figure 9.1.

From the 1960s to the mid-1990s, fishery production witnessed a rising trend. A break in the trend happened in 1996, perhaps as part of the Asian Financial Crisis. Later, the production increased rapidly, and a divergence between total production and capture production became noticeable. Capture production seems to be stabilized since 2005 at around 2 million tonnes, while total production increased mainly due to aquaculture.

In the Association of Southeast Asian Nations (ASEAN) context, Myanmar is a major producer of fishery products, second only to Indonesia (Table 9.1).

Marine capture is the major component of fishery production in Myanmar (Table 9.2, Figure 9.2).

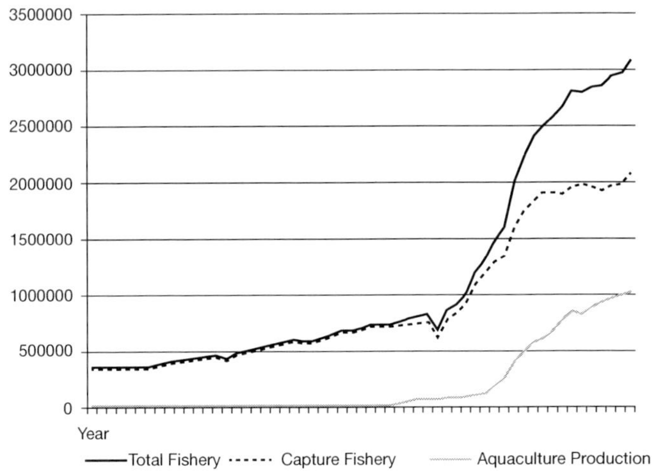

Figure 9.1 Fishery Production in Myanmar (in Metric Tonne)

Source: World Bank.

9.2.2. Fishery Resources of Myanmar

With a long coastline of 1,930 km, Myanmar is well endowed with fishery resources. The fishing grounds are shown in Map 9.1.

The area of the country's fishing waters, including exclusive economic zone (EEZ), is about 486,000 sq. km, and the continental shelf area is 228,781 sq. km. The length of its continental coastline is 2,832 km, divided into three coastal regions, namely the Rakhine Coastal region, the Ayeyarwaddy and Gulf of Mottama (Martaban) region (the Delta Zone), and the Tanintharyi region. Myanmar has extensive inland water bodies of 8.1 million ha, which include natural lakes, reservoirs, river systems and ponds. Its river system consists of the 2,000 km Ayeyarwaddy (Irrawaddy), Sittaung and Thanlwin (Salween) rivers and 2,600 km of tributaries and smaller rivers combined.

In terms of fishing vessels, the data show variation between the different regions of the country. The Rakhine region has the highest number of non-powered fishing boats, but the Tanintharyi region has the highest number of powered fishing vessels. Most of the powered vessels have a capacity less than 5 tonnes to 5–9.9 tonnes (Table 9.3 and also refer typical fishing vessels and a ship-yard in Myiek, Figures 9.3 and 9.4).

Table 9.1 Fishery Products of ASEAN Countries in 2015

Country	Marine Capture		Inland Capture		Aquaculture		Total	
	Quantity (MT)	Value (US$ 1,000)	Quantity (MT)	Value (US$ 1,000)	Quantity (MT)	Value (US$ 1,000)	Quantity (MT)	Value (US$ 1,000)
Brunei Darussalam	3,370	9,303			983	6,165	4,353	15,468
Cambodia	100,984		487,905		143,000		731,889	0
Indonesia	6,065,060	8,031,919	455,270	724,041	15,634,093	8,775,201	22,154,423	17,531,161
Lao PDR			62,635		95,965		158,600	0
Malaysia	1,486,050	2,382,430	5,924	18,353	506,465	804,915	1,998,439	3,205,698
Myanmar	2,854,200	4,852,140	1,463,120	2,267,836	999,630	1,643,071	5,316,950	8,763,047
Philippines	2,094,346	2,710,338	203,366	208,919	2,348,159	2,135,384	4,645,871	5,054,641
Singapore	1,265	9,348			6,896	30,511	8,161	39,859
Thailand	1,317,217	1,486,032	184,101	301,441	928,538	2,331,558	2,429,856	4,119,031
Vietnam	2,839,900		196,500		3,513,300		6,549,700	0
Total	16,762,392	19,481,510	3,058,821	3,520,590	24,177,029	15,726,805	43,998,242	38,728,905

Source: ASEAN Secretariat, Jakarta.

Table 9.2 Fisheries Production in Myanmar from 2012 to 2014

Ecosystem	Production Volume (in Thousand MT) 2012	2013	2014	Change (2012–2014) (%)
Aquaculture	898.96	929.38	964.26	7
Freshwater (capture)	1,246.46	1,302.97	1,381.03	11
Marine (capture)	2,332.79	2,483.80	2,702.24	16
Total	4,478.21	4,716.15	5,047.53	1

Source: Department of Fisheries, Government of Myanmar.

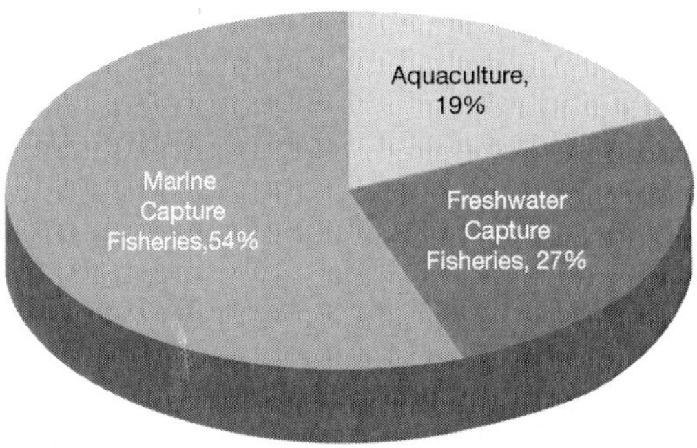

Figure 9.2 Percentage Distribution of Fisheries Production in Myanmar by Subsector, 2014

Source: Drawn by authors based on Table 9.2.

This variation can be understood in the light of the extent of fishing grounds within each region. The Tanintharyi region is well endowed with a large fishing ground in Myanmar.

9.2.3. The Demand Side

According to Southeast Asian Fisheries Development Center (SEAFDEC), about 70 per cent of the fish landing in Myanmar is for direct human consumption, mostly as fresh and chilled, while some are frozen or cured, and about 10 per cent is processed into fish meal (Figures 9.5 and 9.6). According to FAO (2010), domestic demand accounts for 90 per cent of the production, and the remaining 10 per cent is for exports.

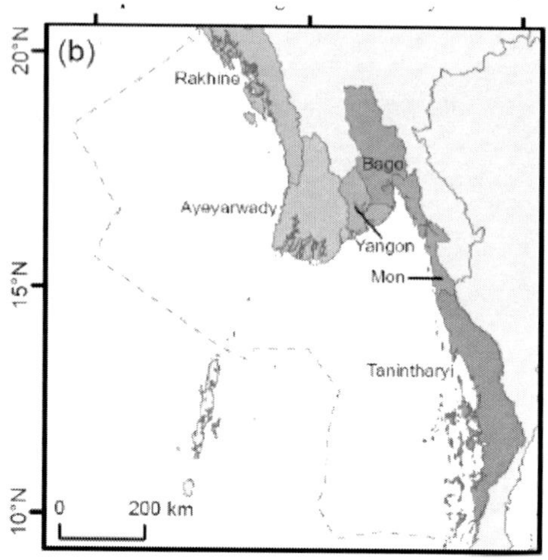

Map 9.1 The Fishing Grounds in Myanmar

Source: Birch et al. (2016) as cited in Leadbitter (2017).

Disclaimer: This figure has been redrawn by the author/s and is not to scale. It does not represent any authentic national or international boundaries and is used for illustrative purposes only.

9.2.4. Major Export Destinations of Myanmar's Fishery

The main markets for Myanmar fishery exports include China, Thailand, Malaysia, Saudi Arabia and Singapore, with China topping the chart (see Table 9.4).

China is the largest market for Myanmar's fishery export in terms of value, but Thailand accounts for the highest volume. Other markets are Singapore, Malaysia and Saudi Arabia. SEAFDEC also reports a similar picture. Composition of fishery export is shown in Figures 9.7 and 9.8.

An interesting trend is the increase in aquaculture for the export market, namely soft shell crabs, which has a ready market in the region.

9.2.5. Fishery Sector in the Tanintharyi–Tanaosri Region

The Tanintharyi region is probably the largest contributor to the overall production of capture fishery in Myanmar, given its location in the Andaman Sea and being open to the Indian Ocean.

Table 9.3 Number of Fishing Boats by Type and Tonnage in 2010

			Power Boat										
					In-board Power Boat								
Country, Sub-area	Total	Non-powered Boat	Sub-total	Out-board Powered Boat	Sub-total	<5	5–9.9	10–19.9	20–49.9	50–99.9	100–199.9	200–499.9	>500
Myanmar	32,824	17,054	15,865		15,865	10,186	2,628	999	810	631	607	4	–
Tanintharyi	12,367	3,700	8,667		8,667	4,906	2,070	647	480	330	234	–	–
Mon	2,091	278	1,813		1,813	905	447	93	85	118	165	–	–
Yangon	323	323	95		95	95	–	–	–	–	–	–	–
Rakhine	14,842	11,267	3,575		3,575	3,358	34	–	97	63	20	20	–
Ayeyarwady	3,201	1,486	1,715		1,715	922	77	259	148	120	188	188	–
Myanmar	29,455	–	–		–	–	–	–	–	–	–	–	–

Source: The authors.

Figure 9.3 Typical Fishing Boat in Myeik

Source: Photo taken by the research team during field survey.

Figure 9.4 Fishing Boats Shipyard in Myeik

Source: Photo taken by the research team during field survey.

According to the Ministry of Commerce, the total border trade between Myeik and Thailand in 2012–2013 was valued at US$125 million with seafood as one of the major export products. It is estimated that about 70–75 per cent of the total fisheries production in Myeik was sold via the Myeik–Thailand border in 2013. The supply chain for fishery products is shown as an example of the complex network now in operation for the Myanmar fishery sector (Figure 9.9).

Figure 9.5 Fish on Sale in Myeik Wet Market

Source: Photo taken by the research team during field survey.

Figure 9.6 Fish on Sale in Myeik Market

Source: Photo taken by the research team during field survey.

The research team found that Ranong was an important landing port for the Myanmar fish industry. Catches landing at Ranong would be purchased and sent to various destinations both within Thailand and Malaysia.

According to a newspaper report, most fish landing at Myeik is destined for foreign markets (Hulst 2015).

Table 9.4 Top 5 Export Destinations of Myanmar's Fishery (2017)

	Fish		Prawns		Other		Total	
Country	Quantity (tonne)	Value (US$ million)	Quantity (tonne)	Value (US$ million)	Quantity (tonne)	Value (US million)	Quantity (tonne)	Value (US$ million)
China	23,953.6	45.16	4,872.7	14.02	49,391.6	102.31	78,217.8	161.49
Thailand	123,353.7	115.52	1,554.1	7.243	24,660	20.40	149,567.8	143.17
Malaysia	1,871.3	2.3	117.17	6.25	10,693.8	25.68	13,682.23	34.23
Saudi Arabia	20,540.8	21.61	11.7	0.02	309.55	0.59	20,862.04	22.23
Singapore	16,301.3	22.4	402.86	1.27	10,345.7	5.98	27,049.9	29.66

Source: Department of Fisheries, Government of Myanmar.

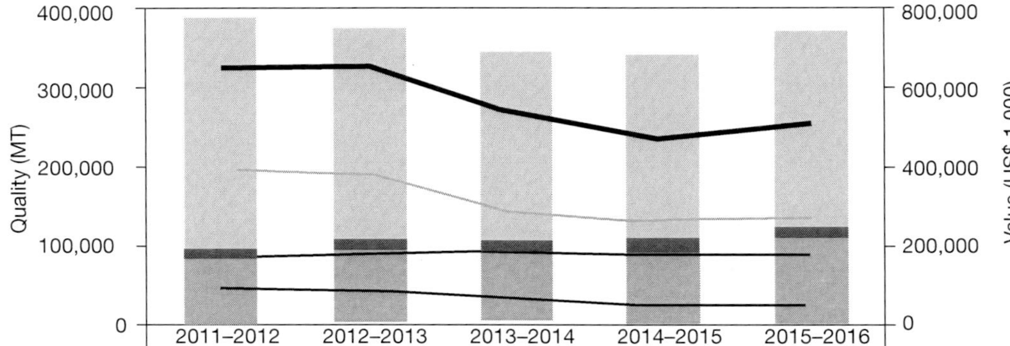

	2011–2012	2012–2013	2013–2014	2014–2015	2015–2016
Fish	283,689	266,465	237,142	225,975	246,971
Prawns	17,995	17,268	16,509	17,527	13,673
Others	85,298	93,113	91,616	94,788	108,326
Total (MT)	396,981	376,846	345,267	338,291	368,971
Fish	396,270	378,050	286,930	258,610	274,250
Prawns	86,190	89,290	61,980	56,890	49,640
Others	171,390	185,500	187,360	166,750	178,740
Total(US$ 1,000)	653,850	652,840	536,270	482,250	502,630

Figure 9.7 Fishery Products Exported by Myanmar in 2011–2016 by Quantity and Value

Source: DoF (2016) quoted in Mar, 2017.

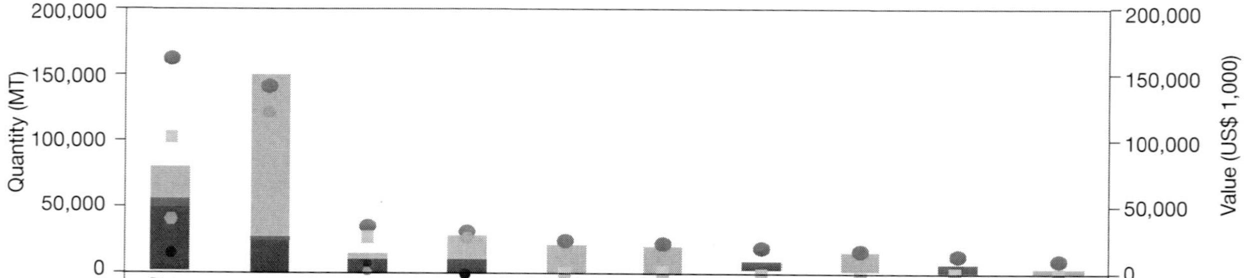

	China	Thailand	Malaysia	Singapore	Saudi	Kuwait	Japan	UAE	UK	USA
Fish	23,954	123,354	1,871	16,301	20,541	20,947	82	13,775	6,789	2,239
Prawn	4,873	1,554	1,117	403	12	4	3,870	330	51	344
Others	49,392	24,880	10,694	10,348	310	36	1,419	84	169	758
Total (MT)	78,218	149,568	13,682	27,050	20,862	20,987	5,371	14,189	7,009	3,341
Fish	45,157	115,525	2,299	22,410	21,609	19,711	153	12,697	11,106	3,503
Prawn	14,020	7,243	6,251	1,269	20	7	13,594	761	232	1,815
Others	102,314	20,402	25,683	5,976	594	75	3,578	329	559	4,713
Total (USS 1.000)	161.491	143.170	34.233	29.655	22.223	19.793	17.325	13.787	11.897	10.031

Figure 9.8 Top Ten Destination Countries for Fishery Products Exported by Myanmar in 2015–2016 by Quantity and Value (Ranked by Value)

Source: DoF (2016).

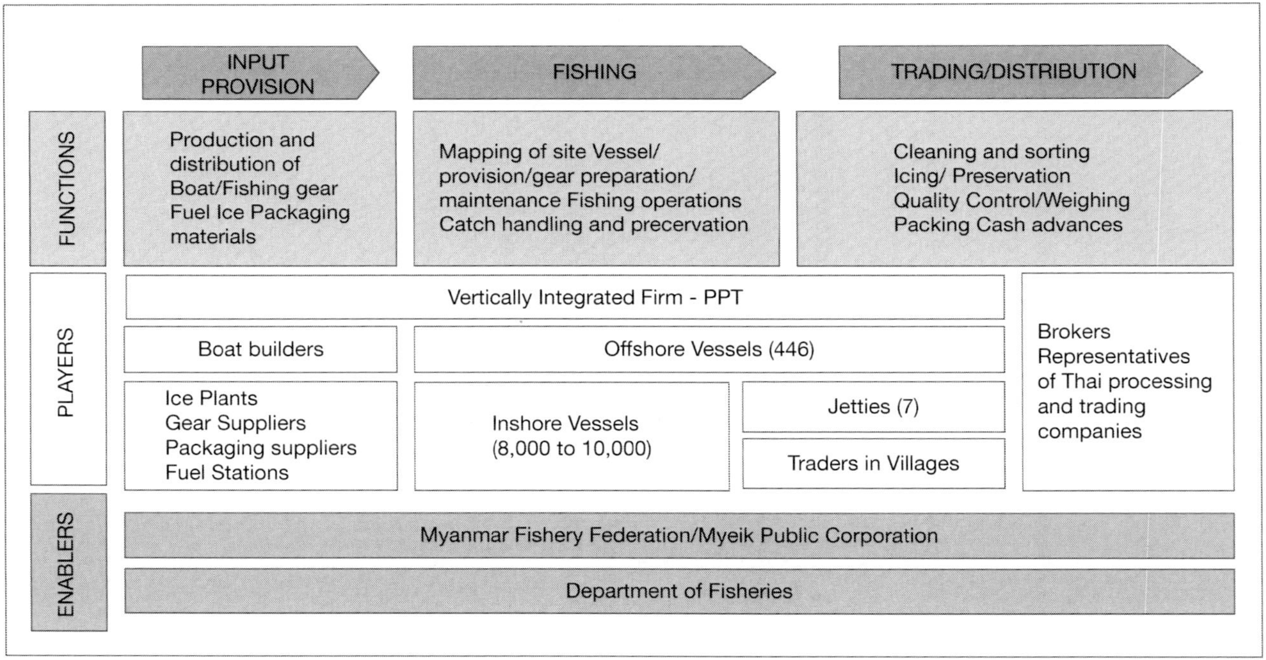

Figure 9.9 Fresh Fish for Thailand–Myanmar Border Trade Value Chain Map—Myeik

Source: ILO (2015).

> Almost none of the fish landing in Myeik is sold in Myanmar. Small fishing boats sell their catch to buyers who transport the fish to Thailand where better prices are paid. Larger fishing vessels transfer their catch to bigger ships that sail to foreign ports. All the best quality fish is exported. Lower quality fish is processed into ngapi (fish paste) or fishmeal for the domestic poultry industry

The Thai data suggest that the border trade in fishery products makes up for a high proportion of the non-natural gas import from Myanmar to Thailand (Table 9.5).

First, we note that most of Thailand–Myanmar trade is border trade, which is natural for countries that share a long common border.

Looking more closely we can see that Thailand has a trade surplus with Myanmar. But in terms of border trade, the reverse is the case; border trade shows a deficit for Thailand. This is explained by the fact that Thailand buys natural gas from Myanmar via the pipeline that comes in at Kanchanaburi.

To get a more realistic appreciation of the characteristics of the trade, we should exclude natural gas from the trade flow; following this exclusion, the data show that for 2015–2017, Thailand has a large surplus with Myanmar. However, for 2018 (January–June), the surplus turns into a deficit because Thailand's export has dropped from around 100 billion baht to just 5 billion baht. This surprising turn of event needs to be further investigated.

Coming to the trade in fishery products, the Thai official data show that for the period 2016–2018 (January–June) fishery products account for around 30 per cent of non-natural gas import from Myanmar, rising from only 10 per cent in 2015. This indicates the importance of fishery products from Myanmar in the total trade.

In terms of the trading channels, we have data for trade by border crossing points located in various provinces. Unfortunately, for each border crossing point, we do not have data according to commodity. Therefore, we can only surmise about the likely routes that the traded products take.

Table 9.5 Thailand–Myanmar Border Trade for 2015–2018 (January–June)

Item	2015	2016	2017	2018 (January–June)
Total trade				
Value	261,872.91	230,139.07	230,422.82	120,953.72
Export	140,687.33	146,534.57	146,084.40	75,830.71
Import	121,185.58	83,604.56	84,338.42	45,123.01
Border trade				
Value	217,964.64	187,964.53	183,037.54	97,265.26
Export	100,819.30	109,339.84	107,681.01	5,626.44
Import	117,145.34	78,624.69	75,356.53	40,988.82
Non-NG import	5,941.58	9,338.89	11,785.84	6,980.24
By province				
Tak				
Value	72,256.07	84,606.78	79,664.08	41,961.70
Export	68,997.00	80,629.03	74,733.00	38,900.64
Import	3,259.07	3,977.75	4,931.09	3,061.07
Kanchanaburi				
Value	112,531.98	70,269.40	64,447.55	3,444.08
Export	1,123.41	694.46	503.40	314.83
Import	111,408.57	69,574.94	63,944.15	34,179.26
Ranong				
Value	18,531.83	19,526.38	25,810.43	11,345.73
Export	16,934.72	15,398.06	20,335.27	8,573.93
Import	1,597.11	4,128.32	5,475.16	2,771.80
Chiang Rai				
Value	12,959.01	12,147.33	11,447.65	7,907.51
Export	12,813.74	11,972.69	11,275.32	7,763.51
Import	145.27	174.64	172.33	144.32

(Continued)

Table 9.5 (Continued)

Item	2015	2016	2017	2018 (January–June)
Mae Hong Son				
Value	1,562.92	1,217.55	1,182.32	1,083.23
Export	855.86	540.91	636.71	590.25
Import	707.06	676.64	545.61	492.98
Prachuap Khiri Khan				
Value	122.83	197.09	485.50	472.67
Export	94.57	104.69	197.32	133.28
Import	28.26	92.40	288.19	339.39
By commodity				
Top 10 items				
Export				
Total	100,819.50	109,339.84	107,681.01	56,276.44
10 items	36,908.89	40,023.84	45,851.95	23,628.39
Share of 10 items (%)	37	37	43	42
Import				
Total	117,145.34	78,624.69	75,356.53	40,988.82
10 items	115,868.16	76,748.25	73,143.78	39,783.09
Share of 10 items (%)	99	98	97	97
Of which				
Natural gas	111,203.76	69,285.80	63,570.69	34,008.58
Aquatic animals	478.36	2,309.99	3,345.70	1,791.50
Squids	88.77	393.55	541.72	329.88
Total w/o natural gas	5,941.58	9,338.89	11,785.84	6,980.24
Fishery products	567.13	2,703.54	3,887.42	2,121.38
Share of fishery of total w/o NG (%)	10	29	33	30

Source: Ministry of Commerce, Thailand.

Relying on descriptive accounts of trade flows at each border crossing point, we can surmise the following.

Tak province: Trade in the export of consumer products for the main Myanmar market and import of general Myanmar goods.

Kanchanaburi: Trade is mainly import of natural gas, and there is very little other imports from Myanmar.

Ranong: Export of general merchandise, mainly cement and machinery for the construction sector in Myanmar. Ranong shows the highest import figure in the non-natural gas sector, and it is likely to be due to fishery products that pass through here.

Chiang Rai and Mae Hong Son: for export of consumer goods from Thailand and very little import from Myanmar.

The total trade volume is still small for Prachuap Khiri Khan. This is because the border crossing is a temporary one. It is also constrained by the lack of good roads between Prachuap and Myeik, which are the main market centres on each side of the border.

However, this is likely to change once the border crossing point is upgraded to be a permanent one, and the roads are improved.

9.2.6. Prospects for the Fishery Sector in the Tanintharyi–Tanaosri Region

Local news reports from Myanmar indicate that efforts are being made to better regulate fishery production in Myeik, so that more fish is traded within the country rather than being sold illegally in foreign ports.

'We are trying to establish international-standard fish markets equipped with jetties that will have the capacity to handle fishing vessels as well as refrigerated warehouses for the storage of supplies,' said U Hla Than, Chair of Pyae Phyo Tun Company, which is planning to build new fish processing factories in new markets.

'Over the longer term we are also aiming to transport the fishery products in refrigerated containers to the Maw Taung border area by truck. We need to take steps to build up the local market' (Aung 2018).

At the same time, from discussion with informants at Ranong, the research team learned that Ranong fishing boats have mostly scaled down their operations. Fishing businesses are also preparing to move to Myeik for investing in fishery-related activities like cold storage and processing. In addition, the production of marine aquaculture is growing (Figures 9.10–9.13).

Figure 9.10 Entrance of a Soft-Shell Crab Farm in Myeik

Source: Photo taken by the research team during field survey.

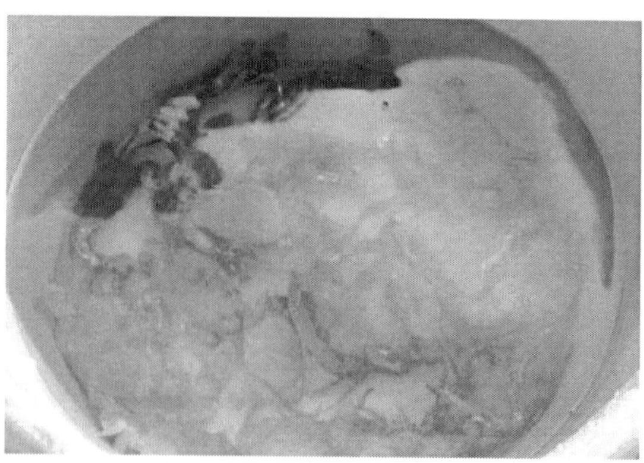

Figure 9.11 Soft-Shell Crabs from the Farm

Source: Photo taken by the research team during field survey.

Figure 9.12 A View of the Crabs in the Floating Feeding Boxes

Source: Photo taken by the research team during field survey.

Figure 9.13 Inspecting the Crabs

Source: Photo taken by the research team during field survey.

It is likely that with improved land transport routes from Myeik to Dan Singkhon and Prachuap Khiri Khan, Myeik will develop into a major trading and processing centre for fishery products.

The major constraints for this development will be supporting infrastructure such as electricity supply, which is still limited in Myeik, and the availability of labour with the necessary skills for the new activities.

- Results for the nine fish categories within the archipelago (including groupers, snappers, butterfly fish and parrotfish) indicate an ecosystem heavily impacted by overfishing.
- Biomass surveys noted many sites have relatively low estimates of fishable biomass (< 3 g/m2). Global estimates of biomass below 30 g/m2 present unhealthy and unstainable fishing states.

Figure 9.14 Extract from Report on Myanmar's Marine Fishery
Source: Howard (2018).

There is also a concern about overfishing in Myanmar. Problems are reflected in reduced catches by local fishermen and in the overall statistics. The FAO (2012) report cites an early (1980–1983) estimate of 1.05 million tonnes of the maximum sustained yield and then compares it with the landing amount being 50 per cent higher; the statistics cited at the beginning of this chapter show production at 2 million tonnes. Clearly, there will be long-term problems that need to be addressed to sustain the fishery sector in Myanmar.

A recent report edited by Howard (2018) expresses deep concern about Myanmar's fishery, specifically focusing on the Myeik area (Figure 9.14).

9.2.7. Fishery in the Context of Thailand, Myanmar and ASEAN Connectivity

There is optimism in Myanmar that fishery has a high potential for development. For instance, a news report states:

> Myanmar exported over 560,000 tonnes of fishery products in 2017-18, the highest in 20 years, according to data provided by the Ministry of Agriculture, Livestock and Irrigation (MOALI). At those levels, the exports are worth $711 million. That could more than double to $2 billion–$3 billion within the next two years, if the right technology, resources and equipment are deployed, said U Htay Myint, chair of the Myanmar Fishery Federation. This includes developing ponds for aquaculture, processing factories and cold storage facilities. The Ministry of Planning and Finance has agreed to provide funds of up to K100 billion to develop the supply chain and modernise the aquaculture process, U Htay Myint said. Earlier this year, MOALI launched dialogues for the drafting a National

Aquaculture Development Plan to preserve the country's fish supplies. (Ko 2018)

This optimism is tempered with the various constraints that have been identified, ranging from resource depletion and degradation and lack of infrastructure to the lack of more advanced technology and technical and business skills. These are also common challenges faced by ASEAN member countries.

In this context, improved physical connectivity would support Myanmar in its development and the overall development of ASEAN through trade and exchanges of labour, knowledge and shared vision for greater prosperity of all.

9.3. TOURISM

9.3.1. Background

The Tanintharyi region covers a long stretch of the southern part of the country on the Isthmus of Kra with a land area of 43,345 sq. km (6.37% of Myanmar). It borders the Andaman Sea to the West, Thailand to the east, the Mon State to the North, and the southern part of Thailand to the southernmost point, Kawthaung. The region's capital is Dawei, while Myeik, another major city, has more inhabitants than the capital; Kawthaung is at the southernmost point. Overall, the region is supported by three districts of public administration: Dawei, Myeik and Kawthaung.

If the beautiful and remote Myeik Archipelago, a cluster of more than 800 largely untouched islands that has huge marine resources, is included in the land area, then the region will be considered even more important in terms of its natural endowments, with potential for the development of tourism and building of infrastructure that can further support development. Along with Myanmar's recent political transition, there is a clear sign that the region has gradually emerged and opened up to neighbouring countries and the outside world.

On the Thai side, the eastern part of the same stretch of land with similar longitude as that of Myanmar, is Tanaosri. The region with a total land area of 46,579 sq. km (9.08% of Thailand) extends to many provinces in the western and southern parts of Thailand, starting with Kanchanaburi, Ratchaburi, Phetchaburi,

Table 9.6 Land Area of Provinces in Tanaosri Region

Province	Land area (sq. km)	Percentage of Thailand's Total Area*
Kanchanaburi	19,483.2	3.797
Ratchaburi	5,196.5	1.013
Phetchaburi	6,225.1	1.213
Prachuap Khiri Khan	6,367.6	1.240
Chumphon	6,009.0	1.171
Ranong	3,298.0	0.643
Total	46,579.4	9.077

Source: Author's own.

Note: *Total area of Thailand is 513,115,020 sq. km.

Prachuap Khiri Khan, Chumphon and Ranong, with Kanchanaburi, the biggest in terms of land area, and Ranong, the smallest of all and indeed the smallest in Thailand (Table 9.6). All these provinces form part of Thailand's Tanaosri region. The Thai side of Tanaosri is much more developed.

The Tanaosri of the Thai side, the Gulf of Siam, is also famous for its seaside resorts and marine and farm products among the locals and even among foreigners who visit beach resorts, starting usually from Cha-am in Phetchaburi to Hua Hin in Prachuap Khiri Khan and down to Prachuap Khiri Khan Township, Chumphon and Ranong. In addition to other kinds of economic activities, tourism seems to be the main core of the basic industries in these provinces, which also provides some trickle-down effects according to the distance and the transport infrastructure that supports the travellers within and outside the region.

9.3.2. Present Tourism Trend and Development

The tourism industry of both countries has developed independently from each other since the land demarcation mark at the physical border separate the landscape of two countries. However, the geography of the two countries makes only one landmass rather than the separate entities that the political division seems to suggest. This is why, the different political regimes of the two countries had a strong impact on the development of tourism from the distant past up to the present. The future, however, suggests this might not be the case given the recent changes that are taking place, particularly in Myanmar, and on how such changes will certainly have a strong impact on the country and a crowding out effect on neighbouring countries like Thailand, with long common borders.

Given the different pace of development in the two countries, tourism in Thailand's Tanaosri is much more developed than that in Myanmar's Tanintharyi. A similar case is with the eastern part of the corridor, which is more developed than the western part. From Kanchanaburi province, the connecting part to Dawei, down to Ratchaburi, Phetchaburi, Prachuap Khiri Khan, Chumphon, and Ranong, which is connected to Kawthaung (Victoria Point), together with the link between Prachuap Khiri Khan and Myeik, the tourism industry has long been developed between these provinces and surroundings, but less connected to the southern part of Myanmar.

9.3.3. Tanintharyi's Tourism: Trend and Development

According to statistics from the Ministry of Hotels and Tourism, 360,835 tourists visited the Tanintharyi region in 2016. In terms of accessibility, it is not very easy to visit the region by road or rail transport as the infrastructure is still underdeveloped. However, travelling by air is easy as its three airports—Dawei, Myeik and Kawthaung—are only a one-hour flight from Myanmar's capital of Yangon. Recently, direct flights began from Bangkok to Myeik.

The Government of Myanmar has designated the picturesque southern state of Tanintharyi as the destination for an inclusive tourism project implemented by the International Trade Centre (ITC) and thus allowed investments in the Myeik Archipelago. Eleven islands, out of the 800 largely untouched islands, are allowed to receive local and foreign investment for the development of tourism in the region. As per the data from the Ministry of Hotels and Tourism, cruise ships carrying 3,201 tourists visited the Myeik Archipelago between January and November 2016. More recently, the Myeik Archipelago has attracted many more tourists, both local

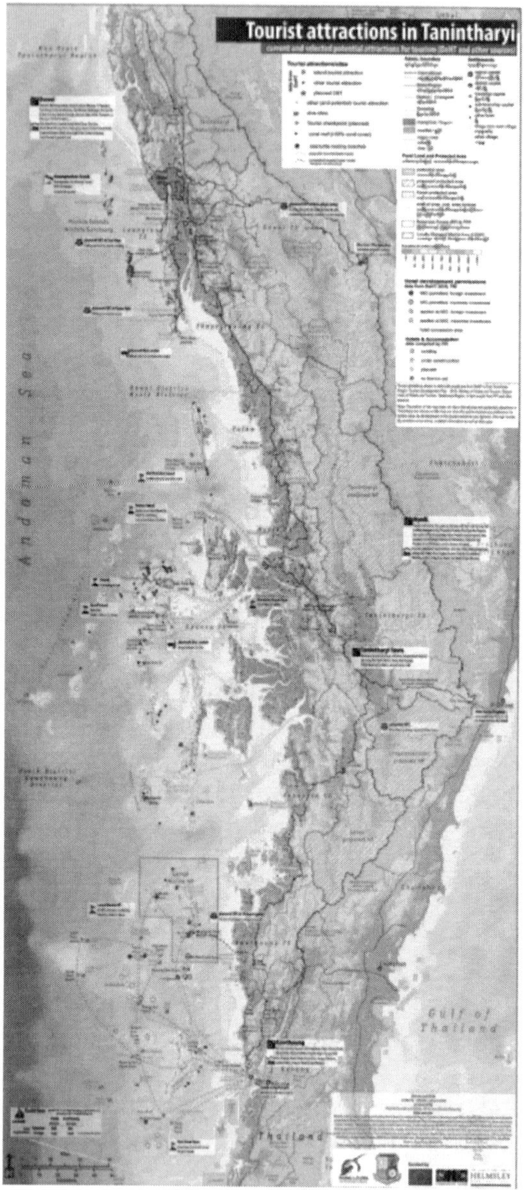

Map 9.2 Tourist Attractions in Tanintharyi

Source: Tanintharyi Tourism Development Committee, 2017

Disclaimer: This figure has been redrawn by the author/s and is not to scale. It does not represent any authentic national or international boundaries and is used for illustrative purposes only.

and foreign, to its islands rich in natural resources, corals and local cultures (Map 9.2).

The government is looking forward to develop tourism in Tanintharyi with an aim to grow and become more sustainable. The big issue here, however, is the kind of infrastructure development that will be needed to support the long-term development. Electricity, land, air and maritime transport and local regulations are some of the hindrances faced when visiting the region.

One of the problems requiring attention is that the best beaches and diving spots in the Myeik Archipelago are quite far away from Dawei, Myeik or Kawthaung. Speed boats are needed to travel to these spots to save time. However, this is not feasible during the monsoon season that could last from May to November. Special licensed boats and permits are needed to go for multiple-day excursions .

9.3.4. Tanaosri's Tourism: Trend and Development

Tourism has been well developed for a long time in Thailand's Tanaosri region, particularly the upper part of the coastal and inland areas. According to the Department of Tourism, Thailand, Kanchanaburi is the most visited province by locals, followed by Phetchaburi and Prachuap Khiri Khan, with much lesser volume for Ratchaburi, Chumphon and Ranong. In 2016, 7.66 million Thai tourists visited Kanchanaburi, while 5.56 million visited Phetchaburi and 4.03 million visited Prachuap Khiri Khan, concentrating much more in the Hua Hin area rather than in the township of Prachuap Khiri Khan. The figures for Ratchaburi, Chumphon and Ranong were 1.62 million, 1.26 million and 0.98 million, respectively (Figure 9.15).

On the other hand, with regard to the number of foreigners visiting the Tanaosri region, Thailand's Prachuap Khiri Khan is the most visited province of all with a total of 0.98 million tourists in 2016, because of the famous town of Hua Hin and its vicinities. Phetchaburi and Kanchanaburi provinces are also preferred destinations among foreign tourists with a total number of 0.48 million and 0.41 million tourists visiting these provinces respectively. The other destinations are Chumphon, Ratchaburi and Ranong with 0.11 million, 0.05 million and 0.05 million foreign tourists

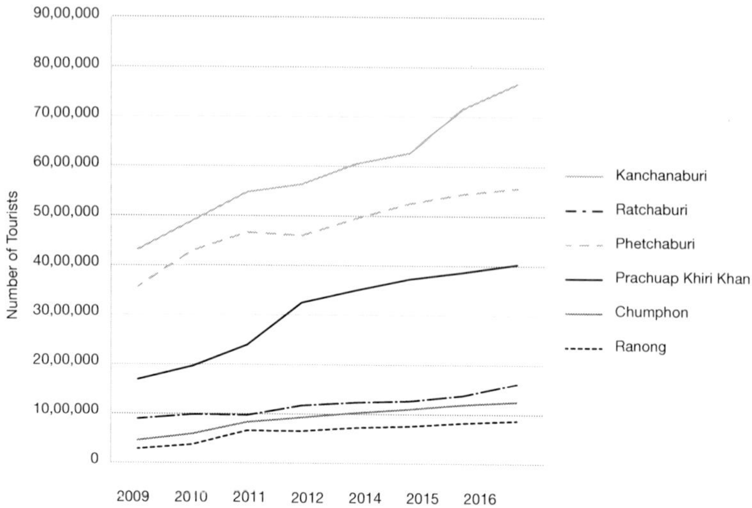

Figure 9.15 Number of Thai Tourists to Phetchaburi, Prachuap Khiri Khan, Ratchaburi, Chumphon and Ranong (2010–2016)

Source: Department of Tourism, Thailand

respectively in 2016. However, the total foreign tourists visiting the Tanaosri region in 2016 stands at 2.1 million, which is 6.4 per cent of total foreign tourists visiting Thailand in the same year (Figure 9.16).

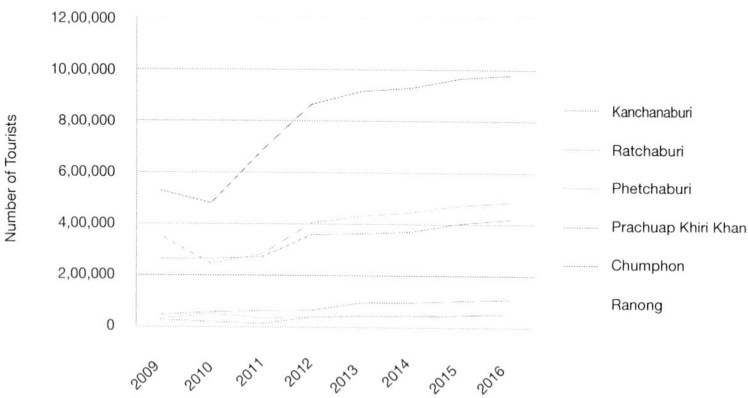

Figure 9.16 Number of Foreign Tourists to Phetchaburi, Prachuap Khiri Khan, Ratchaburi, Chumphon and Ranong (2010–2016)

Source: Department of Tourism, Thailand.

Tourism in Thailand's Tanaosri has been developed for long in terms of infrastructure and other facilities like hotels and restaurants and other amenities, which are well developed to suit the tastes of all kinds of tourists. The upper part of Tanaosri, in particular, Cha-am in Phetchaburi and Hua Hin in Prachuap Khiri Khan, has benefited the most as seaside tourist destinations, as these places are not very far from Bangkok. On the other hand, the lower part of Tanaosri, especially Prachuap Khiri Khan, Chumphon and Ranong, despite their natural beauty, is less developed. However, these areas are receiving more attention recently for eco-tourism and natural beauty (Maps 9.3 and 9.4 and Figures 9.17–9.23).

Overall, Thailand has its own plans to develop further infrastructure to support the development of this region. Tourism could benefit from infrastructural development such as rail, maritime and air transport. However, one needs to define further steps in terms of demand and supply of tourism infrastructure that would be necessary to meet the changing scenarios and long-term trends. In the near term, Prachuap Khiri Khan, Chumphon and Ranong have doubled their efforts to differentiate their natural endowments from other tourist destinations to cater to more local and foreign tourists.

9.4. WAYS TO FUTURE DEVELOPMENT AND THE TANINTHARYI–TANAOSRI TOURISM CONNECTIVITY

It is clear from the discussion above that tourism industry in both Tanintharyi in Myanmar and Tanaosri in Thailand needs a further boost to suit their regional development, but to a different extent, whether it is in terms of job creation, infrastructural needs and private investment, just to mention a few. For Myanmar, it has to play a major role in driving Myanmar's economic development since the start of national reforms in 2011. The Tanintharyi region has been chosen as part of Myanmar's tourism development master plan 2013–2020. For Thailand, it has to develop further infrastructure to support congested destinations like Cha-am in Phetchaburi and Hua Hin in Prachuap Khiri Khan and connect further into the lower parts of Tanaosri, like the townships of Prachuap Khiri Khan, Chumphon and Ranong.

More importantly, both Tanintharyi and Tanaosri need to find ways to integrate tourism and development, based on their relative strengths and complementarities. At present, the tourism

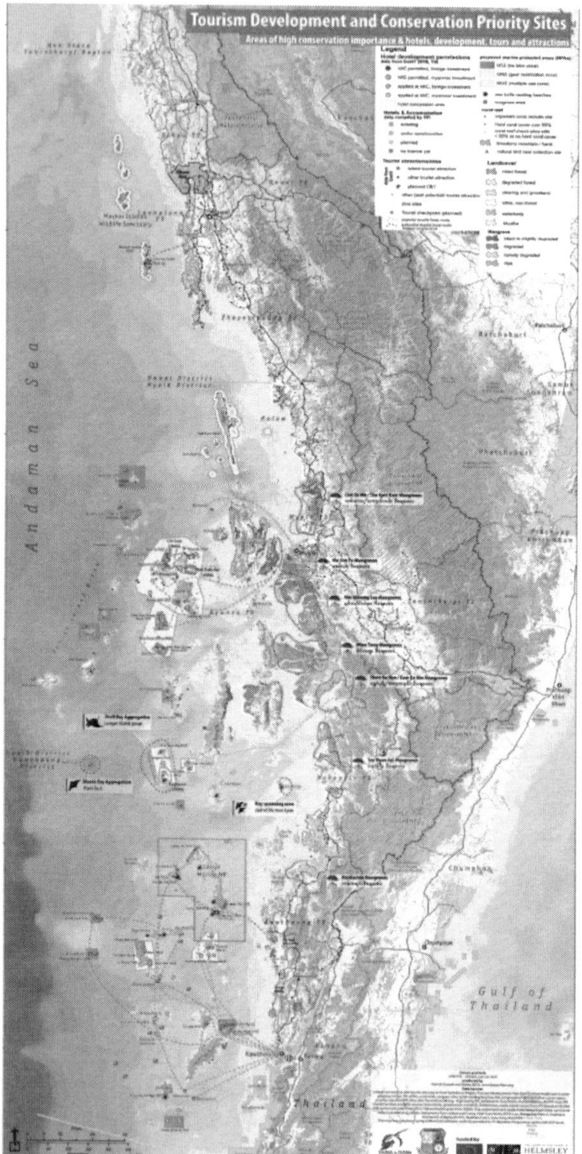

Map 9.3 Tourism Development and Conservation Priority Sites in Tanintharyi

Source: Tanintharyi Tourism Development Committee, 2017.

Disclaimer: This figure has been redrawn by the author/s and is not to scale. It does not represent any authentic national or international boundaries and is used for illustrative purposes only.

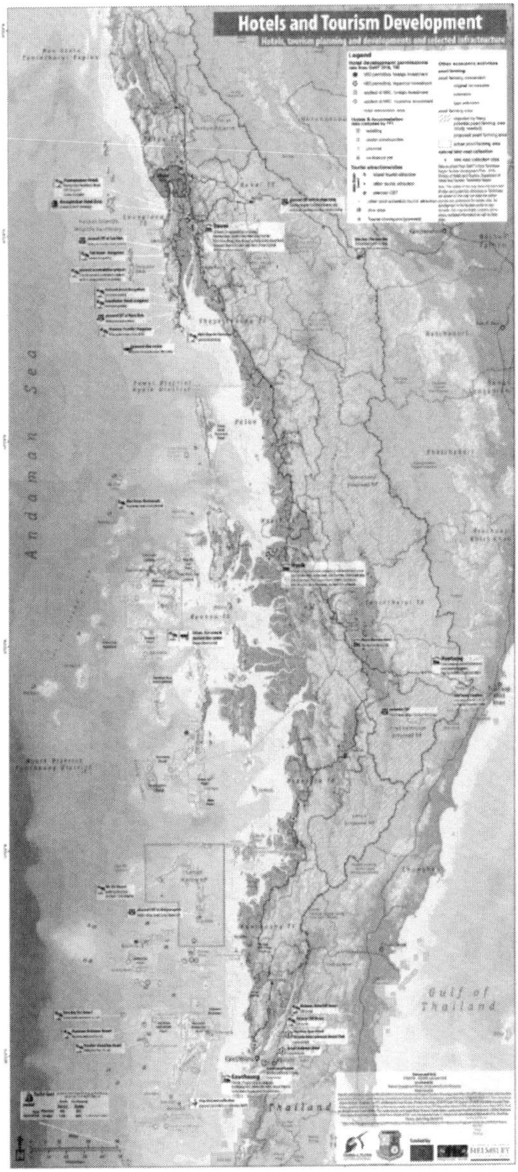

Map 9.4 Hotels and Tourism Development in Tanintharyi

Source: Tanintharyi Tourism Development Committee, 2017.

Disclaimer: This figure has been redrawn by the author/s and is not to scale. It does not represent any authentic national or international boundaries and is used for illustrative purposes only.

Figure 9.17 Landmark of Myeik City: Statue of Aung San

Source: Photo taken by the research team

Figure 9.18 Old Building in Myeik City

Source: Photo clicked by the research team.

industry on both sides of the region has started to make progress in terms of connecting with each other. However, their efforts might not go very far without the support of hard and soft infrastructure and connectivity in the ASEAN context, which seems to be not yet reaching a good level of understanding and implementation in the public sphere of both local and national governments.

Figure 9.19 A Street View of Myeik

Source: Photo taken by the research team.

Figure 9.20 Inside a market at Myeik

Source: Photo taken by the research team.

9.4.1. Tanintharyi's Plan for Tourism Development

The Myanmar government is making efforts to plot a careful and sustainable path for tourism development in the Tanintharyi region. The government has recently formed a Tanintharyi Tourism

Figure 9.21 Roadside Stall in Myeik

Source: Photo taken by the research team.

Figure 9.22 New Construction in Myeik City

Source: Photo taken by the research team.

Development Committee to draw a master plan for sustainable tourism in the region. The committee comprises tourism ministry officials and private sector representatives.

Primary efforts are being made to increase the number of tourists coming particularly to the Myeik Archipelago with less impact on the environment. For instance, plans are underway to draw up a master plan for developing tourism in the region, and especially the Myeik Archipelago, with an aim to create job

Figure 9.23 New Construction in Myeik

Source: Photo taken by the research team

opportunities for local people while protecting the area's national resources and landscape.

The Ministry of Hotels and Tourism, Myanmar, chose Tanintharyi after ITC Geneva, designated this southern region as the destination for an inclusive tourism project. Following the success of an earlier ITC project, which started in 2014 and boosted jobs and incomes while supporting cultural heritage and contributing to peacebuilding in the country's Kayah State, Myanmar government asked ITC to extend its activities to other parts of the country. The project in Tanintharyi will be part of the fourth phase of the Netherlands Trust Fund (NTF IV) portfolio of trade development projects, which started in December 2017 with funding from the Netherlands. The project may take 3.5 years, intervening across the value chain to build business linkages and improve tourism capacity and product quality.

The Tanintharyi region was chosen because of the potential of the proposed destinations as assessed by an ITC value chain tourism project. This region boasts of the beautiful and remote Myeik Archipelago, a cluster of over 800 largely untouched islands with major tourism potential, as well as pristine beaches, unspoiled forests and other eco-tourism sites.

Other efforts are being made to boost tourism in the region's capital of Dawei, which is home to colonial architecture and pagodas. Myeik is a bustling harbour town with cottage industries such as crab farming and other aquaculture activities that have a great potential to earn extra income by organizing properly guided tours. This has to be extended to Kawthaung, the southernmost town at the tip point that is worth a local tour before extending to island resorts. Advantages, as noted by the study, include ongoing efforts by the Japan International Cooperation Agency (JICA) to create a tourism master plan for Tanintharyi.

9.4.2. Tanintharyi–Tanaosri Tourism Connectivity

As a result of the master plan on ASEAN connectivity (MPAC) that was implemented almost a decade ago, connectivity has become 'destiny' for ASEAN's future integration. As a developing region with such a diversity and different levels of development, ASEAN member states are in a better state to organize and become as one rather than living separately like we used to be during the Cold War period. ASEAN's unity in diversity (Acharya 2012) will reinforce ASEAN's strength as it will reflect through the lens of connectivity that will help to generate new visions of how we, ASEAN, organize ourselves in the future.

Tanintharyi–Tanaosri tourism connectivity is no different from the above-mentioned statement as it has to move beyond 'two regions of two countries' into one region, given its geography, with a whole new level of sub-regional cooperation and integration, if the two countries would like to move commonly towards their goals. As long as it is clear to the policymakers of both sides that the regions can be better developed as one, the 'Tanintharyi–Tanaosri region' has the chance to succeed and reach its potential sooner than later.

To move to such tourism connectivity between Myanmar and Thailand, it is first and foremost important that these two countries must have a common understanding and agreement on the greater picture of wholesome development of the 'Tanintharyi–Tanaosri region'; they also need to understand whether this connectivity and integration could foster and in what way future development needs to be made in terms of transportation, communication and infrastructure—roads, railways, airports, pipelines, electricity grids, internet cables and more. Regional infrastructures of both countries as one are morphing the systems of the two countries ranging from divisions to connections and from nations to nodes.

Mapping out connective corridors, like Dawei to Kanchanaburi, Myeik to Prachuap Khiri Khan and Kawthaung to Ranong will help to supersede maps of national borders. By doing this, the sub-regional zone could become an internally integrated Tanintharyi–Tanaosri region, connecting further to Indonesia-Malaysia-Thailand Growth Triangle Subregional Cooperation (IMT-GT), and Greater Mekong Subregion (GMS), sponsored by the Asian Development Bank (ADB). Once this happens, the free movements of goods, services and people coupled with intense connectivity across the region will help thriving townships like Myeik and Prachuap Khiri Khan and its adjacent areas, both rural- and town-based.

With such developments on connectivity and integration, the two countries have to move away from suspicion to infrastructural development to increasing interdependence and then to economic and social integration. When countries are willing to open their territory and trade together, more investment, production and other services like tourism industry could become integrated across the Tanintharyi–Tanaosri region. This is only possible through the shift towards a linked tourism development where optimizing economic and social geography could supersede preservation of territorial sovereignty.

9.4.3. Tourism Sector: Conclusion

Tanaosri and Tanintharyi tourism have long been developed separately. The Thai side's openness has helped the development of Tanaosri tourism to be in line with the overall trend. The upper provinces, namely Cha-am in Phetchaburi and Hua Hin in Prachuap Khiri Khan, are more popular than lower provinces, namely Prachuap Khiri Khan Township, Chumphon and Ranong. Myanmar's situation is very different because of the country's isolation from the outside world for decades. Only recently, and particularly since 2011, Myanmar's tourism has become more open, and this explains the rise of regions like Tanintharyi and Myeik Archipelago on the tourist map.

Now that Myanmar and Thailand are moving to integrate further in ASEAN and globally, the tourism industry of both regions have strong advantages and opportunities to learn and understand from each other and also from the world. On the ground, the tourism industry of both sides of this wider Tanaosri–Tanintharyi region, seamlessly connecting the two oceans, has started to make an appeal and real progress beyond one's imagination, in terms of connecting more people and businesses. These efforts go beyond the governments of both sides, but the future momentum might not be the same if proper guidance, rules and regulations and public infrastructure to support the future expansion of the industry are not provided. That is why, the role of governments of both sides has become crucial to help establish the progress and interests of all stakeholders in the region.

The main issue that lies in the future progress of this wider region is how to frame the common development and integration of both sides to connect in the best possible way to provide, to both countries, well-being of the people, sustainability of the resources and inclusive development. For sure, there will be a great need for all types of connectivity and development. There is a need for creating a master plan for responsible agencies to facilitate coordination among both the countries at all levels—regional to national to local.

Myanmar, for example, needs to strongly recognize and upgrade the importance of the Myeik Archipelago. It also needs to create value chain tourism projects in its own tourism master plan. To succeed with such a framework, it also needs to devise plans to develop infrastructure, both hard and soft, which will support tourism development projects. Thailand, on the other hand, has also realized the need for connectivity infrastructure that it should build to link the southern part of the Tanaosri region better, down from Prachuap Khiri Khan township to Chumphon and then to Ranong, as well as the Tanintharyi region with different important cities, like Dawei, Myeik and Kawthaung. These connectivity plans will help to improve the development of tourism in the whole region.

REFERENCES

Acharya, A. 2012. *The Making of Southeast Asia: International Relations of a Region*. Ithaca and London: Cornell University Press and Institute of Southeast Asian Studies.

Aung, Htin Lynn. 2018. 'Tanintharyi's Fisheries Potential Marred by Illegal Exports'. *Myanmar Times*, 4 May.

FAO. 2012. *Fishery and Aquaculture Country Profiles*. Yangon: FAO.

Howard, Robert, ed. 2018. *Marine Biodiversity of the Myeik Archipelago: Survey Results 2013–2017 and Conservation Recommendations*. Cambridge: Fauna & Flora International.

Hulst, Hans. 2015. 'Fishing for Trouble in Myeik'. *Frontier Myanmar*, 27 October. https://www.frontiermyanmar.net/en/fishing-for-trouble-in-myeik

ILO. 2015. *Value Chain Analysis and Competitiveness Strategy: Marine Capture Fisheries: Myeik and Yangon, Myanmar*. Yangon: International Labour Organization, ILO Liaison Officer for Myanmar.

Ko, Thiha Ko. 2018. 'Fishery Exports Break 20-year Record, Could Double within Two Years'. *Myanmar Times*, 10 April.

Leadbitter, Duncan. 2017. 'Fish Matter'. *Myanmar Fisheries—Situation Report*. Fish Matter https://docplayer.net/97624595-Myanmar-fisheries-situation-report-duncan-leadbitter-fish-matter-pty-ltd-october-2017.html

Mar, Myat Khine. 2017. 'Regional Fishery Policy Network(RFPN) Member for Myanmar'. http://www.seafdec.org/fisheries-country-profile-myanmar/

Myanmar Business Information Center. 2018. 'Tanintharyi Region Economic Overview'. 25 January. http://www.thaibizmyanmar.com/en/thai-myanmar/Non-paper%20-%2025%20Jan%202018%20-%20Overview%20of%20Tanintharyi%20Region.pdf

CHAPTER 10

PEOPLE MOBILITY AND ACCUMULATION ON PRACHUAP–MYEIK CORRIDOR IN THE CONTEXT OF ASEAN CONNECTIVITY

Supang Chantavanich

10.1. INTRODUCTION

Prachuap and Myeik are towns in Thailand and Myanmar, respectively, which have been connected as a corridor since the 15th century. The corridor was an old trade route as well as a war route. With the Association of Southeast Asian Nations (ASEAN) concept of connectivity and the plan and strategy of the Asian Development Bank (ADB) on East–West Economic Corridor (EWEC) in the Greater Mekong Subregion (GMS), this southern corridor can be an example of people-to-people connectivity and tourism development. People who cross Singkhon Pass in Prachuap to Mudong and Myeik in the Tanintharyi region of Myanmar comprise migrant workers, tourists, traders, investors, officials, academicians and researchers. Commodities that are passed through this corridor include construction materials from Thailand and seafood products from Myanmar. State policies on both sides emphasize on the promotion of tourism and trade and improvements in infrastructure and connectivity. The private sector and civil society also play an important role in people mobility. Given the ASEAN policy on people-to-people connectivity, with emphasis on greater Intra-ASEAN mobility, the Prachuap–Myeik Corridor exemplifies such policy with its initiatives to enhance tourism by facilitating the immigration process and provision of information to travellers. Infrastructure, particularly the 180 km route on the corridor, has been developed and renovated, making it faster for commodities and people to commute. Capacity building, especially language skills training and academic/student exchanges, can ensure more people mobility and connectivity. There are strong tendencies that the corridor will develop steadily and expand westward to the Bay of Bengal and link the Pacific Ocean to the Indian Ocean in the near future. Nonetheless, concerns over long-lasting border demarcation conflict and transnational crimes, including smuggling of weapons and drugs as well as human trafficking, prevail on the corridor.

10.2. PRACHUAP–MYEIK CORRIDOR: ITS HISTORY AND DEVELOPMENT

Thailand and Myanmar, formerly known as Siam and Burma, respectively, share more than 2,000 km of borders. The southern corridor is demarcated by the Tenassarim Range, which separates the two countries. The range ends at Sinkhon village near the current border between Prachuap Province in Thailand and Myeik in Myanmar.

Historically, from the 16th to the 19th centuries, Siam and Burmese relations were mainly through trade and warfare against each other (Chutintaranond and Tun 1995, 33). The Siamese capital of Ayutthaya was captured by the Burmese army in 1569 and 1767. The Southern Corridor Myeik–Prachuap was the frequented war route of the Burmese troops in the past. It was less difficult for the army to cross the high Tenessarim Range. Later, during the Second World War, this part of the corridor served the Japanese troops who arrived in Thailand via Prachuap to reach Myanmar, and they occupied it until 1946. Historically, the corridor has been an important old trade route, where commodities from Europe, Persia and India were transported by big vessels from various origins to the Gulf of

Myeik and then continued into the deep and large Tanaosri River to be off-loaded at the Tanaosri Pier (in the old town of Tanaosri). The commodities were then carried by land to Siam and to the rest of Southeast Asia (Collis 1965, 42). As a result, the corridor was a natural pass where local people commuted across the border and trade took place regularly since the 15th century. Myeik and Southern Tenasserim had played an important role in trade and also as a gateway for cultural influences from India and the West (Mills 2006, 35). Myeik was a major Siamese port until 1760, when Burmese troops marched to conquer Ayutthaya Kingdom and its southern towns. Recent developments in both states in the fields of gas and oil exploration and seafood industry can bring back its significant role (Mills 2006, 36). Obviously, Myeik and Prachuap on the southern corridor is not a new route of connectivity.

At present, the major southern corridor immigration crossing is located in Prachuap Khiri Khan Province opposite to the Tanintharyi region. Dan Sinkhon is the temporary border crossing point that links to Myeik. In the past, Dan Sinkhon had been a natural pass where local people commuted, and trade took place regularly before the ADB and ASEAN initiatives on economic corridor and connectivity were launched.

10.3. ASEAN INTEGRATION AND PEOPLE-TO-PEOPLE CONNECTIVITY

Why and how the Prachuap–Myeik Corridor is emerging to become a new major crossing point? The Master Plan on ASEAN connectivity (MPAC 2025) and ADB's East–West Transport Corridor are the two key instruments that drive the connectivity plan in the ASEAN region. The MPAC 2025 designed in 2016 considers connectivity as an important element of ASEAN cooperation and integration. The MPAC encompasses three aspects: physical, institutional and people-to-people linkages, which include education, culture and tourism as the means to achieve the economic, political-security, and socio-cultural pillars of an integrated ASEAN Community.

Since the adoption of the MPAC 2025, progress has been made on people-to-people connectivity with a new strategy to guide future progress, particularly people mobility and tourism connectivity. The MPAC 2025 on people connectivity aims to overcome restrictions on travel for ASEAN nationals within the region and to improve mobility by facilitating travel for tourists, addressing the lack of information on travel options and providing simpler mechanisms to apply for a visa (Association of Southeast Asian Nations [ASEAN] 2016).

Since 1998, the ADB has promoted the notion of the EWEC as a flagship initiative in the GMS. Strategy and action plan were revised in 2001 and 2009 to create a better implementation modality and expanded from transport to include trade, investment and tourism (Asian Development Bank [ADB] 2010). The upper areas of the GMS have already been developed as the EWEC in the 2000s. In the case of the southern areas of the GMS, a need to push for the southern economic corridor is well recognized. One of the new southern east–west corridors, which can link Cambodia, Lao PDR, Myanmar and Vietnam (CLMV) by land and sea, is the Prachuap–Myeik Corridor.

During 2016–2018, the ADB developed tourism assessment strategy and roadmaps for CLMV. It reported the progress on connectivity since 2010. Under people-to-people connectivity, there are notable developments in promoting deeper intra-ASEAN social and cultural understanding. However, ADB indicated that tourism connectivity had not yet been developed adequately due to the barriers that include lack of coordination (harmonization of the system) and lack of capacities (appropriate technologies and skilled labour necessary for implementation; ADB 2017).

In its MPAC 2025, ASEAN has specified three strategic objectives for people-to-people connectivity, which include supporting ease of travel throughout ASEAN, reducing the gaps between vocational skills demand and supply across ASEAN, and increasing the number of intra-ASEAN international students. It also proposes four initiatives to reach such objectives: (a) to enhance ASEAN travel by making it easier to find information, (b) to ease ASEAN travel by facilitating the visa process, (c) to establish new vocational training programmes and common qualifications across ASEAN and (d) to support higher education exchange among ASEAN countries (ASEAN 2016; Figure 10.1). The Prachuap–Myeik Corridor will be examined in the framework of existing people-to-people connectivity, its development and ASEAN objectives and suggested initiatives.

Figure 10.1 ASEAN Connectivity 2025

Source: ASEAN (2016).

10.3.1. People-to-People Connectivity on the Prachuap–Myeik Corridor

Located in the southern part of Thailand and Myanmar, the cross-border connectivity covers Singkhon Pass on the Thailand side and Mudong Pass on the Myanmar side. The distance of the corridor is 180 km. The corridor is situated at the end of the Tenessarim Range, which makes it easier for travellers to cross over. However, the route is mountainous. It is the old route that connected the two countries from the old days, as narrated by Kerr:

> It seems probable that the route followed by the writer is the same as that used in the seventeenth century; excepting only two stretches, one at its eastern end, the other cutting off a bend of Klawng Singkawn. This route is said to be the easiest and quickest way across the peninsula in this region, and it is still constantly in use. The track surveyed for the proposed railway across the Peninsula from Mergui to Prachuap Khiri Khan closely follows this route for a great part of its length. There are other routes to the north and south, but they are more difficult, chiefly on account of the higher hills that have to be crossed. (Kerr 1933, 204)

10.3.1.1. Past Relationships

People from Myanmar and Thailand have crossed the borders to visit each other long before the borderlines were created. Ethnic Mon, Karen and Shan people live along both sides of the borders. They share the same language, culture and social networks within each ethnic group that connect them through the development of the two states. At present, although the people belong to different nationalities, they continue to keep their ethnic, social and family ties. An ethnographic account of a Tai (Shan) town on this border illustrates continued mobility and connectivity mainly through trade (Pawakhapan 2015, 93–97). Evidently, people mobility can be found widely at the local scale. People are engaged in trade and services, including daily commuting workers. Such connectivity can certainly support the framework of ASEAN integration. Short-term tourism to the border areas is popular. People integration is higher between these two countries. Other ASEAN visitors usually connect to this part of the corridor by air rather than by land.

There are four major permanent international immigration checkpoints by land and sea on the Thailand–Myanmar borders (Map 10.1). They are located from north to south of the borders in the following locations:

Mae Sai (Chiang Rai Province)—Tachileik (Shan State)

Mae Sot (Tak Province)—Myawaddy (Karen State)

Phu Nam Ron (Kanchanaburi Province)—Htee Khee (Karen State) to Dawei

Map 10.1 Thailand–Myanmar Corridors

Source: Asian Research Center 2019, adapted from Kosem (2016, iii).

Disclaimer: This figure has been redrawn by the author/s and is not to scale. It does not represent any authentic national or international boundaries and is used for illustrative purposes only.

Ranong Province—Kawthaung (Tanintharyi Region)

Apart from the permanent passes, there are some natural, informal passes that connect the local people. Singkhon Pass that links Prachuap and Myeik is a temporary one.

The Prachuap–Myeik Corridor is unique for its constant people mobility. People who live on the corridor share some ethnic and cultural links. On the Myeik side, villagers who live in the small township of Sinkhon speak Thai. They were originally Thais who lived in Myanmar and became Myanmar nationals. In some other small towns or villages south of Myeik, like Bokpyin and Maliwan, villagers also speak Thai. On the Thailand side, some persons of dual nationality (Thai-Myanmar) can be found in Ranong, particularly local traders of Chinese origin.[1] Like any other border zones, the porosity of the border and people mobility contribute to the existing connectivity. In Sinkhon town and Maliwan village in Kawthaung (Victoria Point) in Myanmar, some people identify themselves as Thai. They are descendants of Thai nationals who were automatically placed into Myanmar territory because of the border demarcation line drawn by the British during the colonial period, although the areas where those people lived were once part of Thailand. During 1927–1957, some of them migrated back to Thailand and lived without legal status in Ranong and Prachuap. Their relatives who lived in Myanmar later sent their children to attend Thai schools and visited Thai hospitals. The National Security Council described the illegal settlers as 'displaced person from Myanmar with Thai origin'. There were 5,000 persons of such status. The new Nationality Law of 2012 finally granted Thai citizenship to this group who live in Thailand (National Security Council 2012). These people are an example of human connectivity on the corridor.

In terms of space and location, Prachuap and Myeik are points that can expand and connect to other corridors. On the Thai side, Prachuap is connected to the Gulf of Thailand, which is a part of the Pacific Ocean. Across the Gulf, one can reach Koh Kong Province in Cambodia. In the 19th century, when Koh Kong was

[1] Based on our team's interview with key informant in Myeik on 22 February 2018.

under Thailand's administration, Prachuap was called by its current name of 'Prachuap Khiri Khan' and Koh Kong was called 'Prachan Khiri Khet'. This reflects the fact that the two provinces, which are located opposite to each other across the Gulf of Thailand, had already been considered as connected under Thailand's administration. From Koh Kong, the corridor can go further to Sihanoukville in Cambodia, Phu Quoc in Southern Vietnam and the South China Sea. On the Myanmar side, Myeik is connected to the Mergui Archipelago, the Andaman Sea, Rakhine State of Myanmar and the Bay of Bengal, which is a part on the Indian Ocean. Further is Bangladesh, and Indian cities of Chennai and Kolkata. The expanded parts cover some of China's Belt Road Initiative (BRI).

On the corridor, people from both countries use the Singkhon Pass as a new land crossing. The attractive tourist spots in Myeik and Prachuap (and its vicinity) are a magnet for people to travel along the new corridor. Trade and employment opportunities encourage more people to cross the border. It is expected that Thailand will consider expanding the permitted area from Amphoe Mueang of Prachuap to the whole province, including Hua Hin and the nearby Phetchaburi Province, as Myeik tourists already cross from Amphoe Mueang to Amphoe Hua Hin casually.

The existing connectivity also sees people who commute regularly on a daily, weekly or monthly basis. They are tour operators and tour guides, traders, investors and workers. The borders become blurred and give way to new categories of border crossing, which are related to nationality and identity.

10.3.2. Immigration and Human Flow

Although Singkhon is a temporary pass, it is equipped with the customs, immigration and quarantine (CIQ) services that are necessary for the mobility of people as well as for animals and plants according to ADB dimensions of connectivity, which includes infrastructure, organization and people. The border was officially opened in 2015.

There are two types of official documents to travel across the Singkhon Pass: *Border Pass* and *Temporary Border Pass*. Border Pass is a document that only local people in Prachuap Khiri Khan and local people in Myeik can obtain to cross regularly. It is valid for

Table 10.2 Number of Outbound People at Dan Sinkhon 2017

Month	Outbound										
	Border Pass					Temporary Border Pass					
	Thailand		Myanmar		Total BP	Thailand		Myanmar		Total TBP	Total
	Male	Female	Male	Female		Male	Female	Male	Female		
January	258	137	1,266	4,205	5,866	656	361	1,647	2,663	5,327	11,193
February	243	140	1,157	3,845	5,385	1,096	425	1,590	2,163	5,274	10,659
March	327	153	1,531	4,601	6,612	1,180	540	2,047	2,893	6,660	13,272
April	275	162	1,399	4,065	5,901	1,331	730	2,317	3,345	7,723	13,624
May	288	130	1,417	4,494	6,329	974	435	2,089	2,770	6,268	12,597
June	319	123	1,188	4,134	5,764	892	433	1,447	2,199	4,971	10,735
July	288	109	1,198	3,839	5,434	984	432	1,481	2,038	4,935	10,369
August	330	125	1,284	3,664	5,403	879	389	1,730	2,308	5,306	10,709
September	313	114	1,311	3,852	5,590	1,972	898	1,805	2,404	7,079	12,669
October	308	113	1,161	3,710	5,292	1,012	561	1,976	3,226	6,775	12,067
November	302	123	1,262	3,767	5,454	748	378	1,959	2,894	5,979	11,433
December	251	158	2,661	5,563	8,633	911	463	3,571	3,724	8,669	17,302
	3,502	1,587	16,835	49,739	71,663	12,635	6,045	23,659	32,627	74,966	146,629
	5,089		66,574			18,680		56,286			

Source: Prachuap Immigration Office 2018.

Labour Report 2016). The professional workers came from the Philippines, England, China, Australia, India, Japan, Myanmar and other countries.

As discussed earlier, most travellers from Myanmar are jobseekers. They come to work in Prachuap as well as in other towns in Thailand. Although the immigration pass allows them to stay only in Amphoe Mueang, many of them travel further to other areas. The ways used to travel legally are (a) to stay only in the authorized zone and find some available jobs and (b) to register as an occasional migrant labourer in the province.

This will require services from individual or networks of brokers who play the role of an employer. The broker facilitates them in the registration process, helps them in all stages of complicated procedures and recruits them to the real employer in Prachuap or other provinces. The services usually cost Thailand baht (THB) 3,000–5,000 per person (Asian Research Center for Migration and Centre for European Studies 2017, 58–59). A high-level source of information from Prachuap indicated that Myanmar migrants who passed Dan Sinkhon would seek to register in the periodical provincial migrant labour in order to become a legal migrant worker and travel beyond Amphoe Mueang. During 2015–2018, the total number of Myanmar migrant workers registered in Prachuap increased from 10,196 to almost 20,547 persons (Table 10.3). It is

Table 10.3 Statistics of Registered Myanmar's Migrant Worker in Prachuap, 2015–2018

Year	*Number*	*% of 3 Nationalities*
2015 (1)	10,196	64
2016 (2)	16,834	45
2017 (3)	14,760	—
2018 (4)	20,547	—

Sources: (a) Prachuap Labour Provincial Report 2015; (b) Prachuap Labour Provincial Report 2016; (c) Department of Employment 2017; (d) MOL Prachuap One-Stop-Service Center 2018.

Note: The three nationalities are Cambodia, Lao PDR and Myanmar.

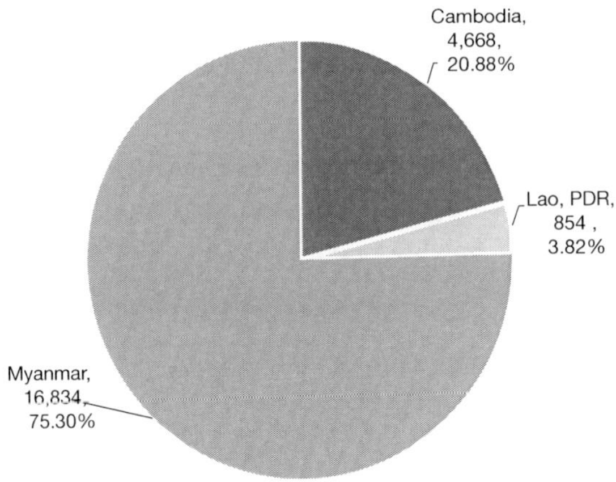

Figure 10.2 Proportion of Registered Migrant Workers in Prachuap, 2016

Source: Prachuap Provincial Labour Report 2016.

high compared to previous years and accounts for 64–75 per cent of all migrant workers from Cambodia, Lao PDR and Myanmar in the province (Figure 10.2). They were primarily irregular and then registered to be employed in the sector of agriculture, sea fisheries, trade, services (including hotel services) and construction (Prachuap Provincial Labour Report 2016). There is still a significant unknown number of irregular migrants from Myanmar who are employed locally.

The mobility of migrant workers from Myanmar to Thailand is considered as a hot issue due to the high number of irregular flows across the borders and the possibilities that such flows are linked to transnational organized crime, particularly human smuggling and trafficking. This also included the case of Rohingya migrants from Myanmar and Bangladesh who were facilitated by transnational criminal networks to come to Thailand and Malaysia during 2014–2015. Some of them became victims of trafficking (Chantavanich 2019a). In February 2019, a criminal network of trafficking was identified in Prachuap. The network was arrested while bringing workers from Myanmar and sending them to Malaysia. All workers came by a natural informal border crossing spot located 12 km from Singkhon Pass (Talk News online 2019).

10.4.2. Tourists

As a new border crossing pass, Dan Sinkhon attracts tourists from both sides. Thai tourists cross the border to visit Tanaosri and Myeik in Myanmar, mainly for sightseeing, culture and island tours. There are approximately 20 Thai tour agencies in Prachuap (including Hua Hin). Some of them operate tours to Myeik. They need to use Myanmar tourist guides because Myanmar law requires so. The number of Thai tourists is around 500 persons per month. With the immigration regulation that requires only an identity card for crossing the Thai border and a permitted seven-day stay, more Thai tourists are visiting Myeik. Tourists usually stay for 2–3 nights in Myeik and the Mergui islands. The programme includes visits to Tanintharyi's old town, old pagoda, market and the old port. In Myeik, Thein Daw Gyi Pagoda, old Chinatown quarter, Myeik Port and market are the popular places for sightseeing. Additional places as requested by tourists include Myeik University, fishing pier or aquaculture. The visit to the islands offers scuba diving, swimming, sightseeing, night camping on the beach and visit to the Moken/Salone (sea nomads) communities on some islands. The sea tours are similar to the Thai ones, but the beaches and the islands are virgin with very few Western tourists. There are more than 10 tour companies in Myeik. Most of them offer island tour packages. In the near future, Thai tour agencies may bring more tourists to the Mergui Archipelago. Great awareness about environment preservation of the sea, the beaches and the islands can be observed in Myeik.

Myanmar tourists, especially the well-to-do people, have started visiting Thailand via Dan Sinkhon. Tourists usually take a one-day or two-day trip. As they cannot go beyond Amphoe Mueang of Prachuap, the trip is limited to the town areas, which include Ao Manao beach, Wa Ko Science Park, Wing 5 Air Force Base with the War Museum and some Buddhist temples. Tour agencies try to offer more spectacular spots in the vicinity of Amphoe Mueang, including the famous Hua Hin sea resort, by bringing clients to the monuments of Thai Great Kings, Huay Mongkol Temple, supermarket and clothes shops in Hua Hin and popular steak and salad buffet restaurants. Tourists from Myeik seem to enjoy the modern lifestyle in Hua Hin than in Prachuap town. In order to go beyond the permitted zone, tour agencies need to inform at the police checkpoints that Myanmar tourists will visit some places near Hua Hin and return to Prachuap Amphoe Mueang within the same day. Such casual practices enable tourists to see more places in Thailand. Licensed guides from Myanmar usually accompany the tour group from Myeik to Prachuap. Once they are in Thailand, they become interpreters to the Thai guides. Licensed Thai guides who can speak Myanmar are not available on the Thai side. Tour programme for the one-day trip starts as early as 3 AM in Myeik town. Tourists have breakfast at Mudong town near the border and then cross Dan Sinkhon at 8 AM. The trip includes visits to places in Amphoe Mueang as earlier described. At 4 PM, the tourists return to Dan Sinkhon and reach Myeik by 9 PM. For the two-day trip, tourists visit the same places like the one-day trip tour and then stay at a hotel in Amphoe Mueang for one night. On the next day, they visit Hua Hin and return to Dan Sinkhon at 4 PM and then go back to Myeik. Approximately 30 tourists from Myeik take this trip on a daily basis.[2]

10.4.3. Traders, Investors and Business Persons

Myeik is an old trade route and old coastal town with a strong tradition of inter-continental marine trade, sea fisheries and dockyard business. The Mergui Archipelago consists of more than 800 islands. Economic activities related to the three industries have continued from the old days until now. Sea and land trades are currently booming. Thai, Chinese, Singaporean, Japanese and Korean traders come to Myeik to explore investment opportunities with local partners. Investors come by land and air. For land connectivity, Thai investors and traders benefit from the geo-economic location with the nearest land link to Myeik. Commodities cross Dan Sinkhon for destinations in Thailand. Construction industry is one significant sector that connects Myeik to Ranong, Bang Saphan, and Prachuap. It enables infrastructure development both within Myeik, and between Southern Thailand and the Tanintharyi region in Myanmar. Businessmen in the construction sector cross the border to Myeik to initiate joint ventures. Seafood exports

[2] Based on our team's interview with key informant in Myeik on 20 August 2018.

from Myeik to Prachuap via Dan Sinkhon valued THB 500 million in 2017 (Prachuap Customs Office 2018). An unknown number of traders and investors from both sides accumulate on the corridor.

10.4.4. Officials, Academicians, Students and Researchers

Since 2016, a significant number of Thai government officials at the national and provincial levels have visited Myeik to discuss possible cooperation. In February 2018, a delegation from the Thai Embassy in Yangon and representatives from the private sector, including banks and chambers of commerce, visited Myeik and Dan Sinkhon. The Thai government is considering the possibility of developing Dan Sinkhon as a permanent pass. But, it cannot be easily decided. There is a plan to build four buildings for CIQ, check post and services in the premises of the pass. Academicians and researchers from Thailand have started to visit Myeik for academic cooperation. Academicians and researchers from branches of Rajabhat Universities on the western borders of Thailand (Ratchaburi, Phetchaburi and Kanchanaburi) have visited and developed academic cooperation with Myeik University. In 2019, a student internship programme to promote Myanmar language learning for Thai students was organized in Myeik. A study of the Moken/Salone (sea Nomads) can be a common topic of interest since there are more than one million Moken in the Tanintharyi region. Tourism and marine science programmes have been established in Myeik University, and there are plans to cooperate with Thai universities. In 2019, a Memorandum of Understanding (MoU) was signed between the University of Myeik and four Thai universities along the western borders adjacent to Myanmar.

10.4.5. Transport and Commodity Links

Myeik has become one of the major suppliers of seafood products to Thailand after the EU issued a yellow card for illegal, unreported and unregulated (IUU) fishing to Thailand in 2014. The National Fisheries Association of Thailand (NFAT) is exploring possibilities to cooperate with counterparts in Myeik since 2016. Seafood products were purchased and brought to Samut Sakhon province to fill the gap due to seafood scarcity on the Thai side. Earlier, in 2016, cross-border trade between Thailand and Myanmar via Dan Sinkhon amounted to THB 18.7 million. Major commodities comprised consumer goods and food products (Prachuap Provincial Labour Report 2016). Chinese traders also arrived at Myeik and become strong competitors to Thai and Singaporeans traders. Another aspect of connectivity is the purchase of Thai fishing vessels at a low price by fishers from Myanmar. Thailand's overseas fishing has almost completely stopped after the IUU crisis. Big vessels of 100++ gross tonne that were left unused in the docks in Samut Sakhon were informally bought by Myanmar counterparts in Myeik at a low cost despite the existing dockyard industry in Myeik.[3] The old vessels bought from Thailand and the new ones manufactured in Myeik are both used for fishing in the Andaman Sea.

With regard to the transportation route between Prachuap and Myeik, most parts of the dirt road have been repaired. The part between Mudong and Maung Khar is the last part being renovated with the financial support from the Myeik Chamber of Commerce under the supervision of a Thai construction company. However, some parts of the road are flooded annually during the rainy season due to heavy rain in the Tanintharyi mountain range, making it difficult to commute. In 2018, Tanaosri town was heavily damaged by the floods that lasted for more than two months. Support in cash and in kind, was sent across the borders by the people in Prachuap to those in Tanaosri. Myanmar government is considering how to solve the flood problem, which is a barrier to connectivity. Flash floods are common in many ASEAN countries. Each government and the local people need to adopt resilience strategies and overcome their limitations. ASEAN governments need to make special efforts to ensure warnings and guidance on flood preparedness. Post-flood relief programmes must be prepared to support local initiatives (Lebel, Chantavanich and Sittitrai 2018, 194–195). The Prachuap–Myeik Corridor can take lessons from other flood cases in ASEAN and try to identify other alternatives for more efficient and faster transportation and connectivity on this corridor.

[3] Based on our team's interview with key informant in Myeik on 21 February 2018.

10.5. STATE POLICIES AND PROGRESS ON CONNECTIVITY

As Thailand's investment and business in Myeik and Myanmar's exports via Prachuap have been rising, it is clear that the connectivity between the two countries through the corridor is expanding continuously. Both countries have adopted policies to enhance such links.

10.5.1. Thailand

Thailand has adopted tourism policies for the southern part called the 'Thailand Riviera'. In its National Tourism Development Plan, Thailand states that it will promote sustainable tourism in the 'Royal Coast', which is the western coastal area of the country. The government is supporting the double-track railway project and speed train from Bangkok to Prachuap. Not only with Myanmar, Thailand is also promoting tourism with China. The China Youth Travel Services (CYTS) initiated a new tour route, that is, Qinghai—Prachuap, in 2018 to bring tourists from Qinghai to Prachuap. A limitation for Prachuap to promote tourism for foreign tourists is that there are a limited number of tour operators speaking Myanmar and Chinese languages. In addition, the Singkhon–Mudong Pass allows only Thai and Myanmar travellers to cross. It does not facilitate the visa process for other ASEAN member states. The limited number of Myanmar and Chinese speaking persons and the restrictions on the visa process require some policy revision. Currently, the local government supports initiatives to train in language skills. It also supports higher education exchange with Myeik. In Yangon, such university exchange programmes have already been held for some years.

In terms of trade connectivity, local investors in Prachuap are discussing a plan to upgrade Singkhon Pass to a permanent pass to boost trade, investment and tourism. The plan includes the promotion of 'Sister City' between adjacent towns that are located on opposite to border, and most of all the integration with the ASEAN Community. At the provincial level, the promotion of tourism to link local identity to the international community is the first goal of Prachuap's development plan. Providing support for trade, investment and tourism across the Singkhon Pass is another goal of the Provincial Development Plan (2018–2021). Actually, such policy has been implemented for some time already. Prachuap Chamber of Commerce and its Myanmar counterpart have initiated investment in the tourism sector since 2016. As a result, border trade became more significant in volume. After two years, economic connectivity is increasing rapidly. In February 2018, the Association for the Promotion of Trade and Investment between Prachuap–Myeik brought 70 traders and investors to visit Myeik and had trade meetings in the sectors of seafood and fisheries, consumer goods, construction materials and interior design, agricultural products, electronic appliances, cosmetics and food supplements, medicine and healthcare services, education services and tourism and Small and Medium Enterprises (SMEs) development. Prachuap also organized a business matching event in September and December 2018 as part of the Prachuap–Myeik Sister City Project. The matching event was jointly organized by the Prachuap-Myeik Trading and Investment Promotion Association (PMTA) and the Myeik District Chambers of Commerce and Industry (MCCI). The third caravan rally to promote the Western Economic Corridor Prachuap-Myeik was held in December 2018. Rally participants were given access to information from the MCCI and were linked with the trade and investment networks in Myeik. Most investors on both sides called for upgrading Dan Sinkhon from a temporary pass to a permanent one. The government is still hesitant to do so due to national security reasons.

The connectivity has expanded beyond the Southern Corridors. In October 2018, a seminar and brainstorming session on 'Cross Border E-Commerce Logistics' was organized in Mae Sot, Tak Province of Thailand. The seminar covered the border trade crossing points of the two countries. The seminar also discussed possibilities to link the trade and investment between Thailand and the Bay of Bengal Initiative for Multi-Sectoral Technical and Economic Cooperation (BIMSTEC). Investment in logistics and Thailand's potential to go beyond the ASEAN region was the major topic of discussion. The Indo-Pacific connectivity led by the private sector may be an input for state policy in the near future.

10.5.1.1. Myanmar

Tourism is currently one of the most significant policy initiatives of Myanmar to improve connectivity. The number of tourists from Thailand to Myanmar via Singkhon Pass has been increasing steadily, while there has been a record rise in the number of tourists from Myanmar to Prachuap.

Myanmar government has developed a plan to promote tourism in the Tanintharyi region, particularly in Myeik. The Ministry of Planning and Finance (MOPF) and the Ministry of Hotels and Tourism (MOHT) have adopted the Myanmar Tourism Master Plan 2013–2020 (Myanmar Ministry of Hotel and Tourism 2013). The Master Plan is the roadmap for strategies to build human resource capacity and promote service quality, improve connectivity and tourism-related infrastructure and build the image position and brand of Tourism Myanmar (Myanmar Ministry of Hotel and Tourism 2013). However, challenges lie in the limited number of registered English-speaking tour guides and insufficient infrastructure. With regard to Myeik and the Tanintharyi region, the government set up the Tanintharyi Tourism Development Committee (TTDC). The government supports the road repair to concrete road from Mudong Town to Thong Khar Village in Tanaosri. In early 2019, the construction of the road has been completed. It reduced travel time between Prachuap and Myeik to 3.5 hours instead of 5 hours in the past. The TTDC plans to promote tourism in the Myeik Archipelago and develop an airport in Kawthaung opposite to Ranong to create more connectivity and allow tourists to visit the archipelago directly (*Myanmar Times* 2018).

The policy on connectivity expands to cover the southern part of Myanmar. In November 2018, China and Myanmar signed an agreement for the development of a deep sea port in Rakhine (*Bangkok Post* 9 November 2018). The framework of the agreement covers the construction of a deep sea port in Kyaukphyu Special Economic Zone in Rakhine State. The sea port and the future highway, which is a part of the China–Myanmar Economic Corridor according to the MoU signed between China and Myanmar in September 2018 will link China's landlocked Yunnan Province with Kyaukphyu and provide access to the Bay of Bengal. It is a part of China's BRI. The new project in Rakhine State illustrates the synergy between ASEAN connectivity and BRI in infrastructure initiatives that can complement each other and avoid duplication and wastage of resources (Jetin 2017).

10.6. FUTURE OF THE PRACHUAP–MYEIK CORRIDOR: IMPACTS AND SUSTAINABILITY

10.6.1. Tanintharyi and Beyond: Regional and Sub-regional Cooperation

How much distance the corridor will cover? Due to people mobility and connections, the areas that will come under the corridor include Dawei, Myeik, Tanaosri town and Kawthaung on Myanmar's side. In Thailand, it will cover Ranong, Chumphon, Prachuap (especially Bang Saphan and Hua Hin) and Phetchaburi. The corridor can go down as far as Phuket in the south following the current routes of tourism and labour migration. Penang in Malaysia is another possibility for the extension of the corridor due to the old trade route among Myeik, Ranong, Kawthaung, Phuket and Penang. It can also go up to Samut Sakhon province, which is the biggest seafood market in Thailand. Currently, all seafood products in Myeik purchased by Thai traders are transported directly to Samut Sakhon. Horizontally, the newly signed agreement between Myanmar and China on the Kyaukphyu deep sea port in Rakhine State will extend its connectivity to Myeik via both maritime and land links. The future highway from Yunnan to Kyaukphyu will connect Myeik to Yunnan faster, and seafood products from Myeik can speedily reach Yunnan and other provinces in China. The southern corridor will be extended based on old and new connectivity routes. Despite its location, China's proliferation is obvious, and Southern China's Yunnan Province will connect to this corridor very soon. The tourism master plans of Thailand and Myanmar affirm sub-regional cooperation. Infrastructure, trade and investment development at regional and intra-regional levels can be observed. More people mobility will follow.

In November 2018, the TTDC drafted a tourism master plan. The plan aims at increasing the number of tourists with a focus on the Myeik Archipelago. The plan targets to create more job opportunities for local people including the Moken (sea nomads called Salone in Myanmar). The committee plans to nominate the Myeik Archipelago for UNESCO World Heritage status (*Myanmar Times* 2018).

Tourism is one of the significant development options. New types of tourism like medical tourism, island eco-tourism, pearl farm and aquaculture (fish, prawn and soft-shell crab) tourism are being promoted by Myeik Tourism Association.[4] On the Thai side, trekking on Lom Muak Hill and parachuting are sports provided by the Wing 5 Air Force in Prachuap. Civil society groups offer programmes to visit fishing villages and learn about the local lifestyle. This initiative promotes villagers' income generation activities. Retiree tourism is currently popular in Thap Sakae District of Prachuap, where more than 5,000 Scandinavian retirees stay annually in their own second homes for six months. This gives new possibilities for tourism development and connectivity based on local needs, interests and potential. More tourists and other groups of people will come to the corridor and may stay longer, leading to people accumulation. Certain levels of cooperation between Thailand and Myanmar can serve as a platform for future regional and sub-regional participation in cross-border migration and economic corridor development.

10.6.2. Security and Political Concerns

While the newly developed infrastructure enables the expansion of the corridor, there are concerns about security and political implications of the connectivity. This includes the people, immigration crossings and related issues covering cross-border security. Culturally, people on both sides feel close to each other due to similar climate and cultural background, including food and festivals. In Mudong, a small border town, there is a Thai Buddhist temple. The villagers speak Thai, but most people in the towns of Tanaosri and Myeik do not. With the new connectivity, there is a need felt on both sides to promote higher language competency in Thai and Myanmar languages. Currently, a private school teaching Thai language is quite popular in Myeik town. On the Prachuap side,

[4] Focus group discussion on 19 August 2018.

very few people can speak the Burmese language. The province needs to develop a Burmese language teaching course to encourage local staff to speak the language. If more people can speak both languages, connectivity and social cohesion will prosper together.

Among the people who live in Myanmar and Thailand, some have got dual citizenship of both countries. An interesting scenario of social, economic and political integration pioneered by this group will take place on the corridor. Migrant workers, both skilled and less skilled, from Thailand and Myanmar are engaged in various economic sectors like tourism and hotels, sea fisheries, aquaculture, construction, wholesale and retail sale, real estate development and dockyard and contribute to people mobility. On the contrary, for decades, the borders have been known for illicit trade like weapons, drugs, forced labour and human trafficking (Boutry and Ivanoff 2009; Chantavanich 2019b; Phongpaichit, Piriyarangsan and Treerat 1998). The porosity of the borders has brought about both positive and negative impacts of people mobility to Thailand and Myanmar.

The security dimension of immigration seems to be the challenge for Thailand. The Thai Army is concerned about the location of the Mudong Pass on the Myanmar side as it is situated exactly at the border demarcation line. The Thai Singkhon Pass is located at approximately 200 m from the borderline leaving an area of 'no man's land' between the Pass and the borderline according to the international standard. The no man's land is usually not owned or controlled by any country and the average distance should be 230 m on each side. The location of Mudong Pass next to the border is a security concern and possibly an impediment to upgrading the Pass to a permanent one as many parties expect.[5] In the recent past, consultation on the demarcation of the common border was occasionally done, and it has been Myanmar government's priority. But, little has been done to officially demarcate the Thai-Myanmar border over the past five to six decades. According to the Anglo-Siamese Treaty signed in 1868, the boundary was delineated in three maps that extend from Ranong area up to Myawaddy–Mae

[5] Based on our team's interview with key informant in Myeik on 20 February 2018.

Sot, which should make it easier to determine the borderlines than in the upper areas (Mizzima 2015). However, the border dispute has not been settled, as in 1999, there were clashes between Thai and Myanmar fishing boats as well as between Thai and Myanmar Naval vessels due to unclear border demarcation (Burmalibrary 1999). The Myanmar–Thailand Joint Border Committee (JBC) has not announced any resolution for border demarcation as of early 2019. The concern over the location of the Mudong Pass remains unresolved.

Whether the pass is permanent or not also affects the duration of the stay and the permitted areas to visit. Myeik authorities want their travellers to be able to go beyond Prachuap's Mueang and to stay for more than four days in Thailand. Thai travellers can go to the Tanintharyi region which includes Tanaosri (Tanintharyi old town), Myeik and Dawei (for a distance of 400 km). The period of stay is 7–14 days. The Myeik Office of Hotels and Tourism will consider reducing the Thai travellers' duration of stay and areas permitted in Tanintharyi if its request to the Thai counterpart is not positively considered.[6]

Another security concern comes from the need to have a commercial airport on the corridor. At present, Thai Air Force Wing 5 is a military airport in Prachuap. On the Myeik side, there is a commercial airport. Myanmar also developed the airport in Kawthaung, south of Myeik, to facilitate foreign travellers to visit the southern part of Myanmar. Needs to push for a civil commercial airport are expressed by the tourism sector in Prachuap who want to attract higher numbers of tourists, especially from China, to Prachuap and further to Myeik when the pass is permanent and international. At present, no discussion on the possibility of developing a commercial airport in Wing 5 is being held.

10.6.3. Sustainability

The Prachuap–Myeik Corridor has great potential to prosper and become a major link of connectivity in the southern corridors of mainland Southeast Asia. People mobility and accumulation on

[6] Based on our team's interview with Head of Myeik Hotel and Tourism Office on 20 August 2018.

the corridor will continue alongside the ASEAN vision on connectivity that includes regulatory excellence, seamless logistics and sustainable infrastructure. Mutual efforts are being made to lessen restrictions on travel between Prachuap and Myeik and facilitate travellers by providing tourist information on the corridor. Cooperation among universities of both the countries on tourist itineraries, infrastructure and services for tourists and capacity building for language skills are examples of existing initiatives. Enthusiasm expressed by the governments, the private sectors and the people on both sides illustrates the commitment of all stakeholders. Master plans on logistics, trade, investment and tourism and their current implementation ensure the sustainability of the connectivity. Few identified security concerns will not stop the links. Geographically, the route Prachuap–Myeik connects the Bay of Bengal and the Gulf of Thailand. There are strong possibilities that the corridor will not only link people in the intra-ASEAN region but also in the ASEAN-BIMSTEC inter-region. Capacity building, including the appropriate technologies, labour and skills which are ASEAN initiatives for people mobility, is taking shape. The dynamism of changes occurs steadily on this corridor due to its geo-economic location, which is synergistic with the Chinese BRI and its maritime Silk Road (Jetin 2017). The joint venture between China and Myanmar for the construction of Kyaukphyu deep sea port in southern Rakhine State will increase human flow and expand the corridor to the west in the near future. The number of travellers on the corridor is increasing every year. However, one has to bear in mind that migration in ASEAN is complex, multifaceted, multidimensional and compounded by sociopolitical and economic changes that are unpredictable (Chantavanich, Middleton and Ito 2013, 8–9). People move on the corridor for various reasons and with different patterns of mobility. Careful design to facilitate the movement of people for tourism, trade, investment and employment will bring about real intra-ASEAN connectivity in a sustainable manner.

REFERENCES

Asian Development Bank (ADB). 2010. *Strategy and Action Plan for the Greater Mekong Subregion East–West Corridor*. https://www.

adb.org/publications/strategy-and-action-plan-greater-mekong-subregion-east-west-economic-corridor

———. 2017. *Tourism Assessment Strategy and Roadmap for CLMV 2016–2018.* Manila: Asian Development Bank.

Asian Research Center for Migration and Centre for European Studies. 2017. *Policy Development on the Problems of Illegal, Unreported and Unregulated Fishing, Forced Labour and Human Trafficking in Sea Fisheries 2016.* Bangkok: Chulalongkorn University.

Association of South East Asian Nations (ASEAN). 2016. *Master Plan on ASEAN Connectivity 2025.* Jakarta: ASEAN.

Boutry, M., and J. Ivanoff. 2009. *La Monnaie des Frontieres: Migrations Birmanes Dans le Sud de la Thailande, Structure des Reseaux et Internationalisation des Frontieres.* Bangkok: Institut de Recherche sur l'Asie-du-Sud-Est Contemporaine.

Burmalibrary. 1999. 'Thai-Burma Accord to End Sea Dispute'. 21 February. http://www.burmalibrary.org/reg.burma/archives/199902/msg00450.html

Chantavanich, Supang. 2019a. 'Thailand's Challenge in Implementing Anti-trafficking Legislation: The Case of the Rohingya'. *Journal of Human Trafficking* 6: 234–243.

———. 2019b. 'Myanmar–Thailand Economic and Political Corridors: From Battlefield to Marketplace'. In *Handbook of International Migration.* London: Palgrave Macmillan.

Chantavanich, S., S. Laodamrongchai, and S. Stringer. 2016. 'Under the Shadow: Forced Labour among Sea Fishers in Thailand'. *Marine Policy* 68 (June): 1–7.

Chantavanich, S., C. Middleton, and M. Ito, eds. 2013. *On the Move: Critical Migration Themes in ASEAN.* Bangkok: International Organization for Migration and Chulalongkorn University Asian Research Center for Migration and Chula Global Network.

Chutintaranond, S., and Than Tun. 1995. *On Both Sides of the Tenasserim Range: History of Siamese-Burmese Relations.* Bangkok: Institute of Asian Studies, Chulalongkorn University.

Collis, Maurice.1936. Siamese White. London: Faber and Faber. p.42.

Department of Foreign Trade, Thailand. 2017.'Border Trade Statistics'. http://www.dft.go.th/bts/trade-statistics/cid/153/-4

International Organization for Migration. 2019. *Thailand Migration Report 2019.* Bangkok: IOM.

Ivanoff, J., M. Boutry, and S. Chantavanich. 2017. 'Adaptation et Resiliences des Pratiques Esclavagistes en Thailande et en Birmanie'. [Adaptation and Resilience of Slavery Practices in Thailand] *Anthropologie et Societes* 41, no. 1: 29–49.

Jetin, B. 2017. 'One Belt-One Road Initiative and ASEAN Connectivity: Synergy Issues and Potentialities'. Institute of Asian Studies, Universiti Brunei Darussalam.

Kaewkuekoonkit, A., and S. Chantavanich. 2018. 'Rohingyas in Thailand: Existing Social Protection in Dynamic Circumstance'. *Asian Review* 33: 5–24.

Kerr, A. 1933. 'Notes on a Trip from Prachaup (Kaw Lak) to Mergui'. *Journal of Siam Society* 26, part 2: 203–214.

Khine, N. K. 2007. *Migration as a Development Strategy: A Case Study of Remittance Flows from Thailand to Mawlamyine, Mon State, Myanmar*. Bangkok: International Development Studies Program, Chulalongkorn University.

Kosem, Samak. 2016. *Border Twists and Burma Trajectories: Perceptions Reforms and Adaptation*, p. iii. Chiang Mai: Center for ASEAN Studies, Chiang Mai University.

Lebel, L., S. Chantavanich, and W. Sittitrai. 2018. 'Floods and Migrants: Synthesis and Implications for Policy. In *Living with Floods in a Mobile Southeast Asia: A Political Ecology of Vulnerability, Migration and Environmental Change*, Routledge Studies in Development and Migration, edited by C. Middleton, R. Elmhirst, and S. Chantavanich. Oxford: Routledge.

Mills, J. A. 2006. 'The Swinging Pendulum: From Centrality to Marginality—A Study of Southern Tenasserim in the History of Southeast Asia'. *Journal of The Siam Society* 85, parts 1 and 2: 35–58.

Mizzima. 2015. 'Thai-Myanmar Border Demarcation on the Horizon'. 10 May. http://www.mizzima.com/news-opinion/thai-myanmar-demarcation-horizon

Myanmar Ministry of Hotel and Tourism. 2013. *Myanmar Tourism Master Plan 2013–2020*. http://tourism.gov.mm/wp-content/uploads/2018/06/Myanmar-Tourism-Statictics-2017.pdf

Myanmar Times. 2018. 'Development of New Airport in Kawthaung Opposite to Ranong'. November 21.

National Security Council. 2012. *Policy on Citizenship for Displaced Thai People*. National Security Council.

Pawakhapan, N. 2015. *Narrative of Mong Tai: Dynamism of a Thai-Myanmar Border Town*. Chiengmai: Center for ASEAN Studies, Chiengmai University.

Phongpaichit, P., S. Piriyarangsan, and N. Treerat. 1998. *Guns, Girls, Gambling, Ganja: Thailand's Illegal Economy and Public Policy*. Chiengmai: Silkworm Books.

Prachuab Provincial Labour Report.2016. Labour Statistics 2016. Online News.

Talk News online. 2019. 'Myanmar Migrants Smuggled to Thailand via Prachuap'. 27 February. https://www.talknewsonline.com/107643/#.XHeZEihHrQZ.lineme

World Bank. 2017. Bilateral remittance matix 2017 (Thailand-Myanmar), Washington, D.C

CHAPTER 11

TANINTHARYI–TANAOSRI BUSINESS DEVELOPMENT

Views of Local Entrepreneurs

Suthiphand Chirathivat and Sineenat Sermcheep

11.1. INTRODUCTION

This chapter aims to find facts of business development on the ground through interviews of home-grown and well-versed entrepreneurs in both Thailand's Tanaosri and Myanmar's Tanintharyi regions. Regardless of whether they are first- or second-generation businesspersons doing business in the region, it is always interesting to learn how they started from scratch, evolved almost from nothing to build up successful business empires and solidly established all sorts of business activities despite their hardships and difficulties in the political and economic environment, more on Myanmar's side than on Thailand's side.

There are preliminary questions abound, like how they had sailed their businesses through such changing business conditions, especially between Thailand's Tanaosri and Myanmar's Tanintharyi regions, in bad and good times. While all the three entrepreneurs are operating their businesses, at least, in the scope between regions of the two countries, it is also interesting to know how they operated all kinds of activities and how they overcame barriers.

For sure, in these quite disconnected regions, there are more multi-dimensional problems to deal with, which require putting real efforts to move the business in the right direction. Seeing opportunities and taking risks is always the name of the game and perhaps more in these particular regions of Myanmar and Thailand. There is no defined model of business in these two regions. The only way is to make devoted efforts and find ways to get things done through the system. The regions have had quite a tough past with conflicts in administration and among different ethnic groups. Ethnics groups still have some control in these areas, especially on Myanmar's side. Therefore, running and expanding businesses at present and in future in the Association of Southeast Asian Nations (ASEAN) mode of integration might be as challenging as in the past. However, we can see from the interviews of the three major entrepreneurs in the region that those who are ready to put in efforts can not only sustain the businesses but also go far enough and succeed.

11.2. INTERVIEW WITH KHUN WANSIN, MYANMAR–THAI ENTREPRENEUR IN MYEIK

The interview was taken on 21 February 2018. Khun Wansin is a Myanmar–Thai entrepreneur in Myeik. His fishing boats' shipyard is located next to the mangroves area, just a few kilometres outside of Myeik. It is one of the major sites for building and repairing fishing boats and has expanded quite significantly in recent years. The site, also his office, can host work for over a hundred fishing boats with sizes varying from 20 to 100 tonnes. The owner seems to be very confident about his future business, in addition to what he has already achieved. He has expanded his business into other business activities like construction materials, aquaculture, fishing, rubber plantation, land development and others (interview with Khun Wansin on 21 February 2018).

Born to a father from Kawthaung, Myanmar and a mother from Kraburi, Ranong, he started working as a dessert seller in Kawthaung. In his twenties, he started repairing fishing boats before starting his own business. He has double nationality, and this has helped him to travel easily between the two countries (interview with Khun Wansin on 21 February 2018).

According to him, firm business connections are strong points for anyone who would like to work in the region. He himself has made many business connections over the years. Among others, he mentioned some of his recent joint business ventures like ice-making, dried fish and cement, with influential local entrepreneurs. He said that he wants to expand his business further. He told us that a Korean firm has recently rented his land to set up a sea-weed factory. He showed us around the mountainous land where he got a long-term lease from government for rubber plantation, construction material plant, etc. (interview with Khun Wansin on 21 February 2018).

With his business in this part of Myanmar, he has been travelling from Ranong to Kawthaung, Myeik and Dawei for over 20 years and knows all the travel routes. He said that the Southern East–West Economic Corridor will make the movement easy, but he believed that maritime connectivity is still crucial for the transport of heavy goods like cement, steel and fishing products. With the recent boom in construction in Myeik, his business is growing as both cement and steel import from Thailand is increasing, but he has to compete with the Chinese. He informed us that the Chinese are coming to be part of the region, and he is well aware and prepared for it (interview with Khun Wansin on 21 February 2018).

Overall, Khun Wansin seems to believe that he still has business advantages and capabilities as he has been working in the region for long. Also, his wife is from Sam Roy Yod, Prachuap Khiri Khan, which gives him another advantage.

11.3. INTERVIEW WITH KHUN SA-NGA (GO FOOK), THAI ENTREPRENEUR IN KAWTHAUNG

The interview was conducted on 8 May 2018. Khun Sa-nga or Go Fook is one of the major businesspersons operating in Ranong. He is into oil trading, energy, ice-making and hotel industries. Given the situation of high demand for energy in Myanmar, he plans to build a power plant in Myeik by using coal as the feedstock. However, the project faced protests from the NGOs because of environmental and social concerns. He explained that his power plant will use modern technology to control the pollution from coal; however, it did not help the situation, and thus, the project was suspended (interview with Khun Sa-nga on 8 May 2018).

He also mentioned that another difficulty in the energy business is price control. The electricity price in Yangon is less than 2 baht per unit, whereas it costs 7–8 baht per unit in Myeik and Kawthaung. People in the southern part of Myanmar may want to pay equal to what people in the north pay, and the government may then step in and control the price (interview with Khun Sa-nga on 8 May 2018Khun Sa-nga).

In the Tanintharyi region, the National Power Grid has not arrived yet at Dawei, Myeik and Kawthaung. Currently, there are small power plants in Myeik that produce energy for the community, but they are unstable. Large businesses must produce their own energy by using electric generators. Alternative energy sources such as solar and wind power can be used only for lighting as they are not sufficient to power heavy machinery in the factories.

Besides the energy business, Khun Sa-nga is in hotel business. He started from oil business and then became owner of Grand Andaman, a hotel with a casino on Son Island (Thahtay Kyun Island). He gets a concession on Son Island and runs the hotel, while his business partner plays a role in casino management. He plans to expand the hotel and turn the extension into a 'green hotel'. He also plays a role in promoting Kawthaung's tourism by promoting new tourist attractions in Kawthaung's area such as Cocks Comb Island and encouraging Tanintharyi's government to facilitate the immigration process for tourists (Interview with Khun-Sa-nga on 8 May 2018).

He believes that the development of tourism in Kawthaung should be in cooperation with the Tanintharyi region. For Ranong, it can be promoted as the province from where you can travel to both the countries—Thailand and Myanmar. Myeik can become a hub for fishery. Kawthaung also has its own fleets, but smaller ones. He suggests that we need to utilize the potential of each area in the regional development plan (interview with Khun Sa-nga on 8 May 2018).

To develop Kawthaung–Ranong and the whole Tanintharyi region, the governments of both Myanmar and Thailand have to improve: first, the soft infrastructure such as laws and regulations; and second, the hard infrastructure by building and improving roads, especially in Myanmar, and increasing energy supply. He also suggests that we should improve transportation in the southern part by connecting the existing routes. For example, we should connect the rail lines between Chumphon and Ranong to transport containers to Indonesia, Bangladesh and the Middle East in the future (interview with Khun Sa-nga on 8 May 2018).

In summary, to develop the southern part of Thailand by connecting it to the Tanintharyi region, we should start with small developments such as building the rail connecting Chumphon and Ranong. This will connect the existing transportation in the west side to the southern part of Thailand. The future line will connect Ranong to Chumphon and then to Ranong port. It will be created for oil transportation and will help in saving transportation time.

11.4. INTERVIEW WITH GO TONG, THAI ENTREPRENEUR IN RANONG AND MYEIK

The interview was conducted on 6 May 2018. Go Tong is a major businessman in Ranong. His businesses cover privately owned fish market, a chicken farm in Myeik, ice-making and construction materials. He started from charcoal making business and then moved to fish trading. His business partner owns boats and ships and does fishing in Myanmar. The fleets transport aquatic animals such as fishes, squids and crabs to the trading place. They are unloaded in an area, and the buyers bid by placing price tags on the stacks that they want. The staff announce the results of the auction by placing the results on the stacks of fish or other products. The fish and other aquatic animals are bought by Thai and Malaysian buyers. Some are sent to Bangkok, Phuket, Malaysia and China (interview with Go Tong on 6 May 2018).

There are fixed periods for fishing in Myanmar's territorial waters. Only 20 per cent of fishing is allowed during the three months of the monsoon season, that is, from mid-May to mid-August. Go Tong mentioned that strict regulations at Ranong's custom office have driven Myanmar's fishermen towards Myeik's fish market. Fishing fleets in Thailand are getting smaller, and approximately 70–80 per cent of Thai fishermen have stopped fishing. Some of the Thai boats were sold to Myanmar. These boats are registered using existing boat licenses of the Myanmar fleet. This is because the Myanmar's government has stopped issuing new licenses for boats (interview with Go Tong on 6 May 2018).

Most of the workers at Go Tong's fish market are Myanmarese. They stay in the building next to the fish market. The owner allows them to go back home during the closing season and gives them money to go to Myanmar. Go Tong also mentioned that most of the Myanmar labourers working in Ranong come from Dawei and Mawlamyine. They tend to work in the restaurants and rubber plantations. Those from Mandalay, Myeik and Kawthaung prefer to work in their own hometowns, and not move to Thailand (interview with Go Tong on 6 May 2018).

He feels that in the next four to five years, the fishery industry will be relocated to Myeik. Myeik is positioned to be the fishery hub for Myanmar. To prepare for this, Go Tong plans to build another fish market in Myeik, in addition to the cement shifting port which is already located there (interview with Go Tong on 6 May 2018).

Go Tong is also into the construction material business. He is a dealer of Siam Cement Group (SCG). Construction material such as cement is sent from the factory in Thung Song, Nakhon Sri Thammarat. He has a privately owned port for cement shipment, and most of the cement is shipped to Yangon, Mandalay, Dawei and Myeik. There has been an increase in demand for cement because of a rise in road, bridge, dam and real estate construction in Myanmar. Even though there are cement factories in Myanmar, the demand for Thai cement is still high because of better quality.

Go Tong also shares his view on the tourism industry and logistics in the Ranong–Kawthaung area. Ranong is famous for its hot spring and diving. Japanese tourists come to Ranong for hot springs. Chinese tourists have also started coming to Ranong, while there is only a small number of Korean tourists. Given the presence of hot springs and nature such as mangrove forest, Ranong has a high potential for medical tourism. However, Ranong still has a limited capacity for tourism because there are many protected areas such as mangrove forests, and not much land is available for construction (interview with Go Tong on 6 May 2018).

The islands in Ranong and Kawthaung areas are famous tourist attractions for diving. Nyaung Oo Phee Island is famous on Myanmar's side. Myanmarese people from the northern and middle parts of the country, that is, Yangon and Mandalay, and Thai tourists like to travel to this area.

There is an increase in demand for flights to Ranong. During the past three to four years, only Nok Air flights were available. Air Asia has recently opened a route to Ranong. Go Tong mentioned that Myeik is not yet ready to become the main port because of electricity shortage and high price of land. Ranong's port has been used mainly for shipping oil and heavy machinery.

Tong mentioned that the development of an international airport will facilitate the development of Ranong.

11.5. CONCLUSIONS: LESSONS LEARNT FROM THE THREE ENTREPRENEURS

The Tanintharyi–Tanaosri region has high potential to become the strategic area for business and regional connectivity. Given the connecting border between the Tanintharyi region in Myanmar and the Western part of Thailand, along with the advantage of linking the Andaman Sea and the Gulf of Thailand, these local entrepreneurs see opportunities to expand their existing businesses and to develop new ones.

From ASEAN's perspective, the local entrepreneurs agree that they are confident about the expansion of their businesses in the future. The key success factors for their businesses are firm business connections, complementarity in businesses and need of inputs from both sides.

An example can be seen from the case of the fishery industry, where the fleet catch fish in Myanmar and sell it at the fish trading place in Ranong, where labourers from Myanmar are hired. The fish and other seafood products are then sold to the bidders, and finally, they are delivered to the customers in Bangkok, Malaysia and China. The resources from both Myanmar and Thailand are utilized together in operating this business.

Another example is the case of construction materials such as cement and steel. Entrepreneurs from both Thai and Myanmar sides ship the construction materials from Thailand and sell them in Myanmar's markets. This expands the market for Thai businesses and facilitates infrastructure development and real estate business in Myanmar. This is one form of ASEAN's single market and production base, and more businesses can cooperate and gain an advantage in the future.

The development of the countries in the region, Myanmar and Thailand, has contributed to further economic expansion of the region; as a result, this opens up more business opportunities for both countries.

To move forward into a more developing and growing region, each local entrepreneur proposes different measures, but all contribute to the objective of seamless connectivity and readiness for business expansion. Physical connectivity via road, rail, port and maritime and institutional connectivity such as laws and regulations, immigration and custom procedures are important factors for higher level of cooperation between Thailand and Myanmar.

Energy is still a challenge for Myanmar's development. The scarcity of electricity is a constraint for large businesses and economic expansion, and thus, the National Power Grid is necessary for further economic expansion for Myanmar and Thailand.

The regional development plan is proposed as a way to develop this area because of the intertwined connectivity of the three districts in the Tanintharyi region (Dawei, Myeik and Kawthaung) and the linkage with Prachuap Khiri Khan and Ranong in Thailand. Each area has the potential to become the hub for different economic activities: Myeik as the fishery hub and Ranong as the transportation hub. The development plan at the regional level can help to identify the competitive advantages of each area and how they can contribute to each other.

From the global perspective, the Tanintharyi region in Myanmar and Prachuap Khiri Khan and Ranong provinces in Thailand have the advantages of rich natural resources and strategic locations. As they are located at the hub where the mainland ASEAN connects to the sea, this connectivity can be extended beyond the ASEAN region, especially to India, China and other parts of the world. This area is a gateway of the ASEAN to South Asia and further to the Middle East. The attractiveness of the region has already bought investors from outside ASEAN, such as a seaweed company from Korea, which is investing in Myeik.

The cooperation between the Tanintharyi region, Prachuap Khiri Khan and Ranong can create high value-added advantage for the region, such as being the fishery hub in the region and providing a unique tourism route across the peninsula, which can be the global destination for tourists.

In summation, the Tanintharyi–Tanaosri region, given the progress in connectivity and infrastructure development in the near future, will be the major economic destination for both ASEAN and the global economy. With rich natural resources, current businesses can expand, and there are many opportunities for new businesses. This is a new and prosperous destination for businesses.

REFERENCES

Interview with Khun Wansin, Myanmar–Thai Entrepreneur in Myeik (21 February 2018).

Interview with Go Tong, Thai Entrepreneur in Ranong and Myeik (6 May 2018).

Interview with Khun Sa-nga (Go Fook), Thai Entrepreneur in Kawthaung (8 May 2018).

PART IV

CONCLUSION

CHAPTER 12

CONCLUSIONS AND RECOMMENDATIONS

Charit Tingsabadh, Suthiphand Chirathivat and Prabir De

The preceding chapters have reviewed various aspects of the Tanintharyi–Tanaosri region of Thailand and Myanmar with a focus on the Andaman Sea coastline in the context of Thailand–Myanmar relations and Association of Southeast Asian Nations (ASEAN) connectivity. In this chapter, we present our conclusions and recommendations for further actions.

12.1. CONCLUSIONS

12.1.1. History and Culture

The historical review comprises three chapters with different perspectives. Thiva Supanjanya's chapter looks at the evidence of connectivity from ancient times, in geological and remote sensing data and in historical documents and local legends. Suchandra Ghosh reviews the archaeological evidence, while David Boggett's chapter looks at a more recent period, that of the Second World War, when the Japanese army occupied the area and attempted to build rail routes from Thailand to Myanmar.

12.1.2. The Trans-Peninsula Route

In terms of geography, Marid town is located at the estuary of the Tanaosri River, with many islands situated across the bay area, protecting the land from natural disasters such as tsunami; thus, Marid suffered little damage during the tsunami of 2004. It is suitable as a port, as has been the case in the past when it was a river port, and ships could travel up to Tanaosri town, the administrative centre located hundreds of kilometres inland.

From the documents related to the founding of Mow Tone town, it was a walled and moated city on the right bank of the Tanaosri River. During the reign of the Thai King Narai (2199–2231 BE), Marid was an important port city on the Andaman coast for the Ayutthaya kingdom, trading with places overseas in the Indian Ocean through the Trans-Peninsula Myeik–Prachuap route. The city declined with the decline of the Ayutthaya kingdom until the Burmese invasion in 2310 BE.

Marid was ruled by the British when Myanmar became a British colony (2367–2491 BE). Throughout this period, Marid was an important trading and strategic military centre for the British, independently administered from the rest of Myanmar, with the idea of occupying the Andaman coastline from Myanmar to Malaysia.

On the eastern coast of the region lies the Prachuap Khiri Khan province of Thailand. King Rama IV of Bangkok recognized the importance of establishing communication along the Gulf of Thailand coast, from Koh Kong at the eastern end of the Gulf of Thailand (now in Cambodia) to this town. The pair of city names, Prachuap Khiri Khan and Prachan Khiri Khet, were bestowed on these places. The location of the town was given by the order of King Rama II, as a defence post against enemies coming through the Singkhon Pass. Prachuap has a popular name of 'the Three bay' city as it is bestowed with an awesome coastline made up of no less than three beautiful bays, namely the Ao Noi, Ao Koh Lak or Ao Prachuap and Ao Manao.

Based on old local legends, the Ta Mong Lai tale reflects the port function of the city, with the names assigned to the different landmarks for navigation purposes. The important one mentioned is the 'Nang Yom Doy', a beautiful girl that foreign seamen long to see.

In summary, it can be said that the Trans-Peninsula Myeik–Prachuap route is an important trade and strategic route connecting the two sides, the Indian Ocean to the west and the

Pacific Ocean to the east, located at about the middle of the Indo-China Peninsula. Historical and archaeological evidence confirm our understanding that the route is an important connecting route even before the Buddhist era to the present. Historical evidence shows settlements along the coastline, located in relation to the Trans-Peninsula Route. In the modern period, Thiva looks at the Japanese wartime attack on the region when the Japanese forces landed on the Prachuap coast. The landing was meant not just to block the communication route to the south of Thailand but was aimed at capturing the Trans-Peninsula Route to the Andaman Sea, and to this day, the road through the Singkhon Pass is called the 'Japan Road'.

Thus, it can be concluded that the Trans-Peninsula Route has been known and used for a long time. Moving to the present period, Thiva considers that the opening of Dan Singkhon as a permanent border crossing point would be the beginning of a new era of the old vision, after having been in use for centuries in the past, to maximize the benefit of trade between the two countries.

12.1.3. Connected Histories

Suchandra Ghosh utilizes the East–West Corridor as a conceptual tool for identifying common cultural processes across mainland Southeast Asia. The choice of the region is from the northern east–west corridor to southern east–west corridor. On the Myanmar side, we have Thaton and Mawlamyine in the north and Dawei in the south, which are the major points of connectivity with Thailand. The Isthmus of Kra was also included in our study to understand the historical and cultural processes. It continued to be a coveted zone from early first millennium CE to early second millennium CE for the monarchs, merchants and monks.

The people of Lower Myanmar and Thailand were linked by three routes: the riverine route between Martaban and Haripunjaya; another from the Gulf of Martaban over Tak and Mae Sot; and a route over the Three Pagodas Pass to Kanchanaburi, Ratchaburi and Phetburi. In northwest Thailand, the Khmer garrison towns, Si Satchanalai, Sukhothai, Phitsanulok and Kamphaeng Phet, were becoming, by the 12th century, centres of silk and ceramic manufacturing, which were to find an outlet in Martaban.

A significant site in the vicinity of the East–West corridor near Mawlamyine was the place called Muttama or Martaban. Archaeological excavations provide a profile of Iron Age to mid-first millennium CE habitation in the lowlands lying between Thaton and the Bilin egress into the Gulf of Muttama. The wave-like and criss-cross design on the pottery is similar to pieces from Sampanago (16.15 n × 97.20 e) some 20 km southwest of Thaton in Thailand; similar shards are seen at Ban Khu Mueang, Amphoe In Buri and Changwat Singburi. The form of Sampanago is similar to the Dvaravati sites of Khubua (interview with Win San 2005).

Noted scholars (Moore and Win 2014) brought together legends and artefacts to define the trading networks of the Mon State in the late first millennium and early second millennium CE. Thaton, located near the Gulf of Martaban, and Mon regions adjacent to the Gulf of Martaban were trading centres. Moving to numismatic connections, Ghosh indicates that Mon–Pegu coins influenced Mon–Dvaravati coinage in Thailand. Thaton's importance in trade with early China is also evident from Chinese sources. Evidence for the connected history with Thailand was the site of Thagara at Dawei, though archaeological evidence was scarce. However, beads, pottery and sculpture of Thagara illustrate the site's local production and trade networks. Beads include finished and unfinished pieces, round and oval spheres, tubes, biconical shapes and flat ovals. Unfinished pieces may indicate that it was also a production centre. Glazed pots underline the peninsula's long trading history with Thailand. Links to 6th–9th century CE Dvaravati cultures of Central Thailand and maritime polities in Sumatra and Java are highlighted by the Thagara local and imported images of the Buddha, beads, urns and pots.

Documentation for Dawei history expands greatly in the 10th century CE when chronicles record a dynasty from Tak ruling at Dawei. Dawei's location attracted conquest by a succession of more dominant powers: not only for Upper Myanmar but also for Lower Myanmar and Thailand. Thus, we have a 10th century line of Thai princes from Tak and later on Ayutthaya rule from 1350 CE.

Ghosh notes that the international demand for forest products and tin helped in the flourishing of the East–West Corridor. Gharuwood is found at Tenasserim in the south which was a large region connected to the Chao Phraya plain at the Maeklong River running south along the coast until it reached Chumphon province. The Kalasin region in Thailand also abounded in gharuwood. This aloe wood, sinking incense or honey incense has been in very general use in India eastward towards Southeast Asia. The forest goods were transported through an intricate network of routes from the inland sites to the coast. There were passes across the Tenasserim (Tanaosri), which were used as ways of transportation across places.

To the south, around Myeik (Mergui), Tanintharyi (Tenasserim) and the many islands off the coast, an early trading settlement is also indicated with the mention of minerals such as tin, lead and iron. Both Dawei and the Myeik–Tanintharyi areas would have been ports of call on a 'Maritime Silk Route'.

Moving further south, it may be noted that though Bengal did not produce tin, we have a profusion of bronze sculptures. Thus, it had to establish links, directly or indirectly, with tin-producing areas. As tin was a trading commodity along trans-Asiatic routes, it is possible that southeastern Bengal received its share of tin from the Isthmian tract. Situated in a strategic location between oceans, the Isthmian tract provided a halting place for traders from both directions. It is called 'crossroads of civilizations'. The region around the Isthmus not only grew as a viable maritime trading zone, but it was also an important centre of Buddhist network which saw a transition from *Mahayana* to *Theravada* Buddhism around the 12th century CE.

In the Buddhism of Southeast Asia, a sacred space is mediated by Buddhist boundary markers known as sema stones, a tradition that can be traced back to the origins of the religion in the region.

The oldest sites in Southeast Asia where archaeologists have found evidence of contact with both China and India lie in the territory of modern Thailand. The array of archaeological finds demonstrates that a swath of mainland Southeast Asia from Lower Myanmar to the eastern part of Thailand was already a crossroad for trade. For the Isthmus of Kra route, we have many sources. For the East–West Corridor, our sources from the past are limited. But even with limited sources, it is possible to weave in a story of the past movements across these multiple routes.

12.1.4. A More Recent Connection

A more detailed look at the Trans-Peninsula Route is provided in Boggett's chapter 'Development of the Thai–Burma Border Areas in the Second World War'.

During the Second World War, the Thai–Burma border areas became of critical importance to Japan, both for supplying its own troops fighting in Burma and for prosecuting the further expansion of the war into India. But, the Japanese military had other reasons to regard the —Thai-Burma border areas as essential to their interests. Only six months after the attack on Pearl Harbour, Japan had suffered a serious naval defeat at the Battle of Midway Atoll. Paradoxically, it was the defeat at distant Midway that forced the Japanese military command to reassess the importance of the Thai-Burma border areas.

Put simply, it was impossible for Tokyo to supply its armies in Burma by sea. This would have involved a long sea voyage through the Straits of Malacca and exposed all Japanese vessels to the serious risk of attack by the British navy in the Indian Ocean. Other means had to be devised to ensure supplies and provision to the Japanese forces in Burma. Shipping from Japan to Bangkok was still relatively safe and secure, due to Japan's continued control of the western Pacific sea lanes to Southeast Asia. It was simply necessary to ensure the transport of sea supplies received in Bangkok, overland through Thailand to Burma. Accordingly, the Japanese would have to develop the local trade routes into a modern communication network capable of supplying their armies in Burma. Several military projects were developed in these border areas:

- **The Thai-Burma Railway** (commonly known as the 'Death Railway'), a 415 km railway linking Nong Pladuk (on Thailand's Southern Railway line, built by the British) with Thanbyuzayat on Burma's Southern Railway.
- **The Kra Railway**, a 90 km rail link from Chumphon to Ban Khao Fa Chi (from where goods were to be transported by boat down the rivers La-Un and Kraburi to Ranong and Victoria Point (Kawthaung).

- **The Khun Yuam–Toungoo (Taungoo) Road**, a full-scale military road for transporting supplies, around 150 km as the crow flies.
- **The Chumphon–Mergui (Myeik) Road**, a roughly constructed road, over a distance of around 200 km as the crow flies, at the very end of the war when the Japanese had few resources to spare. The road was possibly intended for use as an escape route from Burma, rather than a supply road.

All these projects required construction through areas of wild jungle, bedevilled with mosquitoes and other wild fauna, far from any human habitation and medical facilities. Largely forgotten are the considerable achievements in terms of engineering that these projects engendered; so great were the technical innovations that these Japanese military projects rightly deserve to be considered the first modern infrastructure projects in these (still) inhospitable border areas. After the war, all these projects were abandoned. The British regarded Thailand as an 'enemy' country and had no intention of encouraging either trade or human interaction between the Thais and their newly recovered colony. The British army removed the tracks of the Thai-Burma Railway in order to repair the railways damaged by the war in Burma; and then sold the much depleted remains to the Thai government as 'war reparations' for an exorbitant price. The Kra Railway had been abandoned by the Japanese before the end of the war due to heavy Allied bombing raids (the line ran through very exposed territory). The Khun Yuam–Toungoo road is barely passable even by four-wheel drive vehicles or military trucks, and only today is the Myeik Road being considered for possible construction. Boggett also looks at other railways and reminds us of the largely forgotten history of the Kra Isthmus Railway, now being revived by Thailand as a connection to the Andaman Sea. As told by Boggett, the Thai-Burma Railway was not the only railroad constructed by the Japanese military to link Thailand with Burma. The first completed attempt to link the two countries' railroad systems was the much shorter Kra Isthmus Railway, extending some 90 km from the main Southern Line station of Chumphon to the village of Ban Khao Fa Chi on the small River La-Un. From this Thai rural village terminal, goods were to be loaded on to small river boats for trans-shipment along the La-un

River and the larger Kraburi River to Ranong, and thence to the southernmost town of Burma, then called Victoria Point. Today, this sizable Burmese town has been renamed Kawthaung and is known to the Thais as Ko Song.[1] Construction of the Kra Railway was started later than that of the Thai-Burma Railway but was completed first; indeed, this railway had been intended as only a temporary measure to address the problems of transporting goods into Burma posed by the slow pace of the former's construction.

Construction work on the Kra Isthmus Railway began in June 1943, and the line was completed by the end of November of the same year; however, it only operated for some 11 months before intensive Allied bombing of the extensively exposed track forced the Japanese to abandon it and concentrate their efforts on the larger Thai-Burma Railway project. Much of the steel track was at that time removed from the Kra Isthmus Railway to be used on the Thai-Burma Railway and elsewhere. The final connection that Boggett reviews is the Chumphon–Mergui (Myeik) Road. As described by Boggett, towards the end of the war, the Japanese quickly constructed another link in the hope of providing an escape route from Burma for their defeated armies. Several prisoners from the Thai-Burma Railway were used in the building of a road from Prachuap Khiri Khan (some distance north of Chumphon) on the Gulf of Siam through Tenasserim to Mergui (Myeik) on the south Burma coast. The road itself was a very basic affair.

As described by a survivor of the wartime construction effort,

> In effect, the road was little more than a sandy track through the jungle, varying in width from 15 to 20 feet. On either side ran a narrow ditch to help drain away the monsoon waters when they came.... By the end of the first week in July, the accursed road had been completed, and a Japanese lorry drove over it from Mergui to the Siamese coast.

---

[1] The present military government not only changed the country's name from Burma to Myanmar, but it also renamed most of Burma's cities, towns and villages, causing considerable confusion to outsiders unfamiliar with the country. For the sake of clarity, this article retains the old names commonly used in documents covering these events. Wherever possible, the new names have been inserted in brackets.

Nevertheless, his account of the Mergui Road is important for detailing some of the smaller, but now forgotten, Japanese military construction projects.

12.1.5. The Regional Perspectives

Since the Southern East-West Economic Corridor (SEWEC) involves, in the first instance, two countries which share a common border, Thailand and Myanmar, it is appropriate to begin with Myanmar's perspectives on the area. In the ASEAN context, however, the extended western part of the corridor is India, as part of the wider western region. Here, we summarize the two chapters included in this book.

Mu Mu Theint, from Myanmar, argues that 'SEC and EWEC connectivity projects are of strategic importance for Myanmar' since Dawei, Myeik, Kawthaung and Myawaddy are trading hubs and they have to be well connected to outside areas, and the resulting connections would definitely be beneficial for Myanmar, Thailand, India, ASEAN and Asia. Although there are many challenges for Myanmar in achieving positive outcomes on the project, it is better to respond to the opportunities offered by its geographical and natural advantages to have competitive advantages through the global market chain. Therefore, the economic integration depends on guidelines or policy frameworks and strong political desire to set and agree on a common and shared vision to integrate their economies themselves. Her chapter reviews statistics on trade, natural resource and economic activities to indicate that the SWEC is an important area that has the potential to develop extensively if the region is highly integrated into the international trading system through the enhanced connectivity that is the subject of the book. Thus, Theint offers the view:

> Tanintharyi Region is also strategically linked to the East–West Economic Corridor and is logistically important for trade between the Gulf of Thailand and the Andaman Sea. Businesses from Tanintharyi region and Kayin state are mainly based on primary products rather than producing value-added products. Major export products are rubber, natural gas, wood products, jade and gems, and livestock and fisheries. Encouraging formal export is one of the appropriate

> strategies for the country, therefore, it is required to investigate further detail strategic plan to penetrate and to create products as per international conventions related to export control. Capacity-building and training should be provided to enhance the quality of products to meet international requirements. The government needs to encourage local businesses to come up with new export items.

However, Theint also raises a number of issues that could be an obstacle to such a development.

> Implementing effective trade policies to determine how short-term gains from natural resource trade should be efficiently utilised to ensure long-term sustainability... In order to improve trade facilitation, the government need to simplify import/export and customs inspection procedures, eliminating the licensing system, cooperating with finance authorities for faster processing of financial transactions, providing trade credits, etc. Emphasis should be on the signing of bilateral, and if possible multilateral trade agreements with as many countries as possible....

In addition, Theint considers the issues of human and natural resources.

> Regarding socio-economic development, the government should provide educational programmes and increase investment in the human resource within the country. Improvement in electricity infrastructure should also be made... Legal framework for environmental protection should be in place... In terms of land policy, land grabbing and commercial investment in the 1970s and 1980s drove a large-scale displacement of people. Access to land remains a complex and pertinent issue in Tanintharyi even today, as is also evident from the high number of land disputes being led by some Township Administrations.

On implementation issues, Theint has the following observations:

> According to the SEZ registration list, there is a limited number of official registration in DSEZ, Myeik, Myawaddy. The government encouragement is needed to engage a private firm to develop and manage the SEZ, but the state must be an active player in improving transport, electricity, water,

> telecommunications, waste disposal, and other infrastructure to link the SEZ to the global economy.

Theint concludes with the important observations that:

> From the policy perspective, aimed at transforming the SEC and EWEC into economic corridors, it would be more fruitful to concentrate on how aspects linked to the political, institutional and regulatory environment have affected efficiency and effectiveness of stakeholders from different industries who have significant operations in Dawei, Myeik, Kawthaung and Myawaddy ports.... Among the ports, Dawei, Southern part of Myanmar is targeted as an export-oriented port and there is a potential to transform it as the major connectivity point between mainland South-east Asia and South Asia. Thailand-Myanmar ASEAN integration could be enhanced with physical infrastructure development and effective institutional arrangement.

12.1.6. The Wider Context: Looking West to India

Prabir De's chapter provides a more extended scope for considering the SEWEC. Reviewing current India's Look East Policy, the author highlights the possibilities for development that the SEWEC can bring by providing greater connectivity to India in particular and more broadly to the maritime South Asia.

> Greater connectivity between the Bay of Bengal countries can yield numerous benefits. Larger markets can bring about economies of scale in production and enhance competitiveness. Integration of markets can facilitate the movement of production networks and attract more foreign investments along with the benefits of knowledge and technology transfer and opportunities to connect to regional and global supply chains.... India's trade with Southeast and East Asia has increased considerably over the past two decades or so. To facilitate the trade, India's connectivity, although at present at an initial stage of development, may appear as a great facilitator of global integration in coming years.

De makes a specific reference to Myanmar:

> Connectivity improvement in Myanmar is essential for a stronger connectivity between South and Southeast and

> East Asia. In Southeast Asia, Thailand's connectivity with Myanmar is expected to provide cost effective and efficient logistic services to promote trade and development, not only in the Southeast Asia but also between India and Southeast Asia.

With reference to India, De makes remarks that

> In particular, India's relation with Southeast Asia is firmly embedded in culture, commerce and connectivity in the backdrop of the 'Act East Policy' (AEP). India recently celebrated the 25 years of its partnership with ASEAN. India's connectivity projects with Southeast Asia have been perused in three ways: first, physical connectivity projects; second, soft infrastructure to make the physical connectivity smooth and functional; and third, financing schemes to implement the connectivity projects as well as generate new investments. Thailand's connectivity with Myanmar is, therefore, likely to supplement India's connectivity effort and strengthen the India-ASEAN physical linkages in multifaceted ways.

12.1.7. Myanmar–Thailand Connectivity Projects: Regional Cooperation Implications

The following economic and transport corridors are being investigated to strengthen bilateral (between Thailand and Myanmar) and regional (India–ASEAN or Bay of Bengal Initiative for Multi-Sectoral Technical and Economic Cooperation [BIMSTEC]) connectivity.

- Eastern economic corridor from Thailand to Myanmar
- Singkhon/Prachuap border crossing to Myeik
- Ranong to Victoria Point

De makes the following important observation:

> Connectivity projects between Myanmar and Thailand are unique regional cooperation initiatives in terms of geographical contiguity and access to the ocean. The aforesaid envisaged projects are directly connecting Thailand and Myanmar with the Bay of Bengal community. These corridor projects have far-reaching implications in terms of trade, connectivity and regional integration.

To elaborate,

> the connectivity projects have the potential to convert the Bay of Bengal as a Development Triangle … in view of new connectivity projects in the region, the scope for further cooperation is very high … with zero inter-state political or border dispute on continuous basis in Bay of Bengal, countries are motivated to speed up the integration process, both within and across the region.

De makes the following specific proposals with reference to India:

> Port Blair shall be connected with Ranong and Phuket with direct flights. Port Blair has an international airport. While the Port Blair airport does not have adequate resources for night landing facilities of aircraft, by allowing international flights to operate from Port Blair, it can facilitate tourism. Besides, some of the popular tourist places such as Penang and Langkawi in Malaysia, Sabang in Indonesia, etc. can also be connected with Port Blair through cruise and air linkages… Visa facilitation in the form of a regional arrangement should be promoted. India's e-Visa along with Thailand's visa on-arrival experiences may be shared with the region… To handle the increased ocean cargoes, particularly between ASEAN and India, we need to improve the efficiency of existing ports in the eastern coast of India as well as develop existing ports as hub ports in the Bay of Bengal …New shipping routes may emerge between India (Chennai, Vizag and Kolkata) and Myanmar and Thailand. Countries in the Bay of Bengal need to advance the multi-modal physical connectivity (air, rail, roads and waterways) and agree to a Coastal Shipping Agreement in the Bay of Bengal.[2] Greater port connectivity between Colombo and Ranong or Colombo and Dawei would be required to strengthen the port and shipping networks. Besides, we need to design port and shipping plan to connect Port Blair, Ranong, Kolkata, Haldia, Chennai, Vizag, Dhamra, Dawei, Klang, Singapore, Colombo, etc.

---

[2] BIMSTEC Coastal Shipping Agreement (BCSA) is presently being negotiated by the member countries. The BCSA is proposed to deal with cargo ships and applicable up to 20 NM. The First Working Group Meeting of the BCSA was held at New Delhi from 28 to 29 November 2017 at Delhi. Member countries have agreed to complete the negotiation of BCSA at the earliest.

> Tariffs do not appear to be the major barrier to trade. It is the non-tariff issues, which are holding back the growth of trade …. FTA in the Bay of Bengal may certainly activate the production links between the countries, which would ultimately generate regional value chains, thereby more regional trade in circle … the Bay of Bengal countries such as Bangladesh, India, Thailand, Myanmar, Malaysia and Indonesia need to link themselves through production networks and develop regional and global value chains, both in goods and services. Regional value chains (RVCs) should be looked at as building blocks to global value chains. The creation of RVCs will depend on a host of factors. One such factor lies in the ability of firms to capitalise on existing resources and opportunities…. Investment cooperation should be accorded high importance and priority to strengthen intra-regional investment in the Bay of Bengal. India's economic reforms, in the last three years, have resulted in higher FDI flows…. Improved air connectivity is an important catalyst for promotion of tourism and services trade. Bay of Bengal countries should facilitate air connectivity, particularly to link India's Northeast and Andaman Islands with Myanmar, Thailand.

De also points out issues that should be kept in mind, in that they can impact negatively the benefits of enhanced connectivity. These are the 'Non-Traditional Security Threats'.

> Security is indivisible, whether it is the security of sea lanes of communication in the Bay of Bengal region or the persisting challenges of terrorism and transnational crimes. The Bay of Bengal countries face severe security threats like smuggling, human trafficking, fake currency, drugs and piracy, etc. Countries need deeper regional cooperation in strengthening security in Bay of Bengal region, particularly, to stop smuggling, human trafficking, fake currency and drugs.

In addition, a common interest that binds the countries of the region together is 'Disaster Management and Emergency Response'.

> Disaster risks and vulnerabilities have no national boundaries. Any major disaster like Tsunami can have a devastative effect beyond borders. Most of the Bay of Bengal countries have been experiencing weather and vulnerability to natural

> disasters. Several studies have also demonstrated that disasters particularly affect the poorest and most marginalised people, widening social inequalities and harming economic growth.
>
> We need an early warning system for the Bay of Bengal region as well as technical support to the disaster management force.

12.1.8. Focus on the Region

In our focus on the region, we consider the following topics that are important for understanding the preconditions for enhanced connectivity and the existing situation that can be seen as favouring the opportunities for it. The issues are infrastructure, sectoral development, fishery, tourism and trade and investment opportunities arising therefrom. We also looked at cross-border labour issues which are of special importance in the region.

12.1.9. Infrastructure

Wiwat's chapter provides an overview of the infrastructure issues. Over the past few decades, there have been numerous visions and master plans around the Thailand–Southern Myanmar border, but none are spot on. The SEWC somehow finds itself within a huge void between the two eminent organizations, the Asian Development Bank (ADB) and ASEAN, and needs to make its presence relevant in the foreseeable future.

12.1.9.1. Roads within Southern Myanmar

12.1.9.1.1. Mawlamyine–Mudon–Ye–Dawei

This 316 km northernmost section is part of the ASEAN Highway (AH 112). It was mostly a secondary road suitable as a supply route. A 90 per cent all-weather road, it normally took 7.5 to 8 hours to traverse its length.

12.1.9.1.2. Dawei–Thayetchaung–Palaw–Myeik

This 260 km mid-section is also a part of AH 112. It was also a secondary road suitable as a supply route, with an attainable average speed of 30 kph. The time to traverse this whole length was 8 hours. Altogether, there were 46 single-lane bridges and five toll gates. The purpose of toll gates for such a road in such conditions remains a riddle to the author.

12.1.9.2. Roads between Southern Myanmar and Thailand

There are at present two main routes linking Southern Myanmar and Thailand: one between Dawei and Kanchanaburi, and another between Myeik and Prachuap. Currently, these routes are mostly undergoing construction and/or rehabilitation at different stages.

12.1.9.2.1. Dawei–Kanchanaburi via Phu Nam Ron

The 138 km Dawei–Phu Nam Ron road link is part of Myanmar's 196 sq. km Dawei Special Economic Zone (SEZ) development, as per the contract between the Myanmar government and Italian–Thai Development PCL (ITD). Though far from satisfactory, the road has somewhat activated movement of people and revitalized the local economy.

12.1.9.2.2. Myeik-Prachuap Connection

This Myeik–Prachuap connection consists of an approximately 180 km road section between Myeik and the *Special Temporary Checkpoint* of Dan Singkhon opposite the Myanmar border town of Maw Daung, plus some 25 km road length between Dan Singkhon and the Prachuap Central Business District (CBD).

12.1.9.3. Railways: Thailand

Of the 4,000 km railway track in Thailand, nearly a quarter of the length lies in the southern peninsula region. However, these tracks are almost exclusively close to the eastern coast along the Gulf of Thailand. Line connections between the existing tracks on the gulf side to the Andaman coast are being studied, starting with the Chumphon–Ranong Line.

12.1.9.4. Southern Myanmar Rail

The metre-gauge Tanintharyi Line operated by Myanma Railways (MR) runs from Mawlamyine (approximately 310 km north of Dawei) to Dawei. The track running south from Ye, halfway between

Mawlamyine and Dawei, is reportedly treacherous. There are yet no service freight trains from Mawlamyine to Dawei. Rail links between Thailand and Myanmar are either in the process of being considered for resurrection (such as the 110 km Thanbyuzayat—Three Pagodas Pass in Myanmar to connect with the 153 km Three Pagodas Pass–Nam Tok in Kanchanaburi, Thailand), or are in the planning stages. In February 2018, yet another feasibility study final report was presented to the public. The Feasibility Study on Economics, Engineering and Environment on the Chumphon–Ranong rail connection was conducted by the Office of Transport and Traffic Policy and Planning (OTP). Vital characteristics of the line are as follows: 103 km in length, mostly alongside Department of Highway No. 4 between Chumphon and Ranong Port, plus a 5 km spur into Ranong township; single-track; 9 stations; approximately 6,000 passengers in the first year of operation and 12,000 in the year 2030; approximately 33,000 TEUs freight during the first year and 85,000 TEUs by the year 2030; project cost 45,300 million Thailand baht (THB) (approximately US$1,400 M); economic internal rate of return (EIRR) 12.20 per cent.

12.1.9.5. Ports

It is interesting to note here that there are a number of private piers along the Ranong coast just south of Ranong Port. A few piers are used to facilitate boat travel across the Kraburi River.

12.1.9.5.1. Prachuap Pier Co. Ltd at Bang Saphan

Logistically, the port could serve as an intermodal maritime connection terminal for goods transport either from Prachuap or from Ranong via Chumphon.

12.1.9.6. Flights at Dawei, Myeik and Kawthaung Airports

Notable is the only international flight, scheduled twice weekly between Myeik and Bangkok (Don Mueang), which is operated by NewGen Airlines (a Bangkok-based company) and commenced its scheduled operation in February 2018.

Introduction of a bigger plane by Air Asia plus increasing popularity of the province's attractions as well as the greater prospect to travel across the border to Kawthaung and its many pristine archipelagos, such as Cocks Comb Island (The Heart Island) and Nyaung Oo Phee Island, will certainly add a lot more to these figures in the years to come.

12.1.10. Sectoral Development

12.1.10.1. Trade and Investment Opportunities

Myeik is the land of trade and investment opportunities, but it is locked. The factors that make this land full of opportunities are geographic location and abundance of natural resources. Myeik offers many business opportunities, especially natural rubber, crude palm oil, fisheries, agricultural product and food processing industry, birds' nest, pearls, tourism, and last but not the least, energy and mining.

Additional factors that make this region even more interesting are as follows: demographic structure; purchasing power; culture; and history. The workforce of individuals aged 14–65 in the area is still abundant. With the level of economic development that has taken place in the past, the purchasing power of these populations will continue to rise. Another factor that will make the tourism sector in this area even more prominent is the richness in terms of culture and history.

However, to unlock these hidden trade and investment opportunities, cooperation between Thailand and Myanmar is essential for accelerating the implementation. In this regard, the following three dimensions are most important. First, upgrading the status of the Singkhon–Maw Daung Pass to an International Permanent Border Crossing Point with the help of local government and local collaboration is a must. Second, upgrading the physical connectivity (such as seaport and highway) to connect Prachuap Khiri Khan and the Tanintharyi region is also equally important. Better infrastructure in terms of physical connectivity from Myeik to Samut Sakhon will reduce transportation time from 30–57 hours to just 6.5–8 hours and cover a distance of only 480 km (reduction from the current route with 850 km). Last but not the least, institutional connectivity in the form of trade facilitations (such as customs clearance procedures, immigration procedures, standards and commencement) is also the most important in order to make a real connectivity happen.

For private sectors, to utilize these hidden opportunities, there are 10 key success factors to bear in mind for doing trade and investment in this area. These are (a) need to have a business plan and know about consumer behaviour in each market; (b) necessary to have local business allies; (c) study logistics and communication routes; (d) have cash reserves and working capital; (e) study the payment system and foreign exchange transactions; (f) study the business environment; (g) study laws, rules and regulations; (h) workers need to have their skills further developed; (i) cultivate good community relations, where prudent and sustainable investment policy is a must; and (j) learn about external factors beyond your control.

12.1.10.2. Fisheries

From the 1960s to the mid-1990s, Myanmar's fishery production was mostly capture production, slowly increasing over the period. A break in the trend was seen in 1996, perhaps as part of the Asian Financial Crisis. Later, the production increased rapidly and divergence between total and capture production became noticeable. Capture production seems to be stabilized since 2005 at around 2 million metric tonnes, while the total production increased due to aquaculture. In the ASEAN context, Myanmar is a major producer of fishery products, second only to Indonesia. With a long coastline of 1,930 kilometres, Myanmar is well endowed with fishery resources. The Tanintharyi region is well endowed with a large fishing ground within Myanmar. In terms of fishing vessels, the data show variation between different regions of the country. The Rakhine region has the highest number of non-powered fishing boats, but Tanintharyi has the highest number of powered fishing vessels. Most of the powered vessels have a capacity of less than 5 tonnes to 5–9.9 tonnes. The Tanintharyi region is probably the largest contributor to overall production of capture fishery in Myanmar, given its location in the Andaman Sea and being open to the Indian Ocean.

About 70 per cent of the fish landed in Myanmar is for direct human consumption, mostly as fresh and chilled, while some are frozen or cured, and about 10 per cent is processed into fish meal. According to FAO (2012), domestic demand accounts for 90 per cent of production, and 10 per cent is for exports. China is the largest market for Myanmar's fishery export in terms of value, but Thailand accounts for the highest volume. Other markets are Singapore, Malaysia and Saudi Arabia.

According to the Ministry of Commerce, the total border trade between Myeik and Thailand in 2012–2013 was valued at US$125 million with seafood as one of the major export products. It is estimated that about 70 to 75 per cent of the total fisheries production in Myeik was sold via the Myeik–Thailand border in 2013.

The research team found that Ranong was an important landing port for Myanmar fish. Catches landing at Ranong would be purchased and sent on to various destinations both within Thailand and Malaysia. According to a newspaper report, most fish landing at Myeik is destined for foreign markets (Hulst 2015).

Coming to trade in fishery products, the Thai official data show that for the period 2016–2018 (January–June), fishery products account for around 30 per cent of non-natural gas import from Myanmar, rising from only 10 per cent in 2015. This indicates the importance of fishery products from Myanmar in the total trade. Of specific relevance to the fishery sector, Ranong is an import channel for trade: export of general merchandise, mainly cement and machinery for the construction sector, in Myanmar occurs from Ranong, while the cross-border trade data for Ranong show the highest import figures in the non-natural gas sector, and it is likely to be due to the fishery products that pass through here.

For Prachuap Khiri Khan, the total trade volume is still small. This is because the border crossing, the Singkhon Border Crossing point, is currently a temporary one. It is also constrained by the lack of good roads between Prachuap and Myeik, which are the main market centres on each side of the border.

However, this is likely to change once the border crossing point is upgraded to be a permanent border crossing point, and the roads are improved. Regarding the future prospects of the fishery sector, Myanmar local news reports indicate that there is a movement to better regulate fishery production from Myeik, so that more fish is traded within the country rather than being sold illegally in foreign ports. At the same time, from discussion with informants at Ranong, the research team learned that Ranong fishing boats have mostly scaled down their operations. Fishing businesses are also preparing to move to Myeik for investing in fishery-related activities like cold storage and processing. It is likely that with improved land transport routes from Myeik to Dan Singkhon and Prachuap Khiri Khan, Myeik will develop into a major trading and processing centre for fishery products.

There is concern about overfishing in Myanmar as a whole. Problems are reflected in reduced catches by local fishermen and in the overall statistics. The FAO (2012) report cites an early (1980–1983) estimate of 1.05 million tonnes of the maximum sustained yield and then compares it with landing amounts that were 50 per cent higher, and the statistics cited at the beginning of this paper show production at 2 million tones. Clearly, there will be long-term problems that need to be addressed to sustain the fishery sector in Myanmar. Of special relevance is that improved physical connectivity would support Myanmar in its development and overall ASEAN development through trade and exchanges of labour, knowledge and shared vision of greater prosperity for all.

12.1.10.3. Tourism

Of special relevance to the tourism sector is the beautiful and remote Myeik Archipelago, a cluster of more than 800 largely untouched islands. Along with Myanmar's recent political transition, there is a clear sign that the region has gradually emerged and opened up to neighbouring countries and the outside world.

On the Thai side, the Tanaosri region, extending to the Gulf of Siam, is already famous for its seaside resorts and marine and farm products among the locals and even among the foreigners who come to beach resorts, starting usually from Cha-am in Phetchaburi to Hua Hin in Prachuap Khiri Khan and down to Prachuap Khiri Khan township and then to Chumphon and Ranong. In addition to other kinds of economic activities, tourism seems to be the main core of basic industries in these provinces, which also provides some trickle-down effects according to the distance and transport infrastructure that support the travellers within and outside the region.

The tourism industry of both countries has developed independently from each other since the land demarcation mark at the physical border separates the landscape of the two countries. The future, however, suggests this might not be the case given the recent changes that are taking place, particularly in Myanmar, and how such changes will certainly have a strong impact inside the country and the crowding out effect on the neighbouring country like Thailand with long common borders.

12.1.10.3.1. Tanintharyi's Tourism: Trend and Development

According to statistics from the Ministry of Hotels and Tourism, 360,835 tourists visited the Tanintharyi region in 2016. In terms of accessibility, it is not very easy to visit the region by road or rail transport, as the infrastructure is still underdeveloped. However, travelling by air is easy as its three airports—Dawei, Myeik and Kawthaung—are only a 1-hour flight from Myanmar's capital of Yangon. Only recently, direct flights began from Bangkok to Myeik.

The government of Myanmar has designated the picturesque southern state of Tanintharyi as the destination for an inclusive tourism project implemented by the International Trade Centre (ITC), and thus has allowed investments in the Myeik Archipelago. Eleven islands, out of the 800 largely untouched islands, are allowed to receive local and foreign investment to develop tourism. As per the data from the Ministry of Hotels and Tourism, cruise ships carrying 3,201 tourists visited the Myeik Archipelago between January and November 2016. More recently, the Myeik Archipelago has attracted much more tourists, both local and foreign, to its islands rich in natural resources, corals and local cultures.

One of the problems requiring attention is that the best beaches and diving spots in the Myeik Archipelago are quite far away from Dawei, Myeik or Kawthaung. Speed boats are needed to travel to these spots to save time. However, during the monsoon season which could last from May to November, this is not feasible. Special licensed boats and permits are needed to go for multiple-day excursions.

Tourism has been well developed for a long time in Thailand's Tanaosri region, particularly the upper part of the coastal and inland areas. According to the Department of Tourism,

Thailand, Kanchanaburi is the most visited province for locals, followed by Phetchaburi and Prachuap Khiri Khan, with much lesser volume for Ratchaburi, Chumphon and Ranong. In 2016, 7.66 million Thai tourists visited Kanchanaburi, while 5.56 million visited Phetchaburi and 4.03 million visited Prachuap Khiri Khan, concentrating much more in the Hua Hin area rather than in the township of Prachuap Khiri Khan. The figures for Ratchaburi, Chumphon, and Ranong were 1.62 million, 1.26 million and 0.98 million respectively.

On the other hand, regarding the number of foreigners visiting the Tanaosri region, Thailand's Prachuap Khiri Khan is the most visited province of all, with a total of 0.98 million tourists in 2016, because of the famous town of Hua Hin and its vicinities. Phetchaburi and Kanchanaburi provinces are also preferred destinations among foreign tourists with a total number of 0.48 million and 0.41 million tourists visiting these provinces respectively. The other destinations are Chumphon, Ratchaburi and Ranong with 0.11 million, 0.05 million and 0.05 million foreign tourists respectively in 2016. However, the total number of foreign tourists visiting the Tanaosri region in 2016 stands at 2.1 million, which is 6.4 per cent of the total number of foreign tourists visiting Thailand in the same year.

Thailand has its own plans to develop further infrastructure to support the development of this region. Tourism could benefit from infrastructural development such as rail, maritime and air transport. However, one needs to define further steps in terms of demand and supply of tourism infrastructure that would be necessary to meet the changing scenario and long-term trends. In the near term, Prachuap Khiri Khan, Chumphon and Ranong have doubled their efforts to differentiate their natural endowments from other tourist destinations to cater to more local and foreign tourists.

12.1.10.3.2. Way to Future Development and Tanintharyi–Tanaosri Tourism Connectivity

The tourism industry in Tanintharyi in Myanmar and in Tanaosri in Thailand needs a further boost to suit their regional development, but to a different degree, whether it is in terms of job creation, infrastructural needs or private investment, just to name a few. For Myanmar, it has to play a major role in driving Myanmar's economic development since the start of national reforms in 2011. The Tanintharyi region has been chosen as part of Myanmar's tourism development master plan 2013–2020. For Thailand, it has to develop further infrastructure to support congested destinations like Cha-am in Phetchaburi and Hua Hin in Prachuap Khiri Khan and connecting further to the lower parts of Tanaosri like the township of Prachuap Khiri Khan, Chumphon and Ranong.

More importantly, there are missing links on both sides. Tanintharyi and Tanaosri need to be connected to support further tourism, and there is a need to find a way for tourism integration and development, based on their relative strengths and complementarities. At present, the tourism industry on both sides of the region has started to make progress in terms of connecting with each other. However, their efforts might not go very far without the support of hard and soft infrastructure and connectivity in the ASEAN context, which has not yet reached a good level of understanding and implementation in the public sphere of both local and national governments. Primary efforts are being made to increase the number of tourists coming to the Myeik Archipelago in particular, with lesser impact on the environment. For instance, plans are underway to draw up a master plan for developing tourism in the region, and especially the Myeik Archipelago, with an aim to create job opportunities for local people while protecting the area's natural resources and landscape. Elsewhere in the region, other efforts are being driven to boost tourism. For example, there are efforts to attract tourists to the region's capital of Dawei which is home to colonial architecture and pagodas. Myeik is a bustling harbour town with cottage industries such as crab farming and other aquaculture activities that have a great potential to earn extra income by organizing properly guided tours. This also has to be extended to Kawthaung, the southernmost town at the tip point, which is worth a local tour before extending to island resorts. Advantages, as noted in the study, include ongoing efforts by the Japan International Cooperation Agency to create a tourism master plan for Tanintharyi.

To move to such tourism connectivity between Myanmar and Thailand, it is first and foremost important that these two countries must have a common understanding and agreement on the greater picture of wholesome development of the 'Tanintharyi–Tanaosri region'; furthermore, it should be assessed whether this connectivity and integration could foster and in what way future development need to be made, including transportation, communication, and infrastructure—roads, railways, airports, pipelines, electricity grids, internet cables and more. Regional infrastructures of both countries as one are morphing the system of the two countries ranging from division to connections and from nations to nodes.

12.2. RECOMMENDATIONS

Thailand–Myanmar Southern East–West Corridors (TM-SEWC) or the Tanaosri–Tanintharyi regions have often been addressed in bits and pieces by policymakers, but these regions have not yet been integrated in a full-fledged manner as a common region for development and integration. This study aims to prove otherwise and to fill the knowledge gap in this area. To project the future outlook of these regions, the study takes as the departure point that it is time to avoid addressing integration and development of TM-SEWC in a piecemeal or divided fashion.

Viewing from the new dynamics and changing landscape of the Tanaosri–Tanintharyi regions, the study has laid out objectives to look at challenges and opportunities in the TM-SEWC with the belief that a new initiative for both regions at the two sides of the oceans is needed beyond the present policy narrative to discover a much better potential of the regions if they come together. For this, the research has made preliminary and independent attempts to list out the priorities of the regions that need to be addressed in terms of the corridors' impact, trade and investment, resource allocation, sectoral changes and people mobility, to cite a few.

Despite the relatively small size of the land area of Myanmar's Tanintharyi region (6.37% of Myanmar) and Thailand's Tanaosri region (9.08% of Thailand), the regions are well known and rich in natural resources, and if the land area is extended to the seas, the whole meaning of the regions will change tremendously, with people living on both sides of the oceans peacefully and relatively linked back through history and culture. If connected together through the hills and mountains that divide territorial borders, flows of all sorts ranging from people to goods, services and investment, the regions will have great potential to develop and grow not only among themselves but more jointly with the rest of ASEAN and outside world.

12.2.1. TM-SEWC in the Context of ASEAN Connectivity

This is an area where both countries could come closer in the context of ASEAN connectivity and integration despite unsettled issues that remain, for instance, border issues, people migration, customs procedures and so on. The TM-SEWC needs to enhance regional development by integrating in the context of ASEAN connectivity. Government agencies on both sides responsible for such matters should come together to get an agreement first on how they would like to move further together on such an issue.

For instance, the upper corridors of AH 123 Dawei–Myittar (55.5 km) and AH 123 Myittar–Thai Border (103.5 km) have been listed as ongoing efforts that continue from the Master Plan on ASEAN Connectivity (MPAC) 2010 to the MPAC 2025. It has also included the strategy to establish an integrated and seamless multimodal transport system that will include the following: connecting the Dawei Port, conducting a feasibility study on the railway line linking Dawei Port to Kanchanaburi, developing an effective network of ASEAN dry ports in accordance with existing ASEAN initiatives such as the Asian Highway (AH) and Singapore-Kunming Railroad, and building the highway between Kanchanaburi and Dawei.

The next step to reach the ASEAN level is to integrate the TM-SEWC at a later stage, in the context of the Master Plan for ASEAN Connectivity. According to the work plan for the MPAC 2025, each initiative will consist of 3 phases of implementation, namely, Planning Phase, Phase 1 Implementation and Phase 2 Implementation. For this, it is important that the three economic corridors (upper for Dawei–Kanchanaburi, middle for Myeik–Prachuap Khiri Khan and lower for Kawthaung–Ranong) should be submitted as soon as possible for sustainable infrastructure development with the ASEAN Connectivity Coordinating Committee (ACCC) and National Coordinators (NCs), as specified by MPAC

2025. This is to establish a rolling priority list of potential ASEAN infrastructure projects and source of funds.

The project should also be able to reach the ADB for the programmes it takes on sub-regional cooperation, such as the Greater Mekong Subregion (GMS), Indonesia–Malaysia–Thailand Growth Triangle (IMT-GT) and Brunei Darussalam–Indonesia–Malaysia–Philippines East ASEAN Growth Area Brunei Darussalam–Indonesia–Malaysia–Philippines East ASEAN Growth Area (BIMP-EAGA). The role of the ADB is crucial since it provides financing and leveraging resources as well as for generating, sharing and applying knowledge. The ASEAN–ADB cooperation provides direct assistance to ASEAN to support ASEAN integration through sub-regional and country programmes. TM-SEWC should fit well within the scope of ADB sub-regional and country cooperation programmes. Maritime transport also plays an important role in TM-SEWC, which should fit well in the scope of ASEAN connectivity because of the geographic connection of Thailand–Myanmar in the area (ADB 2016, 12–15).

12.2.2. Strategy for Integration and Development

There have been rapid changes in fishing, agribusiness development, tourism, trade and investment, people mobility, construction and infrastructure development in both countries despite the missing links and overlapping development and regulations. This is an excellent time to make a turning point by enhancing the importance of the economic and transport corridors that need to be further developed from within and outside. The major issue is how to address the missing links and overlapping sub-regional economic integration on various dimensions.

12.2.2.1. Trade and Investment

The TM-SEWC has definitely high trade and investment potential that has remained untapped due to trade and investment barriers, structural differences of the economies and uncoordinated development plans; the barriers include border barriers such as customs procedures, standard controls and people mobility and other barriers such as business registration, work permit and resource use and exploitation. Therefore, a large number of obstacles need to be removed to tap trade and investment potential of all sorts in the TM-SEWC, if both countries want to turn these challenges into future opportunities.

Despite recent development and improvement, transaction costs with regard to trade and transport are still high and not very attractive for newcomers who would like to do business in the areas. For example, customs regulations at the border are not uniform among the three corridors, with the lower part, Ranong–Kawthaung, being the most developed; the middle part, Singkhon–Maw Daung, becoming more important due to its connection to Myeik; and the upper part, Kanchanaburi–Dawei section, is yet to be developed further. Non-tariff issues seem to hold back trade expansion that should have grown otherwise.

For instance, ASEAN regional integration and connectivity have not yet been able to break old barriers and serve the regions so far. The countries need to come closer and break old barriers and share responsibilities. To cite an example, Myanmar's Maw Daung Pass has been developed into an international cross-border check-point into Thailand since 2014, while Thailand's Singkhon Pass was upgraded only into a temporary border pass in 2015, which makes it difficult for people, particularly international tourists, to cross the border at this point.

As people from both sides are increasingly getting engaged in all kinds of economic activities, either through trade or through investment, the challenges remain on how these regions could fully apply the scope of ASEAN integration and connectivity to liberalize and facilitate trade and investment, despite inconsistencies in local authorities' laws and regulations in the context of ASEAN regional development.

12.2.2.2. Regional Connectivity

With Myanmar's recent opening up to the world and Thailand's Look West policy, these neglected regions of Tanintharyi–Tanaosri offer unique opportunities to address some of the overall development challenges of the two countries. For instance, transport and logistic costs make it difficult for businesses to move forward for their future development. Underdeveloped transportation and logistics, high transaction costs because of cumbersome administrative procedures, time spent on fulfilling all requirements as per the rules and regulations and unstable and insufficient power supply on Myanmar's side are impediments to smooth trade. None of the master plans around the regions seems to target all these issues.

The TM-SEWC needs to fill a huge void and make its presence felt and relevant between the MPAC 2025 and the ADB sub-regional cooperation programmes, for instance, the GMS and the IMT-GT. The potential of TM-SEWC and some of the most important missing links should be made clear to the policymakers involved. At the same time, the two governments, both national and local, and the responsible agencies should consider seriously on how to address the development and integration of the TM-SEWC in a timely fashion as the authorities of both sides will further deliver the output/outcomes of future development and integration of the regions involved.

Road linkages in SEWC presently need major revamps for speedy rehabilitation. For the north of the corridor, the two-lane road, 132 km, linking Phu Nam Ron in Kanchanaburi to Dawei in Myanmar needs improvement and reconstruction. The middle corridor, linking Dan Singkhon in Prachuap, Thailand and Myeik in Myanmar, 180 km, is undergoing construction and rehabilitation and should be able to support well the future needs of an increase in transport as newly built customs and immigration checkpoint facilities are opening soon. The south of the corridor, between Kawthaung in Myanmar and the province of Ranong in Thailand, is quite well used by vessels across the 5-km-wide Kraburi River mouth. There is a need to consider a friendship bridge at a suitable crossing point in the near future, as economic activities will become more important between the two points of the countries, which can lead to much wider connectivity in these regions and beyond.

Rail linkages in the TM-SEWC are severely lagging behind road linkages in many parts of the two countries. The big question is how to integrate the TM-SEWC into the long-term development and integration of the two countries; in particular, in terms of rail logistic development, the projects to be prioritized and well-integrated with the overall plan need to be determined. Myanmar should consider developing the rail links from upper Dawei down to Myeik and possibly to Kawthaung. For Thailand, the 103+5 km Chumphon–Ranong line with the double-track railway is in the process of being considered and adjusted through EIA. Strategically effective implementation of this will take place within the next few years, perhaps by 2022, which should extend further to cover the vision of the Andaman Rail Line as envisaged by several parties of IMT-GT working groups.

Maritime linkages in TM-SEWC are also underdeveloped and have much potential if a common plan is crafted for future development. For instance, the Ranong Port in Thailand has its own plan to connect to BIMSTEC. However, the lengthy (28 km), narrow (120 km) and shallow (8 m at the lowest tide) channel remains the challenge to be improved to handle larger vessels, in addition to a long period of underutilization. The long monsoon season also causes the Ranong Port to consider collaboration with nearby ports such as Na Kluer Port at Kantang in Trang province as well as nearby port destinations in Myanmar, such as Kawthaung, Myeik and Dawei ports—when these are better developed to handle the greater volume of cargoes. These ports should not rule out their connection to the IMT-GT sub-region. In addition, the Ranong Port, for example, should consider integrating the intermodal role for transportation on the Andaman side with ports on the Gulf of Thailand side across the Isthmus of Kra via roads and rails, where possible.

Air linkages in the SEWC region are presently restricted to only each side of the sea, with a few domestic flights from Bangkok to Hua Hin and Ranong and from Yangon to Dawei, Myeik and Kawthaung. There are attempts to start international flights between Bangkok and Myeik, but still, there are irregular flights when it comes to real operations on this route. Considering the future potential of the Andaman Sea on this side of the SEWC with the newly opened 800+ islands in Southern Myanmar, in addition to quite a few interesting island destinations on the Ranong side, much more air linkages with other towns and cities should be play out well in future development. Looking from the Thai side, for example, the Bangkok–Myeik air link could be considered next as well as more new routes from Hat Yai and Krabi linking to Ranong and Myeik.

12.2.2.3. Sectoral Development

The Tanintharyi–Tanaosri regions have the potential for the development of national resources and natural beauty. These two sectors are examples of integrated development in the future. It is interesting to observe that dynamic changes and changing landscape have already happened on the ground.

While the Thai fishing industry is facing more difficulties at home in terms of addressing illegal, unreported and unregulated fishing (IUU) and other factors, a number of Thai fishing boats and Thai entrepreneurs have already started to feel the pinch and have shifted their operations from Ranong, the most concentrated fishing piers on the Thai side of the Andaman sea, to Myeik, the hub of fishing activities on the Myanmar side, and to Dawei to a certain extent. In such a new circumstance, the Thai fishing industry and distribution on the Andaman Sea, particularly from Ranong, will need to increase international efforts to strengthen and validate the blue economy to achieve practical outcomes and to prepare for such a major shift if it will impact income, jobs and marketplace in the long run.

Myanmar's fisheries, on the other hand, have great potential due to a long coastal line; Tanintharyi alone has a coastline of around 1,200 km and more than 800 islands with rich coastal resources. In the past few years, China has moved very quickly to replace Thailand for the demand for all kinds of marine products, thus creating new dynamics and changing the landscape for future sectoral development. It seems that the Myanmar authorities, including the local district administration of the Tanintharyi region, are still to catch up with the new trends, and there is a need for a clear policy initiative to support both the fishing industry and marine resource exploitation.

Tourism industry will have a very prominent future only when the SEWC region could take common development and integration seriously in the long run. The Thai side of the Tanaosri region has already been well developed, with more development around Cha-am, Phetchaburi, and Hua Hin, Prachuap Khiri Khan; however, the region also has the potential to develop further down to the city of Prachuap Khiri Khan and then down to Chumphon and Ranong. With a better transport network, it will be able to extend the tourist tours beyond the usual destinations.

The Myanmar side of the Tanintharyi region has also become a case in point for development, with the Myanmar's government's recognition to develop further its tourism industry in the coming years. Among the three districts of administration, Kawthaung connected to Ranong will have the chance to develop its island tourism linking the Myeik Archipelago to the Thai side of Andaman beyond Ranong, like Phuket and Krabi, which are already very popular among global tourists. Myeik, as a city and destination to connect to the Myeik Archipelago, could also develop as a tourist corridor, with Prachuap Khiri Khan, if the two cities could come closer for win-win tourism development. Tourism planning for the town and islands should be well integrated for more sustainable development of tourist facilities.

Tanintharyi–Tanaosri tourism connectivity has to move beyond 'two regions of two countries'to one single entity 'one region', given their geography, with a whole new sub-regional cooperation and integration, if the two countries are brave enough to move commonly to achieve such a goal. As long as it becomes clear to policymakers and people of the two sides, Myanmar and Thailand, the 'Tanintharyi–Tanaosri region' could have the chance to succeed and reach its potential of tourism development sooner than later. Mapping out connective tourist corridors, like Dawei to Kanchanaburi, Myeik to Prachuap Khiri Khan and Kawthaung to Ranong, will help to supersede maps of national borders. This can be achieved only through the shift toward a linked tourism development where optimizing economic and social geography could supersede the preservation of territorial sovereignty.

12.2.2.4. People Mobility

Chantavanich in her chapter discussed the population links between the TM-SEWC in the Prachuap province of Thailand and Myeik in the Tanintharyi region of Myanmar. The route from Prachaup to Tanaosri and Myeik has been an old trade road since the 15th century. It links the two countries and two oceans. As ASEAN initiated its integration and people connectivity in 2016, its master plan lays emphasis on tourism and connectivity within

ASEAN through four strategies: enhance ASEAN travel, facilitate visa process, increase capacity building and support higher education exchanges. The Prachuap–Myeik Corridor has always had constant people mobility. In 2017, 94,469 Myanmarese crossed Singkhon Pass to Thailand, and 23,769 Thais crossed to Myanmar. Many of them are migrant workers and tourists. The rest comprised officials, investors, traders, academicians, students and researchers. The improved infrastructure on the corridor facilitates people mobility as well as trade and investments. Both Myanmar and Thailand have developed tourism policies in their national and regional plans during 2013–2020. The plans cover promoting sustainable tourism, upgrading trade and investment relationship, building human resources, promoting service quality, and lastly, repairing roads to reduce travel time.

Proposed strategies for integration and development on the Prachaup–Myeik Corridor can include the promotion of new types of sustainable tourism, such as medical, retiree and aquaculture tourism. Island eco-tourism, artisanal fisheries and lifestyle tourism are also strong points for the region. The development and connectivity can be enhanced by the promotion of academic and economic exchanges plus the integration of local population on both sides.Security surveillance on illicit trades and cross-border crimes, including human smuggling and trafficking, is recommended. Most importantly, upgrading Singkhon–Maw Daung Pass to an international permanent pass will facilitate the visa process and boost regional tourism. The incoming of Chinese travellers and investment in the region will be an accelerating force of connectivity and development with careful consideration and planning by ASEAN.

12.2.3. Strategic Implications from BIMSTEC, IORA and Indo-Pacific

While putting forward the importance of the TM-SEWC or Tanintharyi–Tanoasri regions to policymakers and interested parties involved, it is important to remind such connections to other regional and sub-regional frameworks that are happening around. In addition to the ASEAN Connectivity, MPAC 2025 and the ADB sub-regional cooperation frameworks, there are a few other regional scopes that merit attention to consider their possible linkages in the near future.

BIMSTEC is a unique regional cooperation initiative in terms of geographical contiguity and access to the ocean in which TM-SEWC is becoming a sub-part. BIMSTEC's objective to accelerate growth and social progress in the sub-region through joint efforts could support and complement TM-SEWC development and integration. It brings together a sizable regional economy with a view to develop the region together in a sustainable and inclusive way. For instance, BIMSTEC has made substantial progress in taking steps to energize the grouping's integration and development.

The Indian Ocean Rim Association (IORA) also offers a new collaborative opportunity to develop a long-term strategic partnership for sustainable development of the blue economy, which should also directly impact the development of Thailand–Myanmar Andaman Sea and coastal development, particularly fisheries, marine transport, mineral exploration and exploitation, marine bio-prospecting and coastal and marine tourism. All these activities are associated with the blue economy.

Last but not least, the Indo-Pacific, which involves issues related to security and beyond, with the creation of a broad regional framework will help to cement the development and integration of countries involved in TM-SEWC. For instance, ASEAN as a whole adopted the ASEAN Outlook on the Indo-Pacific at the Bangkok ASEAN Summit in November 2019, as it wants to ensure that the new broadened regionalism will strengthen the efforts of ASEAN done so far, particularly the importance of ASEAN Centrality and the balanced partnerships that ASEAN has maintained with dialogue partners, including China. However, ASEAN will need to consider any future regional and sub-regional cooperation that the ASEAN Outlook for Indo-Pacific might touch upon, like the scope of TM-SEWC.

12.2.4. Infrastructure Connecting the Missing Links

Road and rail linkages in SEWCs are presently either lacking or need major speedy rehabilitation. We present the following ideas for further consideration.

12.2.4.1. A Thailand–Myanmar Third Friendship Bridge for Ranong–Kawthaung

South of the corridor, the watery gap between Kawthaung in Myanmar and the province of Ranong in Thailand is presently quite well served by vessels across the 5-km-wide Kraburi River mouth. Nevertheless, to further facilitate international travel between Ranong and Kawthaung, a Thai-Myanmar third friendship bridge at a suitable crossing point, somewhere upstream of the Kraburi River beyond the Ranong Port, should be contemplated and studied for feasibility.

12.2.4.2. An Andaman Coastal Rail Line: Dawei–Myeik–Kawthaung

Besides the main road link via National Highway No.8, Dawei ought to be better connected to Myeik through the speedy realization of the Dawei–Myeik railway line (especially for freight and passengers)—and even through to Kawthaung at the southernmost tip of Myanmar in the long run.

12.2.4.3. Extension of the Chumhpon–Ranong Rail Link to Krabi–Kantang–Satun–Perlis

To take it even further, south of pristine Ranong lies the touristic province of Phang Nga some 230 km away, and a further 80 km, there is another touristic province of Krabi. If the line could be extended down to these provinces and then 135 km further to Kantang Station in Trang, it would complete an ideal loop to the railway line spanning provinces along the gulf coast. An idea of this Andaman Rail Line through to the province of Satun, which borders with the State of Perlis, Malaysia, has recently been floating within the IMT-GT working groups, especially by the provincial chambers of commerce.

12.2.4.4. More Private Port Development at Ranong

Regarding the intermodal role for transportation from ports on the Andaman side with ports on the gulf side across the Isthmus of Kra via roads and rails (if and when available) envisioned enthusiastically by the Ranong Port, the port should also eye other alternative private ports, such the Prachuap Pier Co. Ltd (PPC) Port at Bang Saphan, besides the ports of Port Authority of Thailand (PAT) in Bangkok and Laem Chabang.

REFERENCES

Asian Development Bank (ADB). 2016. *ASEAN–ADB Cooperation toward the ASEAN Community: Advancing Integration and Sustainable Development in Southeast Asia*. Mandaluyong: Asian Development Bank (ADB).

FAO. 2012. *Fishery and Aquaculture Country Profiles*. Yangon: FAO.

Hulst, Hans. 2015. 'Fishing for Trouble in Myeik'. *Frontier Myanmar*, 27 October. https://www.frontiermyanmar.net/en/fishing-for-trouble-in-myeik/

Moore, Elizabeth H., and San Win. 2014. 'Sampanago: City of Serpents and Muttama (Martaban)'. In *Before Siam, Essays in Art and Archaeology*, edited by Nicolas Revire, and Stephen A. Murphy, 217–237. Bangkok: River Books and The Siam Society.

Win, San. 2005. 'The History of Suvannabhumi in Kyaikto and Bilin Townships, Mon State: Results from Fieldwork (27 April to 7 June 2001, in Myanmar)'. In *Myanmar Historical Commission Golden Jubilee Collected Articles*, 258–285. Yangon: Ministry of Education.

ANNEXURE

Ranong–Kawthaung Field Visit Report

Charit Tingsabadh

This report of the Ranong–Kawthaung study trip is aimed at giving a general impression of the connection between Ranong on the Thailand side and Koh Thong on the Myanmar side, based on the field trip undertaken during the study from 5 to 11 May, 2018. Activities carried out during the trip were (a) observation tours of locations of interest, and (b) interviews with local entrepreneurs about the conditions and experience in doing business with relation to the connectivity between the two countries. The report is presented largely in the form of a photo essay.

A.1. OBSERVATION TOURS OF LOCATIONS OF INTEREST

A.1.1. Ranong Town: Fish Landing Pier, the Wartime Chumphon–Ranong Railway, the Ranong Seaport and Other Attractions in Ranong Town

Ranong town is the administrative centre of Ranong province in Southern Thailand. It is a small centre that is changing fast from a small town on the route from Chumphon to Phuket to become a tourist destination in its own right. The old town of Ranong was built on the economy of tin mining and fishing, but now, tourism is becoming increasingly important, for there are many attractions that can be visited from Ranong town. In addition, it is the border crossing point to Kawthaung town in Myanmar.

A.1.2. Fish Landing Pier

The team visited a fish landing pier to observe the activities of the fish market. Not many Thai fishing boats are active now, since the implementation of the anti-IUU fishing regulations which were introduced following the issue of the 'yellow card' warning by the EU in 2014 to Thailand. The warning was lifted early in 2019, but this effect has reduced the fishing effort by Thai fishing boats. Fish that are landed at the pier are mainly from Myanmar fishing boats. After clearing customs formalities, the fish are sorted into piles of different species, and they are then opened to buyers for auction. Buyers are from Thailand and Malaysia. From Ranong, the sold fish are sent to various destinations in Thailand and Malaysia, but perhaps not so much to China because it is further south than Myeik, which is the main centre for fish sales in this region.

A.1.3. The Wartime Chumphon–Ranong Railway

During the Second World War, the Japanese army attacked Thailand and used it as a base for waging war against the Allied forces. The Japanese army moved south and attacked British Malaya and Singapore. To the west, Japan was mounting a campaign to attack British India through Burma as it was then called. To support the east–west movement of troops and war supplies, Japan built and operated a railway line from Chumphon, on the Gulf of Thailand coast, to the Kraburi River, which marks the border between Thailand and Myanmar. The railway was attacked by bombing by the allied forces, and eventually, it was abandoned. All that remains are a few tracks that can be observed near Ranong town, and a museum located on the banks of the La-un River, at the foot of the Khao Fa Chi hill, which is on the line. The route is now used as a road, Highway No. 4, running from Chumphon to Ranong. For the future, there is a plan to rebuild the railway line from Chumphon to Ranong, ending at the Ranong Port, south of Ranong town, though the exact route will be studied further.

A.1.4. The Ranong Seaport

The Ranong Port is built, owned and operated by the Port Authority of Thailand, which operates the Ports of Bangkok and Laem

Chabang, the main ports of Thailand. The port is used by suppliers in Thailand for shipping goods to Myanmar; some oil rigs are also located there. It is used much below capacity, partly due to the competition from the many private operators located in the same area. There are plans to promote it as the gateway for goods to India and other destinations in South Asia. This port will be the terminal for goods for the new proposed railway line from Chumphon.

A.1.5. Ranong–Koh Song–Kawthaung City

The study team made the border crossing from Ranong pier to Myanmar, entering the country at Koh Song, where there is an immigration checkpoint and a casino and hotel. We observed many Myanmar workers waiting at Koh Song to board the ferry to Thailand. Outward-bound travellers are mainly Thai tourists for island diving tours.

From Koh Song, the team went to the town of Kawthaung on the mainland. The town was built by traders as a staging point for goods. It is now a bustling point of departure for visitors to the islands.

A.1.6. The Islands off the Kawthaung Coast

Famous for its 800+ islands off the coast of Southern Myanmar, some islands have been developed for tourism, such as Nyaung Oo Phee and Bruer, but there are many other islands, and more are being opened up for development by the Myanmar authorities. The developer obtains a licence to operate hotels. Some islands are off limits and are used as military bases by the Myanmar government. We stayed on one island and met a group of Thai tourists enjoying an office outing. There were also other Thai, Asian and western tourists. The activities on the islands are swimming, diving for seeing corals, and other activities to enjoy the easy life. Evening entertainment is provided by the hotel as well as full boarding and lodging.

The island experience is very different from places such as Phuket or Phi Phi islands in Krabi, more like a stay in the National Park in Thailand, but a little bit less spartan.

To reach the islands, there are speed boats and other boats, which are usually provided by the hotel. The journey, depending on the island, may be 30 minutes to 1 hour or more.

Fish Landing Pier

Fish Sorted by Species Ready for the Auction

The Auction (1)

The Auction (2)

Fish Ready for Sale

Fish Sold, Marked by Weight and Buyer

Fish Ready for Delivery to Customer

The Chumphon–Ranong Railway: The Second World War Museum at La-un

The Locomotive at the Museum, a Gift from MacArthur from Japan

The View from Top of Khao Fa Chi Showing the Confluence of the La-un River (left) and the Kraburi River to the Estuary.

Note: The hills on the far side are in Myanmar

Ranong Port: Cargo Ship at Ranong Pier, Carrying Bags of Cement

Ranong–Koh Song–Kawthaung City: Waiting for the Ferry at Ranong Pier

The Ferry Crossing

The Landing at Koh Song

Myanmar Workers Disembarking at Ranong

Street View of Kawthaung

Kawthaung on Arrival

Hilltop Temple at Kawthaung

Approaching Kawthaung: The Islands off the Kawthaung Coast

Signpost from Kawthaung

Island Action

Action Close-Up

After-Dinner Show on the Island

Photo credit: The author

ABOUT THE EDITORS AND THE CONTRIBUTORS

EDITORS

Suthiphand Chirathivat, Professor Emeritus, ASEAN Studies Center, Chulalongkorn University, Bangkok, Thailand.

Charit Tingsabadh, Assistant Professor, Centre for European Studies, Chulalongkorn University, Bangkok, Thailand.

Prabir De, Professor, ASEAN-India Centre (AIC), Research and Information System for Developing Countries (RIS), New Delhi, India.

CONTRIBUTORS

David Boggett, Professor, Kyoto Seika University, Kyoto, Japan.

Supang Chantavanich, Professor Emeritus, Institute of Asian Studies, Chulalongkorn University, Bangkok, Thailand.

Suchandra Ghosh, Professor, Department of Ancient Indian History and Culture, University of Calcutta, Kolkata, India.

Buddhagarn Rutchatorn, Assistant Professor of Economics, Chulalongkorn University, Bangkok.

Sineenat Sermcheep, Associate Professor, Faculty of Economics, Chulalongkorn University, Bangkok, Thailand.

Piti Srisangnam, Associate Professor, Faculty of Economics, and Director, ASEAN Studies Center, Chulalongkorn University, Bangkok, Thailand.

Thiva Supajanya, Assistant Professor, Thai Settlement Institute, Prachuap Khiri Khan, Thailand.

Wiwat Sutiwipakorn, Lecturer, Faculty of Engineering, Prince of Songkla University, Songkhla, Thailand.

Mu Mu Theint, Academic Director, Myanmar Imperial University, Yangon, Myanmar.

INDEX